36 - 1939

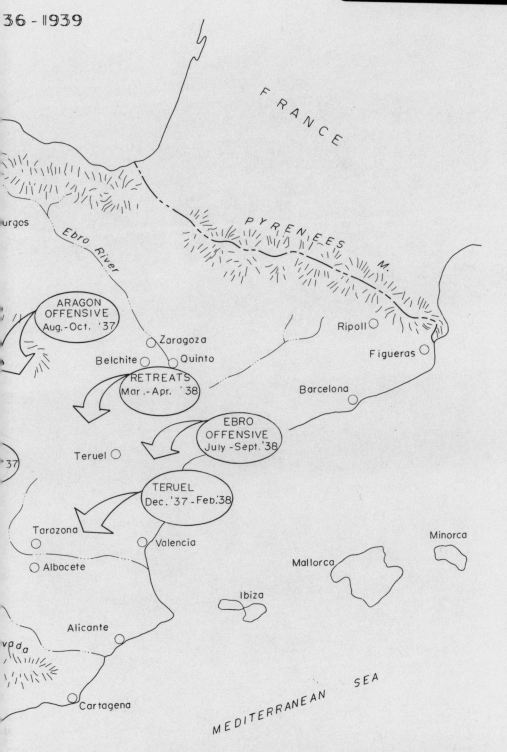

FRANCE

PYRENEES M.

urgos

Ebro River

ARAGON
OFFENSIVE
Aug.-Oct. '37

Zaragoza

Belchite   Quinto

Ripoll

Figueras

RETREATS
Mar.-Apr. '38

Barcelona

EBRO
OFFENSIVE
July-Sept.'38

'37

Teruel

TERUEL
Dec.'37-Feb.38

Minorca

Tarazona

Valencia

Mallorca

Albacete

Ibiza

vada

Alicante

MEDITERRANEAN   SEA

Cartagena

Canadian Volunteers

CANADIAN VOLUNTEERS
SPAIN, 1936-1939

WILLIAM C. BEECHING

Canadian Plains Research Center
University of Regina
1989

Canadian Cataloguing in Publication Data

Beeching, William
   Canadian volunteers : Spain 1936-1939
   1st ed.

(Canadian plains studies, ISSN 0137-6290 ; 18)
Includes index.
ISBN: 0-88977-057-3

1. Spain - History - Civil War, 1936-1939 -
Participation, Canadian, 2. Spain - History - Civil
War, 1936-1939 - Regimental histories. 3. Spain.
Ejército. MacKenzie-Papineau Battalion - History.
I. University of Regina. Canadian Plains Research
Center. II. Title. III. Series

DP269.47.C2B443 1989   946.081   C89-098048-9

Printed in Canada by Hignell Printing Limited, Winnipeg

Dedication

Canadian Volunteers: Spain, 1936-1939 is dedicated to the memory of the Canadian anti-fascist volunteers who lost their lives in Spain in the first armed struggle against fascism. At least 1,448 Canadians answered the appeals for help from the Spanish democrats; 721 fell in the battles to prevent the outbreak of a world war and to preserve democracy. The eternal flame which forever flutters over the tomb of the Unknown Soldier in Ottawa also burns for them.

Contents

Illustrations

Maps

Roll of Honour

Abocheski, George

Abramovic(h), George Yuran

Abramson, S.H.

Adamic, Joseph

Adamic, Michael

Adams, E.G.

Akubec, John

Alarro, --

Alekiuk, Demetro

Aleksic, Petar

Alksnis, Boleslav

Allan, Ted

Allstop, Geoffrey

Aman, Aivan, J.G.

Ambroziak, Peter

Ames, Bruce Clemens

Andersen, Herman (Wade, Orton)

Anderson, Hugh

Anderson, Ivor (Tiny)

Anderson, Sami

Anderson, V.B.

Andreef, John

Andrejev, Ivan

Angel, W. Henry

Anst, Wilfred

Antilla, Erland

Antony, Paul

Ardelsh, P. (Lt.)

Armit, Tommy Burns

Armitage, Joseph

Arnold, --

Asalt, J.

Asemlak, Philip

Ashplant, Arthur

Aspy, W.

Asselson, --

Atanasoff, Nicolas

Aucoin, Thomas

Ausborne, Paul

Aviezer, Elias

Babich, Tony

Bacic, H. Karlo

Backler, Lionel

Backman, Edwin

Bailey, Thomas

Bajuk, Martin

Balderson, J.N.

Bally, T.

Balogh, Mihal

Baltich, Luka

Balwar, Walter

Banik, Karlo

Barak, George

Baranowski, J.

Barcena, Isadro (Frank)

Barilot, --

Barkovitch, --

Barsky, Ben

Bartollota, Charles

Barton, Albert

Bartus, Ignas

Barylas, Frank (Sgt.)

Baryluk, Michael

Basic, Anton

Batic, Luka

Batson, Percy

Batymer, F.

Baxter, Frank

Bayden, J. (Sgt.)

Baynham, R.

Beamish, --
Beanic, Ivon
Beasor, Charles
Beattie, Henry
Beaulieu, Bert (Al)
Beckett, T.
Bedard, Joseph
Beeching, William
Beegachewski, Taras
Beke, Daniel
Belanger, J.H.
Bell, Alf
Bell, Jim
Bell, John
Bellie, J.
Benham, Lionel
Beranic (Bernovich), Ivan
Bereska, Mike
Bergeron, Raymond Edmond
Bertur, Paul
Bespirstis, P.
Bethune, Norman
Bidiuk, Ivan
Bigelia, Walter
Bigelow, Howard
Bigras, Alcide
Bigwood, William
Biles, Norman
Bileski, William
Bilks, Joe (Paul)
Billows, Nicholas
Bilodeau, L. Roger
Binter, Michael
Birsivak, Vaso
Bishop, M. Thomas
Black, James (Sgt.)
Blackley, Harry

Blackman, Frank J.
Blaho, Imrich
Blanc, Jack
Blasek, N.
Blasevic, Marko
Bler, Jack
Block, Joe (Jack)
Bligor, Dine (Yaloucheff)
Bloom, J. Oscar (Alms, Orville)
Bobby, Frank (Costello)
Bodnar, Walter
Bodnarchuk, M.
Bogner, Julius
Bohmer, Walter
Boivin, Edouard
Bojilov, Dimitri (Jimmy)
Bojuk, --
Boland, Duncan
Bolf, Motif
Bollo, Joseph
Booner, Julius
Borics, Jose
Bothwell, Joe
Bowen, Cromwell
Bowzalio, Harry
Boyak, William
Boyko, S.
Brackenbury, Ed
Braden, Roy
Bradley, William
Brais, Napoleon
Bramovic, Jurat
Brennan, William (Sgt.)
Bresevac, Vaso
Briski, Atun
Brkich, Oscar
Brown, G. Allen

Brown, Jim
Brown, Joe
Brown, L.
Brown, O.K.
Brown, R.D.M.
Brown, R.H.
Brown, Robert
Brown, Sam K. (Squeaky)
Brown, William (Pop)
Brownlee, Robert H.
Brozovich, Frank
Brunet, Paul Henri
Brunner, Emeric (E.J.)
Brusic, Anton
Brusovitch, S.
Bubanecz, James
Bubonen, J.
Buccor, Stan
Buchanan, Stan
Buchokowsky, William
Buckovic, Mike
Buckwell, Cliff
Budgeon, Clifford
Budenkewich, Stephen
Budsinovich, Jim
Budzinsky, G. (Jim)
Bukovi, M.
Bulloch, J.H.
Bulova, Walter
Buric, Ivan
Burke, A.P. (Lee)
Burns, Paul
Burton, Albert Ernest
Burton, Yorky
Burtrim, William (Butrimas, Bolis)
Buss, Roy
Butler, Ben

Butrey, Ivan
Butymer, Fred
Butynec, Fred
Bzumik, Manik
Cacic, Tom
Cairmay, Michael
Cameron, John (Jimmy)
Campbell, Charles
Campbell, George
Campbell, Joseph
Campbell, Morrison
Carberry, Dominic (Patrick, Francis)
Carlson, Arvid
Carlstad, Earl
Carreteri (Martin, Tony)
Cecheff, Nicola
Cecil-Smith, Ed (Major)
Chalamanuk, Steven
Chambers, Alex (Scotty)
Charczuk, Steofan
Chardon, --
Chase, Van
Chaudoin, Norman
Chega, Bill
Cherrie, Charles
Chevalier, Alex
Childers, James
Chizyk (Cizik), Nicholas
Chodur, Michael
Chop, Alojz
Chollaux, Armand
Christie, Timothy S.
Christoff, Gregor
Christy, Richard
Cisko, Andy
Clair(e), Leige
Clarke, J.

Clarke, James

Clarkson, Red

Clemens, Ralph

Clement, T.

Cleveland, Ralph

Cleven, Ralph

Cluny, Joshua

Cochrane, James

Cochrane, Thomas

Cockings, William Spencer

Cody, Jack (Wilson, Curly)

Cohen, Saul Bernard

Cohen, Sidney

Coleman, Bryce

Collin, Michael

Conroy, R.E.

Constant, Maurice

Cook(e), --

Cook(e), George

Corak, Ivan

Cowan, Tim

Cowan, Wilfred

Cowie, Charles

Cowstan, John

Cox, Thomas

Cressman, Elmer

Croll, J.W.

Crossley, C.R.

Crozier, Eugene

Cserny, J.

Csoke, Andro

Cullen, M.

Cunningham, Andrew

Cunningham, George

Cunningham, J.T.

Cyurleza, --

Czirmaz, Michael (Mihaly)

Czizmer, Alexander

Czyzewski, J. (Chzewaski, Jan)

Dack, Steve

Dagesse, Perc

Dahl, Eskill (Eskel)

Dames, James A.

Dandy, Jack

Danek, Thomas

Daneliuk, Michael

Danjuk, Pete

Dasovic, Stevan

David, R.C.

Deck, John

Dekan, --

Delaney, Jerry

Delaney (Lachapelle), W.

Demainschuk, Nicholas

Demers, Charles

Demianchuk, Peter

Demidzuik, John

Dempsey, Russell

Denby, John

Dent, Walter (Sgt.)

Dentry, Ernest W.

Derecimovic, Ivan

Derencovic, John

Derrahchuk, Peter

Dettrich, Joe

Dewitt, Thomas

Diamond, Thomas

Dickie, Robert

Dickinson, D.

Dietrich, Jacob

DiPope, Mate

Derkach (Dirkich), Ignatz (Tony)

Djaic, J.T.

Dmitruk, Bartflam

Dobrowolsky, N. (Sam)
Dobson, J.
Doherty, Bill
Dolanchuk, J.
Doley, F.
Dolynuik, Peter
Domitro, S.
Domjnovie, Mile
Douloff, John
Drashner, Anton (Tony)
Dratva, John
Drezel, E.
Drolet, Maurice
Dubel, Vincent
Dudka, John
Dufour, Paul
Dukes, Lawrence
Dulkoff, John
Dumas, L.
Dupak, John (Dupiak, Petro)
Duranciuk, Joe
Dyer, Robert
Dyrow, Michael (Sgt.)
Dziki, Michael
Dzumaga, Michael Stanton
Edgar, George
Edmund, Arthur
Edwards, Ernie
Edwards, Lionel (Capt.)
Edwardson, Ed
Efromov, J.
Elams, Tauno
Eldon, John
Elindiuk (Ellenduik), Nick
Ellis, Wade
Elomaki, Matti
Encott, Charles

Engert, Herbert
Engstrom (Engblom), Ed
Epstien, Hyam
Erdei, Gabriel
Erdeluac, Petar
Evanoff, A.
Evans, Lloyd (Arthur, Floyd)
Evashuk, Max (Ivashchuk, Maxim)
Ewen, Bruce
Ewen, Jim
Fairbanks, W.
Falkowski, Nick
Famrylo, Oleska
Farkas, Alex (Paul)
Faulkner, Percy Howard
Fedorchurk, Michael
Felton, -- (Feltham, D.R.)
Fenton, H.
Ferencz, John
Ferguson, J.
Ferrier, W.H. (Marcelin)
Filkohizi, Emerie
Finnigan, J.
Firmin, John Charles
Fiwchuk, George
Flatoff, Nick
Fleming, Sheridan
Flovecheff, Gregor
Flynn, Richard
Fobert, Cecil
Fogarty, Eugene (Dr.)
Foley, William (Harry)
Foma, Alex
Forbes, Alex
Forby, William
Forrest, William
Fournier, Ed

Fowle, John
Franberg, P. (Elis)
Franchuk, Joseph
Francis, Karl (Carl)
Frantisek, Maxiam
Fredrick(s), William
Friend, Charles (Chuck)
Gabor, Erder
Gabor, Jenei
Gabriel, Michael
Gabriel, Steve
Gahm, --
Gainhorst, T.
Gal, Janos
Gallow, J.
Gangarossa, J.
Garcia, Andrea (A.H.)
Gardiuk, John
Garner, Hugh
Garrow, Clifford S.
Gasgrovaz, John
Gawda, W.
Gawricki, Walter
Gecheff, Nicola
Gee, John Matus
Geng, Joseph
Gibson, Pat
Gideon, Maynard
Gilasen, Harold (Dr.)
Gilian, Andras
Gillbank, Jack
Gilligan, Bert
Gillis, Rod (Kawuza, A.)
Gillstrap, --
Gilmor, William Stewart
Gleadhill, Thomas
Glenn, Joseph

Glow, Jerry
Godin, Emery
Gold, Irving
Goldenberg, Izzy (Budich)
Goldiawicz, William
Goldranic, William
Golgowski, W.
Gombos, A.
Gongora, E.T. (Emile)
Goodison, M.
Goola, A.
Gordon, Joe
Gordon, Robert J.
Gordon, William
Gosselin, Ernest
Gosztini, Frank
Gouette, Ernest
Gougen, Emil
Graham, Walter
Grainger, --
Grant, Lewis Charles
Grasparac, Ivan
Grassl, Adolph
Gray, Arthur
Gregoravich, T. Frank
Grenier, Amadée
Greysdale, Fred
Griffin, Winston
Griffith, John
Grodecki, Danlo
Gruick, Brank
Grujic, Stanko
Grurecrai, --
Guk (Juk), Joe
Gulley, George John
Grigaravicius, John
Gunerod, Ted (Gunrud, Jed)

Gustavsen, A.
Gyurcza, Natzas
Haas, Andrew
Hackett, Fred
Hadazi, Karoly
Hadesbeck, F.
Haferb(l)ier, J.C.P.
Hagerty, B.
Haldane, Marc
Hale, A.
Hall, Harvey
Hallikanen, Einno
Hallowchuk, Mike
Halmberg, Karl H.
Halota, Nikola
Hamilton, Steve
Hamilton, William
Haney, David
Hannan (Kelly), --
Hanni, Matti
Hansen, Hans (Brichfeld, Henrick)
Hanzuik, M.
Harbocin, Nick
Harrison, William
Harrison, William
Harrost, Steve
Harvey, David
Hasiuk, Stepan
Haslit (Haslett), Howard
Haughey, James
Hausbout, Urbane
Hautajarvi, Erno
Hayes, G.
Heany, John
Hebert, --
Heikka, E.
Heinche, Lawrence

Heine, --
Hellund, Walter
Henderson, --
Henderson, Ray
Henderson, William S.
Hendrikson, Suro
Herter, Adam
Hesketh, H.
Higgins, Jim
Hihn, Mike
Hill, George
Hill, Herbert
Hilton, Perry (Wellington, Percy)
Himmelfarb, Victor
Hitchcock, Douglas
Hladka, Mike
Hliva, V.
Hlywa, W.
Hnatkiw, Ivan
Hodge, Robert
Hodgson, Edward (Mark)
Hoffheinz, Art
Holliwell, William (Lt.)
Holmstead, Selwin
Holopainen, Jussi
Hondorf, Michael
Horanic, Pavel
Horduck, John
Hornacek, Mike (Paul)
Horrel, R.A.
Horthovitch, Dragunin
Horvath, Alex
Horvath, Vendel
Hoshooley, Jack
Housianmaa, Oscar
Howard, Allan R.
Howell, Robert

Hrab, M.
Hrodetskyi, Danylo
Hrstic, Petar
Hryszczysrin, Stefan
Hubb, Jack
Huhtala, Sulo
Hurstick, Peter
Hyduk, M.E.
Hylkinen, Waino
Hyppa, Sauli
Hyrnick, Michael
Ibing, Hans
Ilchyshyn, Stefan
Illes, P.
Inge, William
Irving, Edward (Gilroy, Shorty)
Iszciuk (Iszczuk), Steven
Ivanik, J.
Ivanisevic, Nichol
Ivanoff, John (Anton)
Jaakonsaari, Toivo
Jablonski, Walter
Jachems, Ivan (Jacamak, John)
Jacko, --
Jackson, R.
Jacob, Mike
Jacobs, D.
Jacquart, Pierre
Jaczku, S.
Jakovcic, Mike (Mato)
Jakovlavic, Sreto
James, P.M.
Jameson, Clarence W. (Red)
Janas (Jonas), John
Janicki, Eugene
Janik, Stanislaw
Janissewki, Frank

Janneson, Osborn
Jardas, Ed
Jarosziuk, Jose
Jelic, Lazar
Jergovich (Jargonovich), Mate
Jeruche, Eugene
Johnson (Johanson), Arthur
Johnson, J.G. (Johnny)
Johnston, Peter
Jokinen, Heikki
Jones, J.E.
Jones, Norman
Jones, R.
Jordan, F.B.
Jorgensen, J.
Joutsen, Matti
Juhasz, Alex
Junkala, Eino
Kack (Knack), A.G.
Kacki (Kacke), Ivan
Kaipainen, Onni
Kaiserman, --
Kakos, M.
Kalans, Ivan
Kalapaca, Walter
Kalapud, W.
Kalishnikoff, Ivan
Kallin, William
Kaltschmidt, Hans
Kambides, J.
Kandia, Anthony
Kane, James
Kantola (Kanlota), E.
Kaplan, J.
Kardash, Theodore
Kardash, William (Lt.)
Karpuk, Peter

Karrika, Everett
Kaska, Tom
Kasza, John
Katic, Ivan
Keenan, Archie
Keenan, Gordon
Keenan, William
Keitaanranta, John
Kelly, A.E. (Aubrey)
Kelly, Joseph
Kelly, Michael
Kempa, W.
Kennedy, Frank
Kennedy (Lapchuk), Morris
Kenyon, R.J. (Robert)
Kerdiak, Ivan (John)
Kerko, Charles
Kerpaul, Walter
Kerr, Bob
Kesselman, J. (Jehoshua)
Kestick, Frank
Keto, Reino (Lt.)
Kierpaul, Casimir
Kikush, Mykhald
Kipen, Steve
Kiraly, Steve
Kirkics, Ignatz
Kiroff, Istvetan
Kisielis, Luidas (Louis)
Kiss, Andrew
Kit, Nick
Kivi, M.
Kivimaki, Emil
Klaco, L.
Klucetski, George
Knaut, Helmut
Knudsen, A.

Kobal, Andri
Kobaly, Andrew
Kobe, Michael
Kodouice (Kodojoice), --
Kojshak, M.
Kokovskyi, Stephan
Kokura, John
Kolbaska, M.
Kolestar, Geza
Kolniuk, W.
Kolonji, Ivan
Komodowski, Ed
Kondos, George
Koni, J.
Koops, Jan
Kopp, Jordo
Kordian, A.
Kore, John
Koricki, Nikita
Korinski, Joseph
Korniychuk, Stefan
Korody, Alex
Koroscil, A. (Johnson, Andy)
Korpi, Irgo (Lt.)
Kos (Koss), Michael
Koscic, Franjo
Koscma (Kochma), Joe
Koskela, Emil
Koski, Hugo
Kosloff, A.
Koslowsky (Kozlowski), Steve
Kosowatsky, Mortimer
Kostaniuk, Petro
Kostiuk, Vasil
Kostoff, George
Kostur (Koster), William
Kostyk, Fred

Kotnuik, W.
Kotyk, John
Kovacich, Joseph
Kovacs, Steve
Kovelas, George
Kowalchuk, Nesteruk M.
Kozak, Martin
Kozeow, Nick
Koziel, Alex (Alexander, Thomas)
Kozole, Alex
Kral, Otto
Kristian, Emmanuel
Kristiansen, K.
Krizan, Foxel
Krizsan, Tony (Antal)
Kromholz, J.
Krousement, Ewald
Kruth, Nilo
Krysa, Wasyl
Kryshani, A.
Kubinec, M.
Kucherepa, Volodymyr
Kuchny, Mike
Kudebski, M.
Kuebler, Harold
Kulman (Kulmala), Felix
Kumpulaainen, Esko
Kuncho, John
Kuokka, U.
Kupchik, Izzy
Kupusinac, A.
Kurdiak, John
Kurdiak, John
Kuryk, Harry
Kushnier, Allen
Kuzma, Dennis
Kydnia, T.

Kyyny (Kynny), George (Yrgo)
Laaksonen, Valdo
Lacelle, Lionel J. (Leo)
Lackey, Fred
Lacko, John
Lahtovirta, Hugo
Lamont, --
Lamper, J.
Langley, Sam
Lapinskas, E.
Laskowsky, George
Latulippe, Lucien
Lauradin, R.
Laurin, Joseph
Laval, --
Lawrence, Tom
Lawson, Jack
Lazure (Lasure), Omer
LeBlanc, Wilf
Lebzyk, Maxim
Leclerc, J.
Legge, W.S.
Lehtinen, --
Lemal, Arthur
Lenek, Joseph
Lenthier, John Armand (Arthur)
Leppanen, Wiljo
Lerner, Arthur
Leslie, Robert
Levens, H.J.
Levy, Bert (Yank)
Lewis, Alex
Lewitsky, J.
Leye, W.
Lieber, M.
Lightfoot, William
Linardic, Ivan (Ardic, Len)

Lind, Tauno
Linton, Arthur
Liska, Fred
Lisset, John
Liversedge, Ron
Livingstone, Donald
Llewellyn, E.
Loch, Jacob
Lockwood, David
Logovsky, Vasil
Loiselle, John (Regan, Johnny)
Lombart, Herman
Lompik, A. James
Lord, F.
Loser, Creso
Loughran, Pop
Lucas, James
Lukachevich, Ivan
Ludevit, K.
Ludkin, Ernest
Lukac, Simon
Lulic (Bolo), --
Luoma, Emil
Luoto, Frank
Lurgel, M.
Lutesan, Michael
Lynch, Pat
Lyons, Tommy
Lypky, J.
Lys, Jan
Lysetz, Hrytz
MacLeod, Donald
MacNeil, Fred
McAllister, R.
McBride, John
McCallum, Bob
McCallum, James

McCarthy, Cormac
McChesney, Isaac
McClure, A.C. (Alex)
McCrystal, W.
McDonald, A.
McDonald, C.W. (Charles)
McDonald, Tom
McDonald, William
McDowell, James
McElgunn, Francis
McElligot, Pat
McGinnis, Pat
McGrandle, --
McGrath, --
McGregor (MacGregor), Hugh
McGregor, James
McGuire, Patrick E.
McInnis, Neil Henry
McIntyre, T.
McKay, Al
McKay, John
McKenzie, J.
McKenzie, John
McKenzie, Tom
McLaren, B.F. (Slats)
McLaughlin, Bill
McLaughlin, Matthew
McLean, James
McLeod, George
McLeod, Donald
McMann, Francis
McNulty, John
McQuarrie, Roy
McRae (McRoe), Donald
McVicar, Reid (Rod)
Mackenzie, Rod
Madaire, Charles

Madden, Harry

Madeley, Russ

Madsen, Nels

Mafromski, Don

Magid, Aaron (Dr.)

Magul, J.

Magorni, Sedor

Major, Vince

Makela, Niilo (Capt.)

Makela, Utamo

Maki, Juno

Maki, Kalle

Makovcic, Matox

Makura, John

Maleschuk, Paul

Malickas, J.

Malicki, Eugene

Malko, John

Mallen, Thomas

Malone, John

Malson, J.

Mandel, Emmanuel

Maneer, J.J.

Mangel, Dave

Mangotic, Anthon

Malytski, Mykhailo

Manien, J.J.

Mantell, J.P.

Marcelin, Ferrier

Marchuk, Walter

Marier, --

Marinoff, Nick

Marinuik, Walter

Markoff, George

Markowski, George

Markowsky, Andrew

Marsh, Ted

Marshall, A.W.

Marsolin, Zola

Martilla, Helge

Martin, C.

Martineau, Rosario

Martinuik, A.

Martlinseen, Suerre

Martynuik, Tony

Martynuik, Walter

Matesic, George

Mateychuk, N.

Matish, Joseph

Matlack, J.

Matson, J. (Isaac)

Matson, K.W.

Matsuka, S.

Matta, Jean Paul Homer

Mattersdorfer, Fred

Matthews, William

May, Allen

Maynard, R.A. (Roger)

Mazurkevich, A. (Walter)

Mazzar, --

Mazzepa, P.

Medgyesi, Charles

Melajeznik, Mike

Melnick, Alex

Melnychenko, Oleksander

Melville, Pat

Menard, Gideon

Mennel, Morris

Menzies, John (Jock)

Merges, Elmer

Metro, Alexiuk

Meurs, Arnie (Arie)

Meyers, Helge

Meyers, Henry

Mezei, Beri (Ben)
Michie, Thomas M.
Mihaichuk, Mykhailo
Mikkola, Arva
Milan, Sedar
Milas, Nicholas
Miljkovic, Joso
Miller, Alex (Lt.)
Miller, Allan
Miller, John (Jock)
Mironchuk, Mike
Mironuik, Alex
Miscovetz, Sam
Mitchell, Joseph
Modic, Matno
Moffatt, Arthur
Molnar, Jim
Molyneaux, Andrew
Montgomery, Harry
Moore, C.W. (Charles)
Moore, George Howard
Moravski, --
More, Joseph
Morency, Jean B.R.
Morin, François
Moroz, Teudor
Morris, Arthur
Morrow, William
Moses, W.
Moskaluk, Peter
Mowbray, Fred
Mozer, Joseph
Mudry, Harry
Mueller, Ernest
Munnumaki, Uuno
Munnumaki, Walter
Munro, Alexander

Murawsky(i), Andrew
Murisalo, Eines
Murray, Ben
Murray, Edward Charles
Murtch, John
Myers, Nick
Myers, Roy
Myllikangas, Arvi
Nash, Claude A.
Nawallowsky, Stefan
Neilson, C.V.
Neilson, Peter (Lt.)
Neimi (Nieminen), A.
Neimi, John
Nelson, H.
Nelson, Thomas
Nestoruk, Michael
Neufeld, Abram
Nikita, N.
Nikolaychuk, Peter
Nikoloff, D.
Nivirinsky, W. (Nick)
Nolen, Paddy
Norman, S.G.
Norris, Len
Novsol, Yanko
Norrum (Norum), John
Nunemaker, Willis
Nutt, Alexander
O'Brien, John
O'Brien, Sanford B.
O'Connor, J. (Paddy)
O'Daire, Paddy
O'Dorne, Frank
Offer, John
O'Hara, Pat
Ojala, V.

Okonski, Jacob
O'Leary, Earl (Frank)
Olynik, Constant (Mike)
O'Neil, Stewart (Paddy)
Oraschuk, Henry
O'Shea, John
Ostovich, Nick
Ossowski (Osuchouski/Ossiviski), --
Oszesypko, Teddor (Oshchyko, Fedir)
O'Sullivan, Paddy
Oulette, Germain
Ordog, Frank
Ozumaga, Michael
Owen, Darcy
Paake, L.
Pacholorak, Stefan
Pacyna, J.
Padowski, Nicholas
Page, George Henry
Page, John
Paisuta, George
Paivio, Jules (Sgt.)
Pajpak, M.
Pakkala, Franz
Palak, Stanislaw
Palavter, Peter
Panchoff, P.
Pangrac, Martin
Panosuik, S.
Panteluk, Wasyl
Papieanik, Pavel
Papo, Frank
Parker, Charles
Parker, Douglas
Parker, Frank (Reilly)
Paroczai, Alexi
Pascal, Jack A.

Paterson, H.C.
Paton, George
Patrick, E.W. (Dan)
Patrick, O.
Patryluk, William
Patterson, Edward
Patterson, Robert
Patterson, Tom
Paulsen, Harry
Pavelich, Paul
Paveluk (Pawluk), Tom
Pawliuk, Teddor
Peacock, Jack
Pearce, Robert
Pearson, J.
Penn, Marvin
Peneycad, E. (Penny, Ed)
Penrod, J.
Perala, J.
Perce (Perdue), Carl R.
Peressini, Antonio
Perles, Harry
Pesyshanski, S.S.
Peters, R.J. (Bob)
Peterson (Pederson), Ankar Magnus
Peterson, J.
Petijohn, J.
Petkoff, I.
Petrik, William
Petruk, O.
Pike, Florence T.
Piluik, John
Plahkta, Andrei
Plese, H.
Pocik, Steve
Podielzelski, P.
Polich, Stepan

Polichek, John
Polling, Eugene
Pollington, Frank
Pollock, H.
Pomeroy, --
Pongalos, --
Porier, Francis
Potvin, Ed
Pozniac, I.
Prange, Robert (Red)
Pretz, Adam
Princze, Joseph
Pritchard, David
Procyk, Mitchel
Prokopink, Nick
Propkopets, M.
Przedwajewski, J.
Punko, Paul
Purdek, Peter
Puska(s), --
Puttanen, A.
Pyholuoto, Franz
Pyluk, Ivan
Raatikanen, Eino
Rackey, John (Racki, Ivan)
Racz (Race), James
Raisanen, Lauri
Rajki, Matyas (Rayki, Martin)
Rajamaki, A. Bruno
Rakvacs, Joseph
Rally, James
Ramelson, Bert
Ramonovich, Stanley
Rank, Victor
Ranta, Yohan
Rasmus, Matti
Ratkovic, Mladen

Rawicz, Michael
Rayfield, H.H. (Hedron)
Rayner, Stan
Reid, James N.
Reisinen, L.
Renner, A. Henry
Reutta, Len
Reznowski, Ed
Ribas, --
Rickards, Joseph (Rick)
Ricketts, Lee
Righton, Monk
Riley, F.
Rissanen, Laudi
Rivard, Lucien
Robbins, J. (Tom)
Roberts, Tom
Roberts, Harry F.
Robertson, J.K.
Robertson, S.G.
Robinson, Digby
Robson, A.E. (Albert)
Robson, Wilfred J.
Rocziak, Stanislaw
Rodd, W.G.
Roden, F.J. (Frank)
Rodnarchuk, Mike
Rogers, Jim
Rokvacs, Joe
Romaniuk, Alex (Nick)
Romanishin, Dan
Romanovich, Stanley
Romk, --
Ronczkowski, Harry
Roschly, C.C.W. (Charles)
Roschuk (Ruschak), Steve
Rose, Art

Rose, Richard
Rosenberg, --
Ross, Allen
Ross, G.C. (George)
Ross, James (Joseph)
Rovainen, Adolph
Rubics, Frank
Rudzinski, Felix
Ruggeiso, Vincenz Ruggierio
Ruitta, Al
Rushonen, --
Rushton, Harry
Russell, F.M.
Russell, Michael
Russell, Ross
Russell, Thomas
Rutherford, Frank (Francis)
Rutkowski, J.
Ruusaka, Vaino
Ryan, Lawrence
Ryant, Tommy
Ryback, Steve
Rychuk, Fred (Radchuk, Fedir)
Rye (Malinowsky), --
Ryynanen, Toivo
Saari, Toivo
Sakslad, Erich
Salemko, Alers
Salimen, Vileo
Salo, Alex (Albert)
Salvail, Arthur
Samuolis, Anton
Sandiford, F.
Sarvas, Jurai (George)
Saunders, Charles
Saunders, Murray
Sauriol, J.M.V.

Savage, R.
Saxer, Charles M.
Scarpello, Charles (Scanlon)
Schatz, Isaac
Schmeltzer, G.
Schmidt, Joseph
Schneider, John
Schoen, Joseph
Schofield, Ronald
Scott, M.
Sczczyk, Stepan
Sedo (Sedor), Mike
Sekerek, Elias
Semenov (Siminoff), Boris
Seminoff, Walter
Seponen, David (Seppanen, Arvi) (Lt.)
Serdar, P. (Mike)
Sergiwich, Max
Seviceski, Harry
Sezia, Charles
Shapcott, James
Shapiro, Henry (Saul)
Shea, Gerald
Sherwood, William
Sheveliuk, Oleska
Shevshky, John
Shewchuk, Joseph
Shilk, Joseph
Shirley, E.
Shirley, Ed
Shishoff, G.
Shlapak, William
Shpyrka, Paul (Pavlo)
Shumack, Samuel
Shumega, John
Shumekar, John
Sidney, Walter

Sidor, Victor
Sidun, Michael
Sillandaa, John
Siltala, Viljo
Sim, Charles
Simich (Simic), Anton
Simonds, William
Sims, Thomas Patrick
Sipponen, Ilmari
Sirdar, Tony
Sirko, Louis
Sisco, Alex
Sise, Hazen
Siven, Art
Sivestre, M.
Skawulak, D.
Skibinski, Stanley Thadeus
Skinner, Baden (Terry)
Skinner, William
Skoloda, Mike
Skopljek, --
Skup (Scott), Paul
Slater, F.W.
Smi, Joseph
Smichowidi, D.
Smihur (Smibrer), Alex
Smit, Anton
Smith, Jack
Smith, Joe
Smith, Lloyd
Smolko, Jan
Smutylo, Vasyl
Smythe, Daniel
Snisko, Paul
Socha, Frank
Soltesz, Joseph
Sorenson, Henning

Southgate, James
Spamberger, Adam
Spark, Leonard
Sparks, Harold
Spencer, Cyril
Spirka, Pawel
Spiwak, Fred
Spirovic, Djorjije
Staimen (Starman), --
Starnichuk, Peter
Staub, Art
Stavrous, K.
Steele, Jack
Steer, George
Stefanuik, Sam
Stefanyshyn, Mike
Steiner, Sandor
Stemer (Stenner), --
Stenko, Michael
Stern, F.E. (Bertrand)
Stetina, Frantich
Stevens, Pat
Stewart, Douglas
Stillman, John
Stimac, Ivan (John)
Stivic (Stovic), Frank
St. Louis, --
Storgoff, M.
Stoycheff, George
Straub, George
Stromelo, J. (Hromila, H.)
Sueby, André
Suhaida, Frank
Suoniemi, Toivo
Suonieni, Lorio
Suni, Toivo
Suomela, Otto

Sus, Harry
Susia, Gregory
Sustar, --
Swain, Richard J.
Swanson, Harry
Swatak, Frank
Sweeney, Bernard
Swiderski, Gregory
Sych, Andrew
Sypka, Jan
Syurkovics, Istvan
Szabari (Szabali), Gabriel
Szabo, John
Szeder (Serdar/Sedor), Mike
Szewitch, John Luke
Szewirk (Szewezpk), Joseph
Szkara, Vasil (Sakara, Bazil)
Szlapek, Mike (Hyniak)
Szlemko (Salemko), John
Szuesko, Paul
Szpryka, Paul
Sztumic, Stefan (Samuel)
Szucs, Andrew (Suchy, André)
Szumik, S.
Szysz, Gabriel
Tait, James
Takacs, George
Tandaric, Amil
Tarasoff, William
Tarkowski, William
Tarnawskyi, M.
Tashakowski, Frank
Taylor, George
Taylor, Jack (Muni, Erlich)
Taylor, Lawrence
Taylor, Norman
Taras, --

Tazzaman, A.A. (Arthur)
Telec, --
Tellier, Lou
Terno, Vangel
Tesowick, Joseph
Thant, Helmut
Thirkettle, Frank
Thomas, George A.
Thompson, Frank
Tiska, --
Tissets, Harry
Toika, Taavettei
Tomasi, Mike
Tornikowski, Eino
Torosenko, Phillip
Toth, Steve
Tough, William
Tourninen, Sulo (Viljo)
Trakalo, Walter
Traynor, Thomas (Paddy)
Trier, Martin
Triteran, Mike
Trudeau, Hector
Tuovinen, Hekki
Tuho, Tevi
Tupper, Patrick
Turkowsky, William
Turnbull, Joseph
Turner, Robert
Turner, William
Tymus (Tynas), Steve
Udden, Svens
Ugren, Charles
Ulasic, Ivan
Ulkoff, John
Urichuk, P.
Usher, John

Usher, R.E.
Valent, Louis
Van der Brugge, Adrian
Vandzille, Andy
Varchuk, P.
Varga, Andreas
Varro, Frank
Vasas, Zoltan
Vaselenchuk, Mike
Vasileff, Tom (Tanas)
Vasky, Alfred
Vasovic, Vakosin
Vassilov, Norman
Vasylchyshyn, Hryhoriy
Veikkola, Vaino H.
Velichko (Velechko), Mike
Vidakovich, M. (Lt.)
Viitamemi, Hugo
Vinchewskyi, Stan
Vinsky, Albert
Vitez, Joe
Vlasick, Nicholas (Ivan)
Voimla, Ralph
Volaric, Mato
Vozniuk, Daniel
Vukelic, Stepan
Waichuk, I.
Walker, Fred
Walsh, --
Walsh, J. (Red)
Walter, P. Joe
Walthers, Charles (Sands)
Wandzilak, J.
Warga, G.
Waselenchuk, K.M.
Washington, George
Wasylchyshyn, Gregor

Watchman, David
Watec, J.
Watson, Stanley
Watts, Charles
Watts, Jean
Watts, Jim
Waywood, Walter
Webster, Henry
Weibe, Bernard
Weir, Robert
Weldon, John
Wellesley, Arthur
Welsby, Frank
Wesber, Frank
Wesson, Neil
West, Wilfred
Wharmby, James
Wheatley, --
Whitehead, Bill
Whiteside, Fred
Whitfield, Frank
Wilk, Frank
Wijatyk, Antoni
Williams, John D.
Williams, Walter F.
Williamson, Edgar W.
Williamson, William
Willoughby, William
Wilson, James
Wilson, John
Wilson, Leslie Warren
Wilson, William
Windhewski, S.
Winkleman, J.A.
Witczak, T.
Wittaneimi, John
Wladstan, Ganda

Woiner, Peter (Voiner, Petra)
Wolek, John
Wolfe, J. (Sam)
Wolfe (Woulfe), James
Woloncewicz, Vincent
Wood, J.K.
Wood, Frank
Woodman, Walter
Woods, --
Woods, Durrutti
Woolgar, Stan
Wosniuk, Danilo
Yachemec, John (Yacemec, Ivan)
Yakimchuk, N.
Yanitskyi, Yevhen
Yarash, Bill (Ilych, William)
Yarashuk, Joseph
Yardas, Edward (Lt.)
Yarrington, George
Yarysz (Yardz), Theodorz
Yaskiw, John
Yates, James O.
Yaworsky, Stanley

Yurchyk, Paul
Yurinchuk, W.
Yurischuk, Prekop
Zacharuk, Dimitro
Zagog, Sylvester
Zaharik, Jack
Zahornasky, Andy
Zak, Stephen
Zakharchuk, P.
Zaluski (Zaluki), G.
Zaremva, Jim
Zatawni(k), Theodore
Zaviskyi, --
Zayjak, --
Zdanauskas, Ed
Zdones, S. Ed
Zgar, Mia (Zagar, Mike)
Zemek, Jan (John)
Zepkar, Peter
Ziemski, John
Zigorevich (Zygarewicz), Kormil
Zubac, Turon (George)
Zubor, Suros

Acknowledgements

More than ten years ago the Canadian veterans of the International Brigades decided that their history had to be written, a history that would explain why they had volunteered and what they had done when they went to Spain to join in the bloody civil war which overtook that country in 1936.

Two highly respected veterans, Fred Mattersdorfer and Paddy McElligott, formally proposed that steps be taken to produce a history and that I be asked to write it. I readily agreed to undertake a task that was, for me, a labour of love.

Where to begin? The first task was to gather information from archival materials, other histories and interviews with veterans, and to combine it into an account which would tell what ordinary Canadians did when history confronted them with formidable tasks.

I began my work in the National Archives of Canada (Ottawa) where John MacAdam Reynolds introduced me and showed me the ropes. His work in the mid-1960s in obtaining oral history from the veterans for the Canadian Broadcasting Corporation was of much value. I found that the bulk of the archival material was in the National Archives of Canada and the Metropolitan Toronto Library. These two collections are now augmented by a third at the Canadian Plains Research Center at the University of Regina.

Walter Dent and Ross Russell taped and interviewed some veterans; I visited as many as time and money would permit. John and Betty Beeching searched the archives in British Columia and drove me around for interviews. The early writings of Edward Cecil-Smith, and those of Bill Brennan in preparing the 1938 book on the 15th Brigade, provided a good foundation on which to begin the work.

While searching through the archives I often wondered why we had been so late in producing our history, why earlier attempts came to naught, and why Ron Liversedge's early attempts to write about Spain gathered dust on shelves. In 1939 there had been a decision made to write a history and there were veterans with talent and ability who could have produced it. Moreover, memory had not yet faded in those early years, events and exploits now forgotten or barely remembered were still vivid, and archives had not been lost. More of us were alive to fill in the picture. I concluded that a partial answer is that the first bloody battles against fascism in Spain had been overshadowed by the drama and magnitude of the mighty battles in World War II, which came all too soon after the fall of democracy in Spain.

While I have never heard it said, I also concluded that the Left movement which gave birth to us had, and still has, a problem in estimating our place in history, a problem which in part is a lack of appreciation of the role of past history in shaping the present, and the result, as well, of an approach which all too often reflects the ego of new leaders anxious to leave their own mark on history. As well, there has been the persistent stigma attached to what was, in spite of the nobility of its purpose, a losing cause. However, the Canadian veterans who persevered in their efforts to maintain an organization, and who wanted to have a history written, never accepted negative verdicts about their place in history.

On the positive side it is now possible to stand back after all these years and examine that episode, taking into account both the good and the bad, while preserving its essence—an approach so well expressed in the words of Goethe: "Take from the hearth of the past, not the ashes, but the fire."

I completed the manuscript in 1987, but getting it published remained a problem. Dr. James N. McCrorie, Executive Director of the Canadian Plains Research Center, University of Regina, was eager to do anything he could to assist. He and Gillian Wadsworth Minifie, his Manager of Publications, helped me to begin the process of submitting the manuscript to book publishers.

Although there were no rejections from publishers, the indications were that the process of getting the book published would be a long one, a problem of concern to the few aging veterans who remained. I therefore asked Dr. McCrorie if the Canadian Plains Research Center would consider publishing it, to which he enthusiastically agreed.

Dr. McCrorie, who has a keen interest in the role people play in making history, was responsible for arranging in Regina the first seminar of its kind to be held in Canada about the war in Spain and the role of the Mackenzie-Papineau Battalion. William Alexander, who had commanded the British Battalion in Spain, came to Regina from England and played a prominent role in the seminar.

The manuscript was then read by experts and academics, including William Alexander and University of Regina professors Lorne Brown, Joseph Roberts and James McCrorie. All had suggestions for revisions and editing and all agreed that the book must be published. William Alexander's wise counsel, particularly on both military and political matters, was invaluable.

This history owes a great deal to the support of many veterans and the constructive and frank criticisms of my early attempts made by Elsie Beeching, John and Betty Beeching, Donald and Sylvia Currie, Mark and Marion Frank, and Karen and Charles McFadden. I, and the veterans, owe much to Elsie Beeching who read over my first efforts, took part in some of the interviews and meetings, and kept nudging if the work slackened. In innumerable ways she made it possible for me, often under difficult circumstances, to persevere. I also owe a very special thanks to a brave and clever Catalonian, Captain John Nebot, and his wife Mercedes, who filled in much background material.

I am also grateful to the staff of the Canadian Plains Research Center. Dr. James McCrorie, who gave unselfishly and unstintingly of his time and abilities to bring to the final draft his accumulated wisdom and knowledge. He worked hard in redrafting detailed military data into more understandable accounts, which summed up the essence of the struggle for the ordinary reader. Gillian Wadsworth Minifie's design for the book was excellent, and Brian Mlazgar, whose skills are not limited to computers and typesetting, pounced on errors and quickly spotted inconsistencies, contradictions and confusion.

Above all else, I thank my fellow comrades-in-arms who made this story live by clothing the skeleton of history with the flesh and blood of perseverance in a noble cause regardless of the odds and consequences.

If *Canadian Volunteers* helps those who read it to understand the continuity of history, if it fosters a spirit of internationalism and an understanding of the need for each individual to be responsible for and to take actions in the interests of all people, then it will have achieved its purpose.

If, in spite of all efforts to eliminate them, errors and inaccuracies have crept into this history, I as the author assume full responsibility for them.

William C. Beeching
Regina, Saskatchewan

Permissions

Permissions to quote from the following previously published materials are gratefully acknowledged:

Chapter 3, note 1, page 34. Published by permission of Transaction Publishers from *The Struggle for Madrid*, by Robert G. Colodny. Copyright 1958 by Transaction Publishers.

Chapter 4, note 10, pages 74-75. Reprinted from *The Marxist Quarterly* by permission of Progress Books.

Chapter 7, note 7, pages 175-77. Reprinted from the *Toronto Star* by permission of the Hemingway Foundation.

Chapter 8, note 11, pages 197-98. Reprinted with the permission of *Saturday Night*.

Preface

On 18 July 1936 the Spanish army, led by General Francisco Franco, rebelled in Spanish Morocco, plunging Spain into a bloody, three-year civil war. In the end the democratic republican government was overthrown, and Franco established a fascist dictatorship which would last until 1976.

The Spanish conflict, although not unprecedented in the brutality it generated, nor in its outcome, was nonetheless unique in the international response it provoked. The western democracies of Great Britain, France, the United States and Canada refused to come to the aid of the democratically elected Spanish republican government, despite its repeated pleas for assistance, and despite the open intervention of Hitler and Mussolini on the side of Franco and the Falange. Yet the Spanish agony kindled an emotional response among men and women throughout the western world which, in depth and commitment, had never been seen before 1936. Flouting the official neutrality of their governments, volunteers from Argentina, Cuba, Austria, Bulgaria, Czechoslovakia, Finland, France, Germany, Hungary, Eire, Italy, Norway, Poland, Rumania, Sweden, Switzerland, the Union of Soviet Socialist Republics (USSR), Yugoslavia, Great Britain, the United States and Canada went to Spain to fight for the republican cause. In the case of Great Britain, the United States and Canada, the volunteers defied laws designed to keep them at home; anti-fascist volunteers from Germany and Italy risked their lives and the welfare of their families to fight for democracy in Spain.

Although exact figures are unobtainable, it has been estimated that at least 35,000 men and women joined what came to be known as the International Brigades. By 31 March 1939, when Madrid fell and the republican cause crumbled, at least 20,000, or 57 percent, of the international volunteers had been killed in action or murdered in prisoner of war camps. Of the 1,448 Canadians known to have fought in Spain, 721 never returned home.

What were the issues in the civil war in Spain which aroused the conscience and concern of so many people around the world? In particular, why did the fascist revolt against the legal Spanish government stir passions in Canadians, who had neither familial nor cultural ties with the Spanish people? These questions are important, for in Canada we have been discouraged from raising them. The painful truth is that following the triumph of fascism in Spain, the Canadian government harassed the surviving volunteers; proposals to aid in the return of the volunteers were obstructed, and when they did return to Canada, they were treated as dangerous subversives, not as farsighted heroes who had seen the danger which fascism posed to world peace. Upon the outbreak of World War II in 1939, the veterans were prevented from enlisting in the Canadian armed forces. As recently as 1984, a Canadian government refused to introduce legislation providing surviving veterans of the Mackenzie-Papineau Battalion with a pension.

The record of the Canadian academic community has been no less shameful, and the subject of the Spanish civil war has been studiously avoided by Canadian historians and social scientists. Only one book (in 1969) has been written about the Canadian volunteers, and that by an American professor of English literature. Perhaps it is the fact that our role in the Spanish tragedy, if known and publicly acknowledged, would tarnish and undermine our sense of national self-respect. It may have been this possibility which prompted Greg Clark of the *Toronto Star* to write, as he observed the returning veterans disembarking in Halifax in 1939, "I don't recollect ever seeing soldiers who inspired in me so strange a mingling of reverence and humiliation and embarrassment at meeting their gaze."

Why, then, did more than 1,400 Canadians go to Spain to risk their lives in the defence of a people they had never known? The answer is simple, even if it includes a number of complex considerations. We must recall the state of the western world in 1936. The Great Depression was at its peak, and millions of men and women had been out of work for over six years. Savings had been wiped out by currency depreciation, and in many countries, including Canada, unemployment insurance and public welfare programs had yet to be instituted. Many of those who had been fortunate enough to own their own homes were unable to make mortgage payments and lost them; tenants unable to pay their monthly rent were evicted. Millions of people worldwide lived on handouts and the dole. Lasting economic recovery was nowhere in sight.

The Great Depression was not merely an economic catastrophe, for the very magnitude of the economic dislocation created an international political crisis of explosive dimensions. On the left, Communists and social democratic parties proclaimed that capitalism was in its death throes, a statement that was increasingly credible amongst impoverished, unemployed men and women. Talk of revolution and communism, or parliamentary reform and socialism, was on the political agenda. In the centre and on the right, liberal and conservative parties appeared unable to initiate policies which would end the Depression, rebuild the economy, and restore some measure of public confidence in capitalism.

There were two notable and troublesome exceptions. In October 1922 Benito Mussolini was named premier of Italy, and formed a coalition government. By 1927, Mussolini and the Fascists had destroyed parliamentary institutions, curtailed universal suffrage, restricted freedom of the press, abolished labour unions and the right to strike, and declared all political parties illegal, save their own. A new secret police terrorized the population; labour leaders, civil rights activists and left-wing politicians were arrested, imprisoned, and in many cases murdered.

If these ruthless measures troubled liberal capitalists—business leaders with a strong commitment to democracy and parliamentary forms of government—they were forced to consider three points urged upon them by their more right-wing counterparts. However unpleasant Mussolini and his methods might be, it was argued, Italian fascism had been strikingly successful in reducing unemployment in Italy. Fascism had also guaranteed the provision of a disciplined labour force obliged to work for low or reduced wages. Finally, although businessmen viewed government meddling in the economy with distaste, they felt it was an acceptable price to pay for the preservation of capitalism. The record was clear— with one stroke fascism in Italy had destroyed democracy and revived capitalism.

On 30 January 1933 Adolf Hitler was appointed chancellor of Germany. Like Mussolini before him Hitler initially presided over a legal coalition government, but through a careful manipulation of electoral success, propaganda, and sheer terror, he was soon able to assume dictatorial powers. Trade unions were outlawed, civil liberties were suspended, the Jews were persecuted, the powers of the German states were abolished, and all political parties except the Nazis were outlawed. However, despite his anti-business rhetoric of the 1920s, Hitler promptly revived capitalism, favouring the German capitalists who had financed his rise to power. As well, Hitler courted the German officer corps and the landed gentry from which it was largely drawn. These actions were not lost on businessmen in other western societies and indeed American capital would develop sound business relations with the Nazis. Many prominent western political figures, including Mackenzie King, Joseph Kennedy and King Edward VIII (soon to become the Duke of Windsor), were not unfavourable to the Nazis, while important members of the British establishment, such as Neville Chamberlain, Lord Halifax and Lord Cameron of Lochiel, were to go to great lengths in an effort to accommodate Hitler's regime.

What then was the international situation in 1936? The western world was in economic chaos. Capitalists were shaken and uncertain about their future, workers were destitute and unemployed, and the savings of the middle classes had evaporated. Suddenly a revolt by the army in Spain threatened to bring yet another western country under the yoke of fascism. The Texas Oil Company, mindful of fascist support for business in Italy and Germany, supplied Franco and his followers with petrol, while democratic governments in the west, impressed by the fascist economic record, refused to interfere in Spain. On the other hand, the disregard of the Fascists for civil liberties alarmed more thoughtful members of the working class in countries such as Canada. Fascism, they argued, was a cancer upon the body politic. In the words of Norman Bethune, "The time to stop fascism is now, and the place to stop it is Spain."

Spain in 1936 was a nation deeply and bitterly divided along class, regional and ethnic lines. But even this is a simplification as there were divisions within the divisions. For example, while most Spanish workers were hostile to capitalism, their political objectives were not uniform; workers in Catalonia favoured autonomy, while their counterparts in other regions favoured a strong central government. Not surprisingly, such divisions were expressed in the political arena, and again the working class serves to illustrate how fractious Spain was: there was not one but several trade union movements (Unión General de Trabajadores and the Confederación Nacional de Trabajo); not one but several working class political parties (Socialists, Communists, Partido Obrero de Unificación Marxista, Anarchists). The only consolation that could be drawn from this deplorable situation was that capitalists, landowners and clergy were equally divided.

Spain is a dry land with poor soil, except in the northwest. Agricultural practices in 1936 were traditional and often primitive. As well, the Spanish countryside was racked with bitter class divisions. Approximately 50 percent of the cultivated land was in the hands of absentee landowners known as *latifundia*, who were primarily controlled by capitalist entrepreneurs. Only 6 percent of the large estates remained in the hands of the nobility, while Church lands had been disentailed for almost a century. The *latifundia* employed day labour which, combined with small holders, accounted for 4.5 million people, or 54.5 percent of the labour force. Their wages were pitifully low, they were seldom employed for more than

130 days a year, and they had no security in employment; their families endured extreme poverty. Concentrated in southern Spain, the landless peasants were ripe for revolution. There were independent farmers in Spain, particularly in Galicia and the north, but their holdings were small, their land was poor, and in many cases they fared little better than the landless peasants to the south. Their hunger for land and their hatred of the large estate owners cannot be overstated.

The urban sections of Spain were equally divided. Approximately 75 percent of Spanish industry was located in Catalonia, but relations between capital and labour throughout Spain were hostile. An extreme example of this animosity occurred in October 1934, when unemployment and deplorable working conditions drove the miners of Asturias to revolt against the mine owners and the state. Within three days, much of Asturias was in the hands of the workers, who proclaimed a revolutionary soviet. The government in Madrid, ironically, sent General Francisco Franco to suppress the insurrection. He was ruthlessly successful, killing 1,500-2,000 miners, wounding 3,000 more, and taking 30,000 political prisoners. By November the miners had been crushed and the power and privileges of the mine owners restored.

The growing and bitter division between labour and capital, between absentee landowners and landless peasants, was compounded by the fact that Spain was not an ethnically homogeneous nation. Catalonia enjoyed a long history of independent wealth, culture and traditions reaching back to the Middle Ages, and the depression of the 1930s revived in many Catalonians a desire for independence from the central rule of Castille. Separatist tendencies in Catalonia were matched by an even stronger desire for independence among the Basques, a distinct ethnic group numbering 600,000. The Basque region was comparatively wealthy, the centre of shipbuilding, trade and the Spanish steel industry. While the powerful Basque banking houses favoured economic and political integration with the larger Spanish republic, most Basques saw Spanish control as economically, linguistically and culturally suffocating. The Basque separatist movement had become so powerful by the 1930s that it encouraged smaller separatist movements in Galicia and Valencia.

One cannot understand Spain in the 1930s without referring to the Roman Catholic Church. With the exception of the Basques, Spaniards were intensely anticlerical, and less than one-third of adults were practicing Catholics. Although many rural priests lived no better than their impoverished parishioners, the church hierarchy was wealthy, conservative and politically powerful. When church lands were entailed in 1837, the clergy was compensated in cash. By the twentieth century the Catholic Church had become one of the principal industrial and commercial capitalists in the nation.

These were the divisions facing Spain when King Alfonso XIII abdicated in 1930 and a new republic was formed the following year. The new prime minister was Niceto Zamora, a liberal. His government introduced a broad, four-point program: the separation of church and state and the introduction of secular education; support for the trade unions; the break-up of the large estates, with higher wages and job security for landless peasants; and a measure of self-government for Catalonia. While these four principles were widely acclaimed by those they were intended to serve, the government was slow and often ineffectual in carrying them out. Zamora at once lost the support of many of his allies, and was distrusted by his opponents. In 1933 he lost power to the Catholic Party. Supported by various class factions on the right, the new government halted the break-up of the estates, restored religious instruction, suppressed workers' strikes, and withdrew the modest measure of Catalonian self-government. The brutal suppression of the Asturian miners in 1934 not only aroused international indignation, it spelled the end for the Catholic Party. President Azaña called an election for 16 February 1936, and the results were the Popular Front with 4,654,116 (34.3 percent) votes and 263 deputies, the National Front with 4,503,505 (33.2 percent) votes and 133 deputies, and the Centre with 526,615 (5.4 percent) votes and 77 deputies.

Since the electors voted for alliances rather than parties, the breakdown of popular vote by parties cannot be determined. The distribution of seats by parties in the Cortes was as follows:

Socialists	88
Republican Left (Azaña)	79
Republican Union	34
Esquerra	22
Communists	14
CEDA	101
Agrarians	11
Monarchists	13
Carlists	15
New Centre Party	21
Lliga	12
Radicals	9
Basques	5
Falange	0

Azaña formed a government composed of representatives from the Republican Left, the Republican Union and the Esquerra parties, and relied on Socialist support in the Cortes to remain in power. The government went about implementing the provisions of the Popular Front Pact in an atmosphere of mixed jubilation and fear. The Institute of Agrarian Reform was initiated, an amnesty for the Asturian miners was declared, obliging employers to reinstate dismissed workers and compensate them for lost wages, and the minister of education revived the 1931-32 secular education program.

Capitalists reacted vigorously. The *peseta* fell, and financiers began to remove their wealth from Spain, often leaving the country themselves. Mine owners in Asturias closed their mines, forcing the Madrid government to assume control. Clashes between left and right spilled into the streets, with kidnapping, political murders and sabotage commonplace.

It will never be known whether the Azaña government could have found the means to weather the storm and successfully implement its reforms. On 18 July 1936 General Franco, the officer corps and the larger part of the army revolted. They were supported by the Falange, the church, the landowners and capital. The Spanish civil war had begun.

Canadians Volunteers is an account of the participation of Canadian volunteers in the Spanish civil war. The work was commissioned by the Veterans of the International Brigades: Mackenzie-Papineau Battalion of Canada. It was researched and written by William C. Beeching, who volunteered to go to Spain in 1937 and served as a scout with the Lincoln-Washington Battalion.

James Napier McCrorie
Regina, Saskatchewan
July 1989

One

The Call To Spain

Within a month of the outbreak of the civil war in Spain, sixteen Canadians crossed the Atlantic to attend a world peace conference in Brussels. There is no record to indicate that any of them supposed that their concern for peace would lead directly to the participation of Canadians in the Spanish civil war.

The conference was convened by Lord Robert Cecil of Chelwood in the hope of drawing public attention to the deteriorating international situation, particularly in Europe. The agenda of the conference was dedicated to the pursuit of peace; the deliberations, however, were to be dominated by events in Spain.

During the conference a number of Canadian delegates were invited by Spanish loyalists to visit Spain before returning to Canada. It was hoped that the Canadians would gain a better understanding of the civil war if they visited Spain and saw for themselves what was happening. Among those who accepted the invitation were Tim Buck and A.A. MacLeod. The visit was to prove decisive.

Tim Buck at this time was the leader of the Communist party of Canada. While at the front in Madrid with troops commanded by Enrique Lister he was invited by José Díaz, the general secretary of the Communist party of Spain, to attend a meeting in the railway town of Aranjuez to discuss the creation of a new military formation to be known as an international brigade. At the meeting André Marty, a representative of the Communist party of France, reported that Hitler and Mussolini's support of Franco had already attracted more than two thousand volunteers to the loyalist side, many of them refugees from Germany and Italy. At present, foreign volunteers were attached to the Fifth

1

Regiment and other militia units. Marty reported that the Communist International had decided the time had arrived to facilitate the formation of an international brigade, which would fight as such, yet be an integral part of the Spanish Republican Army, subject to its laws, discipline and command.

At the conclusion of the Aranjuez meeting Buck travelled to Paris where he wrote and published a leaflet, "Defend Democracy in Spain, Tim Buck's Message from the War Front," which was distributed across Canada. In it he argued that Franco's military insurrection against the duly elected Spanish government was part of a larger "international offensive against democracy." Prophetically, he saw the outbreak of the civil war as a "definite state in the desperate drive for the new world order," a drive which, if not arrested, would end in world war.

Buck appealed to Canadians to support the republican cause, to send food and medical supplies, and to pressure the Canadian government to support the Spanish republican government at the League of Nations in Geneva. He called on workers to prevent shipments of materiel from reaching the Spanish fascists. Above all, Buck imparted a sense of urgency to the cause of the Spanish people. He declared that the defence of Spanish democracy deserved "all the energy of our party and of every friend of peace and progress." He concluded his appeal with the words: "I call upon all Communists and progressives in Canada to join hands to save the Spanish people from a Hitler-like fate of torture and oppression. I am returning to Spain again. Will send you first-hand information."

Most Canadians at the time knew little about Spain. Apart from first-hand accounts from the front, Canadians had to depend on the newspapers, and to a lesser extent the radio, for news about the progress of the civil war. By the autumn of 1936 the conflict was making the headlines, but media coverage was neither balanced nor objective.[1] Some members of the media had dubbed the republicans and their supporters as "reds," "atheists" and "destroyers" of church and clergy alike; Franco was depicted as the "defender of the Faith" while his forces were described as "patriots" and "nationalists."

Thus when Buck had been asked at Aranjuez whether Canadians could be called upon to support the republican cause, his reply was somewhat cautious. He knew, of course, that many Canadians would quickly reach the same conclusion as he had on the nature and significance of the civil war in Spain, but how many was another matter. Buck informed the meeting that he believed at least 250 Canadians could be expected to volunteer for service in the new international brigade,[2] and those back in Canada who were already taking steps to organize support for the republican cause approved of this figure. In a very short time, Canadians were to demonstrate that their mood had been underestimated.

In late autumn of 1936, Tim Buck and A.A. MacLeod returned to Canada from Spain. The Canadian press corps covered their arrival, since anyone who had visited the Spanish front was "news." Within a few days of their return, the Communist party organized a public meeting in the Mutual Street Arena in Toronto, where Buck was invited to give a full report of his visit to Spain. He recalled:

> To our amazement the arena was packed literally to the roof and people were still outside. There was a terrific amount of enthusiasm and right there in that meeting it was decided that we should launch a campaign for volunteers to go to Spain.[3]

It is clear that public appreciation for the republican cause, and public understanding of the threat posed to world peace by Franco's insurrection, was broader and deeper than had been supposed. Close to twenty "aid to Spain" committees were set up across Canada, located in most of the major cities and scattered throughout the countryside. This broad movement of support embraced the Co-operative Commonwealth Federation (CCF), the Communist party, individuals of liberal persuasion, progressive individuals in the universities, and large sections of the trade union movement and the farmers' movement, particularly on the Prairies. Eventually this spontaneous movement coalesced around two main committees—the Committee to Aid Spanish Democracy, and the Friends of the Mackenzie-Papineau Battalion.

The Committee to Aid Spanish Democracy worked to provide support to the Spanish people and assumed responsibility for financing and maintaining the Canadian Mobile Blood Transfusion Unit. It was chaired by Graham Spry, then chairman of the Ontario wing of the CCF. The Friends of the Mackenzie-Papineau Battalion was established on 20 May 1937, about forty days prior to the organization of the battalion itself in Spain. The committee was designed to deal directly with the problems of the men of the battalion, to provide supplies, including two ambulances, and to publicize the battalion's military feats. It became the battalion's civilian support force in Canada.

Those who served on and worked for these committees did so at considerable personal sacrifice, as it soon became evident that there were forces in Canada determined to go to great lengths to discredit the Spanish republican cause and to give what aid and encouragement they could to the triumph of fascism in Spain.[4] In Québec, Maurice Duplessis's Union Nationale government was open in its hostility to republican Spain and its support for Franco. The Québec government introduced the Padlock Law, which in the name of suppressing communism was designed to undermine the trade union movement, curtail freedom of speech, prevent freedom of assembly, and discourage organized public support for the Spanish republican government.

A number of fascist-oriented groups existed in Québec, including the Knights of Jacques Cartier, the National Social Christian Party, the National Socialist German Workers Party, the *Deutsche Bund*, the *Arbeiter Gemeinschaft*, the *Fascio*, the Italian United Moral Front, and *Dopo Lavore*. Adrien Arcand, a professional journalist and French-Canadian nationalist, became *der fuhrer* of the fascist movement in Québec. The editor of *Le Fasciste Canadien* was also the editor of Duplessis's newspaper, *L'Illustration Nouvelle*.

4

All of these organizations published newspapers and some conducted military training in violation of the criminal code. The Archbishop of Montréal issued a pastoral letter approving such training because, he believed, the authorities were not doing enough to curb communism. Cardinal Villeneuve, not to be outdone, commended the students of the Université de Montréal when they threatened to riot if Alfred Costes, a Communist member of the Spanish Chamber of Deputies, was allowed to speak on campus.

In Ontario swastika clubs appeared, while in Manitoba the Canadian Nationalist Party operated out of Winnipeg. Both were violently anti-Communist, and attacked Jews and interrupted public meetings sponsored by voluntary organizations of a liberal or progressive nature.

In the early 1930s, approximately half a million people of German descent lived in Canada. Hitler's Nazis set up a foreign division with the idea of uniting all Germans in foreign countries and German societies were set up to act in the interests of Nazi Germany. The North American fascist agency was called the Friends of the New Germany and was later renamed the German-American Bund. The work of the Bund caused a deep division within the German-Canadian community, many of whose members were bitterly opposed to Hitler and nazism.

Agitation and support for Franco by right-wing groups in Canada made it risky, at times, to stand up for the republican cause. Conversely, it had the effect of galvanizing support among men and women who refused to be intimidated. An illustration of this can be found in the stand taken by the Trades and Labour Congress of Canada. Meeting in Montréal in 1936, the congress debated then passed the following resolution:

> this Congress wishes to express to the workers of Spain our appreciation of their splendid fight in defence of their liberties and especially of their democratic institutions and government, constitutionally elected and . . . this Congress places itself further on record in the interests of

5

international solidarity as expressing to the Spanish workers our sincere interest in their struggle and extends to them our wholehearted support in the fight for justice, freedom and peace and our hopes for an early and victorious finish.[5]

Within a year the Canadian government was to display a different assessment of the Spanish situation. Yielding to right-wing pressure in general and Premier Duplessis in particular, Prime Minister Mackenzie King and Minister of Justice Ernest Lapointe followed Great Britain's lead by prohibiting the recruitment of volunteers to serve in the international brigades then being organized in Spain.[6] On 31 July 1937 the government passed an Order in Council, making the Foreign Enlistment Act applicable to the Spanish civil war. Prime Minister King eventually defended the decision in the House of Commons:

> The conflict which began in July, 1936, has been particularly destructive . . . because of the intervention of outside govern- ments in the struggle, the Italian and German governments directly assisting the insurgents and the soviet government assisting the government. There was imminent danger of the conflict spreading into a war of isms, of class conflict and of conflict of national strategic interests.

> On the initiative of the governments of France and Great Britain a non-intervention committee of twenty-seven European states was formed to endeavour to prevent or restrict outside participation in that war. The committee has not succeeded in pre- venting continued extensive participation by outside states.

> . . . in order to prevent Canada from being drawn into this European struggle by the recruiting of Canadians for service in Spain, an order-in-council was passed in July applying the Foreign Enlistment Act to the Spanish conflict as had previously been done in the United Kingdom and administratively in the United States, and in early August the issue of passports to Canadian nationals proposing to go to Spain for the purpose of participating in the conflict was prohibited . . . The purpose of both

6

measures was to prevent Canada being drawn into foreign conflicts by the actions either of manufacturers of munitions or organizers of recruiting.[7]

The order in council imposed a $2,000 fine or two years' imprisonment, or both, for violation of the Foreign Enlistment Act.

At the Aranjuez meeting Tim Buck had cautiously suggested that 250 Canadians might volunteer to serve in Spain. In fact, 1,448 Canadian volunteers went to Spain, in spite of the organized opposition of the right and the official opposition of the Canadian government.[8] Why were so many prepared to go?

It has been suggested, mistakenly, that the men volunteered simply because they were unemployed and had nothing else to do. In truth, the motivation of the volunteers was complex, and for those who were out of work when they volunteered, unemployment was but one of several reasons for going to Spain. When the men who went to Spain recall their reasons for doing so, it becomes clear that theirs was not an "economic" act based on rational calculation for self-gain. No one supposed that going to war, with the risk of being killed or seriously wounded, was somehow preferable to being unemployed. If there was one consideration common to all volunteers, it was that they were conscious anti-fascists, following an ideal. Above all else, they believed that if fascism could be stopped in Spain, a second world war could be prevented.

Many volunteers gave up jobs to go. Paddy McElligott, a miner, and Walter Gawricky, a woodworker, quit their jobs and paid their own fare to Spain. Ed Cecil-Smith, who would become the commanding officer of the Mackenzie-Papineau Battalion, was employed, as were many others too numerous to mention. Of the unemployed who volunteered to fight in Spain, most were active in the struggle at home to overcome unemployment. Ron Liversedge estimates that five hundred of the volunteers had taken part in the On-to-Ottawa Trek that had been organized by The Single Unemployed Workers Union in 1935. In his words:

> I think that the terrible life of the Canadian unemployed during the depression of the thirties, the box cars, the flop houses, the demonstrations for relief, seeing the police clubbing men, women and even children unconscious on the city street for asking for food, the twenty-cent-a-day slave camps, the "On-to-Ottawa-Trek," all this had conditioned the men who volunteered to go to Spain to make the decision without much soul searching . . . Also the men were by this time politically conscious, all understanding what fascism meant for the common people, and fully aware that if the fascists won in Spain then the second world war was on. It is important to understand too, that the volunteers believed that their example would influence the people of Canada to bring enough pressure to bear upon the government, to force diplomatic, and economic action on behalf of the Spanish government, and aid in the defeat of the fascists.[9]

In their minds going to Spain provided the opportunity to directly participate in a struggle for a new social order in which unemployment and all the other scourges from which they suffered would be forever eliminated.

The consciousness to which Liversedge refers is reflected in a resolution sent to Prime Minister King by the Winnipeg Single Men's Unemployed Association:

> the organized unemployed single men of the City of Winnipeg pledge to support your government in any actions that will aid the Spanish government and its people and in turn offer to mobilise a voluntary militia of 1,000 men for active service in Spain.

> Today we are idle men. We do not want history to record that we remained idle at a time when international fascism hammered humanity with blows that struck at the very roots of civilization. We yearn to carry through the worthy mission of helping to defend a world's people from impending destruction.

We ask your government to assist us with provision of transportation and supplies.[10]

The volunteers had an internationalist outlook which led them to see the struggles of the working people of other lands as an integral part of their own struggles for a better life. They understood and accepted the need for collective security to stop fascist aggression and war, and seized the opportunity to act in Spain before it was too late. Participation in the war against fascism was a great, dramatic moment in their lives. In part it was a search for adventure, but it was more than that. Their participation in the struggle of the Spanish people against fascism reaffirmed what had driven the volunteers to enlist in the first place.

It might appear that the recruitment of volunteers to serve in Spain was an easy matter, but such was not the case. The campaign to organize support for the Republican side took place in the face of government opposition and hostile surveillance by the Royal Canadian Mounted Police (RCMP), in the midst of an economic depression.

In the autumn of 1936 three prominent Spaniards sailed to Canada to launch the organization of a campaign to inform Canadians of what was taking place in Spain, win political and moral support for the republican cause, and recruit for the formation of the international brigade. They were Señora Isabella Palencia, member of the Cortes, delegate to the League of Nations, and Ambassador-elect to Sweden, Señor Marcelino Domingo, former minister of education and leader of the Left Republican Party of Spain, and the Reverend Father Luis Sarasola, a Catholic priest, scholar and historian.

The three delegates travelled first to Montréal, where their first Canadian meeting was scheduled for the Mount Royal Arena. It had to be cancelled due to the direct intervention of the Duplessis government and Mayor Reynault of Montréal. The organizing committee was forced to reschedule the meeting for the McGill Student Union building, on Sherbrooke Avenue near University Street. The doors of the building were guarded by members of the Scarlet Key Society, an exclusive

9

student group, who turned out in flashy red and white Martlet sweaters. The preceding day John MacDonald, editor of the *McGill Daily*, earned the distinction of being the only Montréal newspaper to defy the Duplessis government, under the ironic headline: "Duplessis—Our Savior."

Duplessis was quick to capitalize on the fact that prominent Canadian Communists were active organizers of the growing campaign of support for the republicans in Spain, and this was undoubtedly the case. Accurate estimates on the number of Canadian volunteers who were Communist sympathizers cannot be provided from surviving records, but Len Levenson, an American who served with the Mackenzie-Papineau Battalion, believes that 63 percent of American volunteers were either members of the Communist party or the Young Communist League. Nevertheless, members of the Communist party did not dominate the campaign for Spain. Supporters and leaders of the CCF, members of the Liberal party, and progressive men and women of other political affiliation all worked for the Spanish republican cause.

There was no shortage of volunteers, but those responsible for recruiting them did not always have the resources to send large numbers to Spain at any one time. The civil war had broken out in the middle of the Depression, and this made it difficult to raise the necessary funds to send the volunteers to overseas; most people simply did not have the money to spare. Only the ingenuity of the organizers enabled so many Canadian volunteers to reach the front.

Tim Buck recalls in his memoirs that it was possible to get a reduced rate and one free ticket for every twenty if a block of twenty passages was booked. The recruiting committee therefore never sent less than twenty or more than fifty volunteers to Spain at any time. However, even here the government made its disapproval felt. Tim Buck and Ron Liversedge stated that trouble developed in obtaining passage with Cunard lines, and concluded that government pressure on Cunard's competitor, Canadian Pacific Steamships, was to blame. Liversedge wrote:

10

It seems that the [recruitment] committee was having some trouble with the Canadian Pacific Steamships, the Company had started to claim that there was no space available whenever an agent from the committee went to book space for a group. It was felt that only strong government pressure could be responsible for the C.P.R. refusing fares.[11]

At times the volunteers who were going to Spain were able to remain anonymous, while on other occasions everyone in town seemed to know who was going. In either event, the volunteers had to leave Canada clandestinely in order to escape the surveillance of the RCMP and the provisions of the Foreign Enlistment Act. There were no rousing send-offs, no bands or grand speeches. The men quietly boarded trains like any other citizen going about his business. They had little money and only a few could afford to patronize the diner. The irony of this did not escape Ron Liversedge:

It seems almost humorous in retrospect, that one in offering to risk one's life in a noble cause, had to be careful not to run afoul of the law in doing so.[12]

It was necessary to have a passport despite the fact that it would be stamped "Not Valid" for travel to Spain. The cost of each passport was $5.00 and the application for it had to be cosigned by someone of authority who declared that he or she knew the applicant. Ron Liversedge described the problems that arose:

I had a problem in getting somebody to sign my application form, as the person who signed was supposed to have known the applicant for a number of years and to vouch for his worthiness. I tried a few people, but to no avail, then I tried a minister of the Gospel, who was outspoken in his denunciations of fascism. He said that he was sorry, but that he would be writing a lie if he did sign my application, and this he could not do, but "how about Dr. Telford" he said with a cute smile. I had been reluctant to go to Dr. Telford as I knew that he had signed quite a lot for the boys up to that time, but I had to get that passport so up to Dr. Telford's office I went. As soon as the good Dr. saw me he said, "My god, not another one, I've signed enough to get me locked up already." I said, "Oh, come on Doc, in for a penny, etc.," and he smiled and signed. Dr. Telford was a member of the C.C.F. and was to be later the Mayor of Vancouver, his sympathies were with the Spanish people. I was thinking that somebody in the Passport Department must be wondering at the sudden interest in the Paris Exhibition on the part of all these single young men in Vancouver, and how it was that Dr. Telford knew them all.[13]

While some of the actual details of the RCMP surveillance would not be confirmed until the 1970s, the RCMP, government officials and politicians were already examining the very problem Ron Liversedge described. Documents in the Public Archives of Canada in Ottawa reveal the lengths to which the police and sections of the civil service were prepared to go to prevent volunteers from going overseas, and to punish those who went and the organizers who helped them get to Spain.[14]

The reason for this harassment was not, it would appear, the violation of the Foreign Enlistment Act. RCMP Commissioner S.T. Wood, in a letter to Dr. O.D. Skelton, the undersecretary of state for external affairs, wrote: "When the time comes some of these volunteers will be fully prepared to carry out in Canada what they learned in Spain of guerrilla warfare and the building and defence of barricades, etc."[15] And in a letter dated 8 July 1937 Commissioner J.H. O'Brien wrote:

> our officer commanding at Regina, Sask., reports that a feeling prevails among the loyal spirited foreigners at that point that recruiting for the Spanish government should be prohibited as it is felt that these youths are being sent to Spain, largely for the sake of gaining experience in practical revolutionary work and will return to this country to form the nucleus of a trained corps.[16]

Ironically, these fears expressed by senior officers of the RCMP were never shared by the volunteers, whose faith in democracy would have embarrassed professional defenders of law and order. Moreover, unlike some senior police officers, the volunteers knew perfectly well that a socialist revolution is never the result of an armed coup by a few individuals. But

12

these fears, this reasoning and this government policy made the recruitment of volunteers to serve in Spain a difficult undertaking, and young men bound to fight for democracy in Spain were forced to leave Canada like thieves in the night:

> These Canadian boys, some of them with familiar English, Scotch, Irish and French names and some with names less familiar, but now made forever glorious in Canadian history have shamed us who let them steal out of their native land as if bent on some criminal enterprise. But it was for Canada they crossed the sea and dared and suffered and (some of them) died.[17]

NOTES

1. For an analysis of Canadian press coverage of the Spanish civil war, see Mary Biggar Peck, *Red Moon Over Spain* (Ottawa: Steel Rail Publishing, 1988).
2. William Beeching and Dr. Phyllis Clarke, eds., *Yours in the Struggle: Reminiscences of Tim Buck* (Toronto: NC Press, 1977), chapter 27.
3. Ibid., 267.
4. A fuller account of the rise and fall of fascism in Canada during this period can be found in Lita-Rose Betcherman, *The Swastika and the Maple Leaf* (Toronto: Fitzhenry and Whiteside, 1975).
5. Quoted in Frank Ryan, ed., *The Book of the XV International Brigade* (Madrid: Commissariat of War, 1938), 7.
6. A discussion of the British imposition of the Foreign Enlistment Act in that country can be found in William Alexander, *British Volunteers for Liberty: Spain 1936-1939* (London: Lawrence and Wishart, 1982), chapter 3.
7. Canada, House of Commons, *Debates*, 24 May 1938, vol. 3, 3186-87.
8. The number of Canadian volunteers is customarily given as 1,237, a figure arrived at by the Friends of the Mackenzie-Papineau Battalion Committee. However, when Lee Burke, a veteran of the battalion, was given the task of compiling a list, he came up with 1,438 names. He checked the names with the American and British lists, and removed obvious misspellings and aliases. In the course of research for this book, an additional ten names came to light. It is estimated, therefore, that 1,448 Canadians volunteered to serve in Spain. It can be assumed that figures for killed, missing and wounded must also remain estimates, as no systematic records were kept. At the end of the war, the Friends of the Mackenzie-Papineau Battalion accounted for the return of 729 volunteers. It may be presumed that at least 719 volunteers were either killed or missing.
9. Ron Liversedge, "Memoir of the Spanish Civil War" (unpublished and undated manuscript in the possession of author).

10. National Archives of Canada (hereafter NAC), W.L. Mackenzie King Papers, #183645-46. Single Men's Unemployed Association, Manor Hall, Winnipeg, Manitoba, 8 September 1936. Signed by James W. Baker, D. Grainger and Mitchi Sago.
11. Liversedge, "Memoir of the Spanish Civil War."
12. Ibid.
13. Ibid.
14. NAC, External Affairs, RG 25 Vol. 1802, File 631-D, Part I.
15. Ibid.
16. Ibid.
17. Salem Bland, from his Introduction to Lieutenant William Kardash's pamphlet, "I Fought for Canada in Spain" (Toronto: New Era Publishers, 1938), 3.

Two

Going To Spain

The procedure followed in going to Spain was rather simple. The centre in Toronto, located in the Seamen's Union Hall at the corner of Queen and Spadina, was informed of the number of volunteers arriving from across the country. Tickets were purchased for them to go to Toronto by train. Volunteers from British Columbia and the Prairies, if they were without funds, were given a small amount of spending money. In those days, trains stopped at divisional points every 150 miles for fuel and water; there was always a restaurant at the station, where a cheap but good meal could be had.

The volunteers were instructed to take essential clothing, to give themselves the appearance of tourists, and to keep their baggage to a minimum. Many of them bought imitation leather suitcases, commonly sold for less than $2.00 in bigger department stores, and packed their meagre belongings in them.

The volunteers usually went first to Toronto where they stayed for several days, attending meetings where they discussed what was involved and were advised to go home if they had second thoughts. They were given a medical examination by Toronto-area doctors who provided their services for free. The volunteers were then given one-way tickets to Spain; some paid their own fares. The men were told who would be responsible for their group and were warned not to disclose their destination, not to drink, and generally to behave in such a manner as not to draw attention to themselves; the need for circumspection and self-discipline was urged on everyone. The trip across the Atlantic was uneventful, and in spite of these warnings the other passengers inevitably soon knew who the volunteers were and where they were going.

France was the gateway to Spain. Officially, the United Front government of Léon Blum made it as difficult as possible to move supplies and volunteers into republican Spain, indifferent to the fact that Hitler and Mussolini were openly supplying Franco's forces. However, the Blum government was no more successful than other western governments in imposing its will on the people. Various foreign nationalities, including Canadians, openly maintained offices in Paris for the express purpose of helping the volunteers to enter Spain. The sheer volume of volunteers moving through France en route to Spain would not have been possible without the cooperation of large numbers of French men and women, including civil servants.

Shortly after docking at Le Havre, the group leader would inform the volunteers that French immigration officials would ask each man where he was going and what he intended to do. The men were instructed to give a credible response, usually stating that they were tourists on their way to the world's fair.

Each volunteer was informed that he needed a minimum of $30.00 in order to enter France legally. The group leader then passed out sufficient money to make up any shortages. Each volunteer was warned that the money belonged to "the committee," having been collected from Canadians for the people of Spain, and that every penny had to be returned to the group leader as soon as customs was cleared.

The French customs officials undoubtedly had a fairly clear idea of what was going on, for it would have been difficult not to suspect that the groups of twenty or thirty young men, dressed similarly and with almost identical sums of money, were destined for the battlefields to the south. However, in most cases the French officials closed their eyes to the situation. For example, Orton Wade (Herman Andersen) of Winnipeg, who led a group of western Canadian volunteers to Spain, opened his black cardboard suitcase, which contained nothing but a bottle of gin, and a pair of clean socks and underwear. The customs official studied it, then looked at Wade. For a moment the two men stared at each other, then the official, without a hint of a smile, closed the suitcase, marked it with chalk, and signalled for Wade to pass through.

There were times, though, when volunteers travelling to France from the United States were singled out for special treatment. Wally Dent and Lee Burke sailed to France from New York, and Burke recalls:

> We arrived at Le Havre and on disembarking, we were divided from other tourists and lined up by Interpol [sic], when we had to show how much money we had and answer to our destination. They announced that the Spanish border was closed and if we had any intentions of going to Spain our return passage would be paid to our homes. Imagine! They were going to pay us to keep us from fighting fascism! Depression and all, money is no problem for governments for such worthy causes. No thanks! No takers.[1]

In Wally Dent's case the American ambassador met the vessel when it arrived in France in February 1937, questioned all suspected volunteers, and offered to pay for their immediate return voyage to the United States. Again, there were no takers.

There was usually a wait for the Le Havre express to Paris. On it, the French *Sûreté* collected all passports and checked them against their master lists of criminals and undesirables. This procedure occupied almost the entire trip to Paris. The passports were returned just before arrival.

Paddy McElligott, a group leader from British Columbia, recounts that while waiting to board the Le Havre express his volunteers got into a "coconut shy game" and won a large number of bottles of wine. Believing that trouble should be nipped in the bud, McElligott made a deal with the man who ran the game to exchange five bottles of wine for one bottle of brandy. The loot was thus reduced to a few bottles of brandy, which he locked in his suitcase and stowed on the baggage rack. Confident that the situation was satisfactorily resolved, McElligott went to another car to attend a meeting. Before long the volunteers in other coaches were startled to hear a rousing chorus of "Hold the Fort for We are Coming" originating in the coach McElligott had vacated. His suitcase had quickly succumbed to the lockpicking abilities of one of the British Columbia volunteers, and their anti-fascist militancy was rising in direct proportion to the quantity of brandy consumed.

The French anti-fascist movement was responsible for getting the volunteers through France, and set up an entire underground railway to do the job. In Paris the volunteers were accommodated in hotels and *rentier* quarters, the owners of which were usually sympathetic to the cause. They ate their meals in dining rooms run by the trade union movement, which daily provided free meals and a small amount of spending money. Many of the men took advantage of this interlude to visit the city, and the world's fair in particular.

When there were spaces in the south of France the volunteers were given a railway ticket and told to lighten their load of personal belongings to the minimum; surplus baggage was stored in a depot in Paris. In the smaller cities and towns of southern France the men were given various lodgings—much the same as in Paris but without the trade union dining room—and were told to wait.

OVER THE PYRENEES

When a sufficient number of volunteers had been assembled, and when the guides considered it possible to cross the Pyrenees, the men were picked up by bus and driven to a rendezvous. Sometimes they were dropped off close to the assembly points, at others they were left at designated locations from which they made their way to a peasant's home, where they were given a meal before setting out for the rendezvous.

Often the buses were stopped by the police, who would eye the baggage rack piled high with identical packages tied with string. On these occasions the driver would be asked where he was going, and would reply that he was driving a sightseeing bus hired by a group of tourists. Usually the police waved the bus on. The men were instructed that at times like these only a designated spokesman would answer police questions. If arrested, each volunteer was told to give only his name and address, and to state he was a tourist.

After dark the volunteers gathered at the assembly point where they met their guides, who were said to be shepherds and rumoured to be smugglers. The guides provided the volunteers with *alpargatas* (rope-soled sandals which laced to the ankle) for climbing purposes. The men were warned that they must maintain absolute silence and refrain from smoking, since the French border patrol was armed and often had dogs; it was understood that if the border crossing was to be a success, the guides would have to be obeyed at all times. The volunteers were told that if someone were injured during the difficult climb he would not be abandoned, but help might not be immediately forthcoming. Jimmy Higgins remembered the events of his successful climb:

> Two guides then took charge of the group. Both spoke English, French, and Spanish fluently. We formed a half circle while they, very quietly, gave us some idea of what to expect in the next six hours. We would have to follow their instructions if we expected to get across. There was to be no smoking until the guides said so. No talking. No unnecessary noise. We were given rope-soled slippers. We were to keep as close as possible to the man ahead of us. It was at this stage that I really began to understand the meaning of discipline, and how important it was to carry out an order . . . After the guides had satisfied themselves that we understood the instructions, we were ordered to follow in single file . . . No time was to be lost. We had to be in Spain by daylight. It was already midnight. For the first half hour we took a downward path. When we had to halt, the guide would raise his hand. Each of us repeated the motion, so that the man behind could get the signal and pass it down the line . . . At times we had to scale eight feet of perpendicular rock. In an hour and a-half we had climbed the peak and word was passed back to keep off the skyline.[2]

The climb was the first real test which faced the volunteers, one for which they could not have prepared. Forced to maintain a brisk pace over dangerous terrain, with only the occasional blink of a signal light to break the darkness, the men were exhausted by the time they reached the Spanish side, their determination and fortitude taxed to the limit. Bill Brennan vividly described the dangers which he faced:

> As we left France and went higher into the mountains you could see, for miles around, the lights of cities and towns stretched out far below . . . We trudged on over a mountain goat path. If it had been daylight and we could have seen the precarious path, many of us would never have made it. We trudged on, panting and gasping for breath, tired and worn out. Some couldn't keep up with our pace. They were left behind to make their own way over alone, later when they regained their strength. Others slipped and fell. Far below—a yell, then the soft echo of a thud, or of splashing water. We stopped and listened. No sound. We went on.[3]

When the fall was not fatal, the victim was hidden and told to wait until he could be rescued. Some of the volunteers lacked the stamina to make the journey without assistance, particularly those who were frightened of heights. All, however, were sustained by the knowledge that Spain and the chance to join the struggle against fascism lay just ahead. Those who won through were greeted by a sight of breathtaking beauty, as Tom McDonald described:

> The walk across the mountains is one that I will never forget . . . It took fifteen hours of steady going before we reached our objective. Late at night when we were starting down from one of the highest peaks, we seemed to come to the shore or a large sea. There were lights shining in several places on the shore of this sea and it was truly a wonderful sight with the moon shining down on its surface. We entered this sea and continued down the sides of the mountain, for it was a sea of clouds and I had never been that high in my life before.[4]

After the seemingly endless, nerve-wracking hours, the path began to turn down towards what appeared to be an ordinary

20

house. There a lean, weathered Spanish border guard welcomed the volunteers to Spain. To the young men from the drought-stricken Canadian Prairies, the surrounding countryside in the early morning light was particularly striking. As Tom Bailey of Moose Jaw declared, "It was heaven to us from the bald-headed west."[5]

Very few of the volunteers understood Spanish, but this made little difference. Smiles, handclasps and cigarettes were easily exchanged; some volunteers got coffee at the border posts in the early days of the war. But most were anxious to move on, and the border guard would point through the hazy morning light to a road leading south, winding like a ribbon through the fields. The volunteers were on their way.

Most of the Canadians made the climb over the Pyrenees to Spain, but Murray Saunders of Alberta was an exception. By an oversight he and an American volunteer were left stranded in Perpignan. Fifteen men had been taken to an empty warehouse and told to wait. In the days that followed the volunteers were taken from the warehouse, four at a time, to make the trek over the mountains, and finally only Saunders and the young American remained. They waited for several days, until they were out of money and food, and still no one came. They considered their dilemma, and concluded that they had no choice but to forge on. Saunders recalled their journey:

> We had to get out of there. We couldn't go back because we had no money and we would end up in the bucket [jail] if we didn't do something. So we set out. I pointed to the mountains and said, "I know Spain is over there so let's go." We walked along the road leading to the mountains and finally came to a tunnel, south of Perpignan. "I'm going over the top," I said, "no more tunnels for me." After several hours we got into a shepherd's shelter. The heat was oppressive. After resting, we went on. We knew we couldn't stop. We saw a white house and headed for it. Some guy began to holler at us, but we couldn't understand what he was yelling about. It was because we were walking through his grapes. He was leery of us. "No guns. No guns," I said. He gave us a bowl of soup and some

21

bread. "*España?*" he asked. So I said, "*Viva la Republica.*" The man took us outside, pointed and said, "*España.*" We walked a long way. We heard a whistle but saw no one, so we stopped and looked around, then we walked again. I told my companion to get behind a rock if he heard the crack of a rifle. Then an old shepherd appeared, complete with staff and a sack. "*España?*" he asked us. We told him yes. He beckoned us to follow, and soon we could see Port Bou below us. There was hardly a light. The old shepherd left us with a soft "*Salud!*" We continued down a pass to a viaduct. I knew we were in Spain because of the bullet scars on the buildings. We met up with some soldiers who took us to the Socorro Rojo [International Red Aid] head-quarters and from there we were taken to the fort at Figueras.[6]

The first Canadian to go to Spain was E.W. Williamson, and his passage to the beleaguered republic differed from that of all those who followed—he went on his own as a stowaway on a Spanish ship with the full cooperation of the ship's crew. Born in Manitoba, Williamson had worked since he was thirteen as a longshoreman, steel erector, lumberman and fisherman, and had taken part in the On-to-Ottawa Trek with the single unemployed. At the time of the Spanish generals' revolt he was living in England. Upon reading accounts of the revolt in the newspapers, and without further delay, he made his way to Cardiff, Wales on 18 July 1936, where he stowed away on a Spanish ship. He arrived at Port Bilbao on 19 July, and the next day enrolled in the militia.

On 21 July Williamson was in action at San Sebastian fighting against the Requette and Falangist troops. On 1 May 1937 Williamson transferred to the International Brigades. He took a fast boat from Bilbao to France, climbed over the Pyrenees, joined the 15th Brigade and saw his first action with the International Brigades at Brunete. He was withdrawn in December 1938.

In all, this distinguished anti-fascist saw two years of frontline duty. Rejected by the British armed forces in World War II, he served with the Free French in the continuing battle against fascism.

Some men never got to Spain, and died before they had a chance to fight. Ron Liversedge witnessed such a tragedy. In Marseilles he had joined a group of volunteers of different nationalities. They intended to sail to Spain aboard the *Ciudad de Barcelona* and were told the trip would take about four days. Liversedge recorded the events of the passage:

> On the evening that we sailed, May 28th, 1937, there were two hundred and forty-five volunteers in the ship. A large portion of the cargo was flour, and before we sailed, somebody amongst the longshore men had ruined the flour by pouring black liquid through the cargo hold. After we left Port and got out to sea some of the crew took us all and distributed us around the ship in the various passenger quarters. George Sarvas and I were given a double cabin in the first-class quarters. Twin beds, running water, reading lights, from the ridiculous to the sublime. After dark we were all allowed out on deck, but no lights were allowed. All the ship carried on the outside were the two running lights. It was rather eerie, trying to move around the crowded deck in pitch dark, listening to conversations going on all around in a dozen or more different languages. We found out that all of our original fifteen from Toronto were on board, and there were other Canadians also, but we didn't find out about them until later, when I found out personally in a very strange manner. Late that night before we turned in, a bunch of us gathered in a sort of lounge one deck down where our cabins were. We had a sort of small impromptu concert, people sang songs in their various national languages, Tiny [Anderson] met the Secretary of the Danish Communist Party and the Secretary of the Danish Young Communist League. There was one New Zealander and two Australians who entertained us with an exhibition of wrestling. Next morning, May 29, 1937, we all slept late, and then we had coffee and bread. Around noon we entered Spanish waters. The ship was sailing just a few miles off the Spanish coast, which appeared to be three or four miles away. Many of us were up on deck. A couple of times a plane would fly from the land, circle around the ship almost at masthead level, we could see the red

markings of the plane, and the pilot would wave at us from the open cockpit, and we all waved our clenched fists in salute. At about two o'clock in the afternoon we were told that we were about forty miles from Barcelona, and would be arriving there around five. I went down to the cabin to have a rest before we got to Barcelona, and I was barely settled on the bed, when the terrific explosion occurred. The ship seemed to literally leap from the water, settle back with a shudder which could be felt distinctly, and then noiselessly to be coming to a stop. As I sprang from the bed and automatically started to tie on a life belt I thought that a shell from a big naval gun had landed right on deck. I was mistaken, we were torpedoed by an Italian submarine . . . As I left the cabin I grabbed the second life jacket, and meeting George Sarvas at the cabin door I gave him the life jacket, told him to put it on and get up top right away . . . When I reached the deck, a horrible sight hit me with a shock. The ships [sic] stern was already under water and she was slowly turning over to the port side. All around the ship was a mass of floating wreckage; barrels, crates, cases, planking, canvas, wooden bedsteads, and amongst all this debris, were bobbing heads, and floating bodies, and around the bodies the sea crimson with blood. Hanging on the starboard side of the ship and resting on the ships [sic] plating was a lifeboat, its rope lines stuck in the davit blocks. In the life boat there must have been fifty men all standing up, and one man was hacking away at the lines with an axe. When the line was finally severed, the boat plunged down into the sea, and it was so over-loaded that it went straight to the bottom. All I had to do was step from the ships [sic] rail into the sea. It was a truly terrible experience, and I started to try to swim away from the ship, at the same time looking back in fascination at the fast sinking vessel. All at once there appeared on the foredeck, Karl Francis, one of our group, he was using the ships [sic] rail to pull himself hand over hand, up to the very peak, where he clasped his arms around the little jack mast. Men in the sea were yelling for Karl to jump, but he was frozen with shock, and then the ship quietly sank and that was the last of Karl. It was over in five minutes from the time the torpedo struck. A seaplane came out and started dropping depth charges into the water, but the submarine was miles away by that time, and when the

24

depth charges burst under water, it felt as though our legs were being blown off. The seaplane landed on the water, and I could see Tiny Anderson swimming and pulling Joe Schoen towards the seaplane, and time after time Tiny swam back into the debris and pulled a man over to the seaplane. When the pilot had the body of the plane filled with survivors he opened up his motors and taxied the few miles to the beach. He didn't come back. Slowly pushing my way through the debris, I came upon Syd Shostick, a small boy from New York who was supporting a two hundred pound Finn, Sankari, who was a none [sic] swimmer. Syd shouted to me to help him with his burden, and that took my thoughts away from myself, and I took one side of Sankari. Things were happening all around us, some men were singing the International as they sank under the water. There were some terribly mutilated bodies floating around. What kept them afloat I don't know. When the torpedo exploded it had blown the engines right up through the decks. We could see some fishing boats away over picking up men, but there was a big area of wreckage between us and them and we seemed to be drifting seaward. After awhile we came across some planking and gathered some together with some canvas we constructed a sort of small, loose raft, and were successful in hauling Sankari onto it. Syd said, as I had the life belt on I could try and swim through the wreckage and look for a fishing boat. Swimming through the wreckage I came up behind a man who was hanging onto the end of a wooden bed. As I approached him I said "how are you making out." He understood and said "not so good" and then as he turned his head he said, "Good Lord, are you here too." He was Ellis Fromberg from Vancouver, and was one of another group of Canadians whom our bunch didn't know were on the ship. Ellis was in bad shape, no life belt, a none [sic] swimmer, and had cramps in his arms. Luckily there was more lumber around and I gathered enough to keep us afloat. I had lost touch with Syd and Sankari but they made it. After two hours we saw the nose of a fishing boat pushing aside the wreckage. I waved and they saw us. There were three fishermen on the boat, they pulled the two of us on board, put us in a little hold in the centre of the boat, and when they couldn't find anyone else took us right on to the beach, at the little town of Malgrat . . . [7]

Joe Schoen, who became a lieutenant in the Mackenzie-Papineau Battalion, was another survivor of the *Ciudad de Barcelona*:

> After a week's stay in Marseilles we boarded a ship, the *City of Barcelona*, and sailed on a Saturday evening, headed for Barcelona.
>
> Next day, shortly before noon, about a mile from shore, we were torpedoed by an Italian submarine. The boat sank in less than five minutes. No one had a chance to launch a life boat. Tiny, the first mate, and I nearly got a boat up and over but before we could launch it, it was already half full of water. I waved goodbye to Tiny and jumped overboard and dog-paddled away from the boat. Tiny Anderson saved my life as well as others that could not swim or who were wounded.
>
> Some fellows swam to shore. Others were picked up by boats that came from shore. Being a Sunday, there were a lot of people on the beach. After Tiny reached me with a life buoy and I was getting my breath a government seaplane dropped a couple of depth charges on the submarine. We were very close to where the explosions took place. The waves were enormous so we certainly had a wild ride.
>
> I did not expect Tiny or anyone else to help me but he got more life buoys and debris. Altogether there were fifteen of us hanging onto something.
>
> The plane that dropped the charges landed and picked us up. Tiny and the two pilots and myself helped the rest of the fellows onto the wings, Tiny in the water and the pilots and me pulling them up.
>
> We lost one, the mate from the boat. He was unconscious and a very heavy man. Even Tiny was so tired that we just couldn't get him onto the wing.
>
> The plane taxied to shore where we were met by hospital staff, also trucks and ambulances to take us to the hospital.

Out of the 240 volunteers on board the ship, 60 were either killed by the explosion or drowned.

This was the town of Malgrat, about forty miles north of Barcelona.

Those of us who were able to travel were outfitted with new clothing. The President of Catalonia came to Malgrat to greet us and express his regrets for the traumatic welcome we experienced and for the loss of the lives of so many volunteers.

We left for Barcelona that evening by train. We had to travel after dark because of air attacks. When we arrived in Barcelona there was still some fighting going on between some of the Anarchists and the Loyalist Republican forces. We were confined to barracks because of this. We could hear the shooting pretty well all night.[8]

SPAIN: FIRST IMPRESSIONS

For those who climbed over the Pyrenees, the first major destination in Spain was the old Napoleonic fort at Figueras. Tired, hungry and thirsty men waited by the roadside for trucks to transport them south. The drive to the fort was uncomfortable, as the volunteers had to stand in the moving trucks, and tense their aching muscles to compensate for unexpected curves in the road. They were soon to discover that this ordeal would be repeated many times in the future.

The arrival at the fort was something of an event in itself, for few of the volunteers had ever seen a fort, except in pictures. Now they were to spend a few days in one capable of accommodating 100,000 men. Ironically it had held 30,000 imprisoned Asturian miners defeated by Franco in 1934, and now it had been converted to shelter those determined to defeat him.

The new arrivals were taken to the dining room and given their first meal of *garbanzos* (boiled chickpeas), cooked with onion and a bit of olive oil; many were never to get accustomed to the strange flavour of olive oil. They were also served a hot liquid that passed for coffee. There were always those who complained, but this was to be standard fare for the duration of their stay in Spain.

The men's names were listed, and they were assigned beds and issued blankets. They were told that they were free to explore, but not to leave the fort. The men marvelled at the thick stone wall of the fort, which could accommodate two cars driving side by side. They also stood in front of the cells in which the Asturian miners had been held in fetters not long before. There was water in the moat and there is a persistent story that one group of Canadians from British Columbia threw a cook into it. The walls of the fort were covered with names, slogans and drawings by earlier groups of volunteers, which gave the men a sense of belonging to a large movement.

The men slept on straw—those who were not too excited or too tired to sleep. In the night bombing could frequently be heard in the distance, the first real sound of war. For many it brought home the reality of the adventure upon which they had embarked, and aroused the first sense of danger, that ever present companion of the soldier.

TRAINING AT ALBACETE

By 1937 all of the volunteers were being taken from Figueras to the International Brigade training base at Albacete, a railroad division and manufacturing centre located between Madrid and Valencia.

There were a total of six international brigades; the first five being numbered from 11 to 15. For some reason the sixth international brigade was known as the 129th, and was composed of Yugoslavians, Czechoslovakians, Bulgarians, Albanians, and Rumanians. English-speaking volunteers were usually assigned to one of the three battalions of the 15th International Brigade—the British, the Lincoln-Washington, and eventually the Mackenzie-Papineau. Because recruiting was uneven and not always sufficient to maintain battalion strength, newly arrived Canadians might find themselves assigned to reinforce the Lincolns or the British Battalion. It was not unusual to find Americans with the Mackenzie-Papineau Battalion, even in positions of command.

Spanish was the language of communication, and learning to speak it was another common bond uniting the thousands of men from diverse nationalities. The Spanish poet, Rafael Alberti, caught the mood and spirit of the time and place:

> You have come from very far,
> But what is distance to your blood which sings without boundary or frontier?
> From one country and another, from
> the large one, from the small one
> . . . you have come to join us,
> because our roots are in the same dream,
> because it has
> nourished us all.

The training base at Albacete had opened on 20 October 1936 when the first volunteers were assembled to form the 11th International Brigade—the first brigade to take to the field later in the year in the defence of Madrid. By 1937 the number of volunteers had risen dramatically, and it was necessary to include the towns and villages surrounding Albacete in the training program. British, American and Canadian volunteers were located at Tarazona.

The trip from Figueras to Albacete was slow, giving the volunteers an opportunity to add to their initial impressions of Spain. On the one hand, all were overwhelmed by the beauty of the countryside; on the other hand, there was evidence everywhere of the bitter civil strife. For many Canadians it was the first time they had seen the devastation and ruin caused by war. They were soon to learn that under these conditions it was impossible to obtain the variety and quantity of food to which they had been accustomed in Canada, even during the severest days of the Depression.

Upon their arrival at Albacete, the volunteers were taken to the bull ring. There, they were outfitted with whatever uniforms were available and separated into groups to reinforce undermanned units. Frequently the clothes were ill-fitting, if not shoddy, while the assignment of units often made little sense to the volunteers. Lionel Edwards was one of the many Canadians who was trained at Albacete:

> A beautiful sunny morning in the bull ring where we had arrived the day before. We formed lines to be interrogated as to our qualifications. In front of me was an American named Joe who, when asked as to what experience he had, answered "I ran speed boats."
>
> "Excellent," replied his interrogator. "Obviously you will fit into the infantry." And thus American Joe was immediately on his way to the battlefield of Jarama.
>
> When asked about my experience in Canada I replied that I had only some knowledge of accountancy.
>
> "Very well, you will be assigned to headquarters." It was a strange transfer, but orders are orders, and I thus checked into the headquarters of the International Brigades. My duties were to censor mail and the official language was strictly and only French.
>
> My office comrades were the strangest assortment of odd people gathered anywhere.
>
> Comrade Einsel was an Esthonian who, as a former opera star, regaled us with constant arias. He had also been a chess champion of Berlin in 1922.
>
> Salem was an Egyptian who had been a merchant in the South Seas and now, of all things, was aiding the re-education of fascist prisoners now in our hands.
>
> A jovial little German named Hans had run a bar in Hamburg. But, it being a red rendezvous, made it a target for the Nazis and Hans got out just in time. He then took up bootlegging in Cuba but repented of this type of career and then joined the International Brigades.
>
> The most amazing character was Jacosta, a Corsican who fluently spoke seven languages and imperfectly some others, besides being able to read Sanskrit. His command of French dialects was such that intelligence used him for interviewing prospective volunteers.

In his spare time he was re-writing a simplified French grammar.

He helped me with my Spanish and this meant rising very early in the morning and after breakfast on those delightful little *churros* we headed for the early morning market looking for luscious blood oranges of which I was told there are twenty-two varieties in the world.

Jacosta and his friends had carried out a most unusual act. They had hijacked a freighter out of Rio [de] Janeiro, Brazil, and then sailed it to Republican Spain as a donation. The ship was loaded with ammunition. I believe that Jacosta was the most extraordinary man I ever met.

I must not forget professor Bateman, a Belgian, who took pity on me and at times spoke English.

In my collection of memorabilia I actually had in my possession the original written order issued by the Military Council of Madrid, naming Emil Kleber, a naturalized Canadian of Austro-Hungarian origin, to the command of all the International Brigades in the siege of Madrid. This with some few precious dollar bills vanished completely a year-and-a-half later when a German shell exploded beside me and only my pack and its contents saved my life.

An unusual incident occurred at this time. A small counter-uprising took place in a village near Albacete. It was quickly put down with no loss of life and the ringleader, a village priest was arrested. His abode was searched and, amid a pile of rubbish and other debris, an old but dirty painting was discovered. It was brought back to the headquarters and an art expert examined it minutely. "Very dirty," he said.

Apparently a masterpiece of art is usually verified by knowledge of the artist's brush strokes. Believe it or not, it was found to be an El Greco and was turned over to the Prado, the treasures of which were at that time under the directorship of the great artist, Pablo Picasso.

After a few weeks I requested permission to go to the front and was then assigned to an infantry unit.[9]

And so it was for most Canadian volunteers. Their short training period was followed by assignment and reassignment; sometimes it made sense and sometimes not. The men barely had time to get their bearings in the unfamiliar surroundings before they were shipped to the front.

NOTES
1. Lee Burke, written account to the author, no date.
2. Jimmy Higgins in Ed Cecil-Smith, "The Mac Paps," an unpublished draft history (circa 1939-40), NAC, M6 E-173 Vol. 1.
3. Bill Brennan in ibid.
4. Tom McDonald in ibid.'
5. Tom Bailey of Moose Jaw, Saskatchewan. This excerpt was taken from a handwritten account dated 8 June 1938 and collected by Maurice Constant, who was gathering historical materials concerning the Spanish civil war.
6. This account was adapted from an interview with the author at Okotoks, Alberta, in 1982.
7. Liversedge, "Memoir of the Spanish Civil War."
8. Joe Schoen of Winnipeg, written account. When he speaks of the shooting in Barcelona, Schoen is referring to an attempted *putsch* by the *Partido Obrero Unificación Marxista* (POUM) along with the Federación Anarquista Ibérica (Anarchists) on 3 May 1937. At the beginning of the war the Anarchists were not part of the popular front but wanted to form a revolutionary committee with the Unión General de Trabajadores (UGT). They later changed their position. The fighting was over in Barcelona by mid-May—the time about which Schoen is writing—but there may still have been some shooting.
9. Lionel Edwards, written account, 28 November 1984.

Three

The Defence of Madrid

By August 1936 the victory of the republican forces seemed assured. The Spanish people, poorly armed and almost alone, had fought the rebellious generals to a standstill. However, the reverses suffered by Franco led to ever-greater intervention by his allies, Hitler and Mussolini. By the late autumn of 1936, with German and Italian support, Franco's forces held the south of Spain. They concluded that the capture of Madrid would ensure a quick victory over the republic and would bring rapid recognition to the fascist cause by the Western democracies.

The battle for Madrid became the first major engagement in which foreign volunteers and the International Brigades played an important, and in this case a decisive, role. The battle began in late summer of 1936 and ended with the defeat of the fascist forces at Guadalajara in March 1937. It included the initial defence of the capital from a frontal attack, followed by major engagements at the Jarama valley to the east and a republican diversionary offensive at Brunete to the west.

THE ASSAULT ON MADRID

Franco's initial assault on Madrid was a success and by 4 November the Madrid Getafe airport was in fascist hands. General Varela announced that Madrid would fall within the week; not to be outdone, General Mola publicly declared that the capital would fall on 7 November—the date of the Russian revolution. Burgos radio began a program called "The Last Hours of Madrid" and announced the order of a victory parade, the names of the military bands which would play, and the areas within Madrid which had been assigned to the ʼalange to rout out and arrest dissidents. General Mola ɔoasted that on the appointed day he would drink his afternoon coffee outside the Café Molinero on the Gran Via. Madrid was isolated, starving, and short of arms and medical supplies. Collapse appeared inevitable, yet incredibly Madrid did not fall.

On the morning of 8 November Fernando Valera, a young republican deputy, delivered a resounding call to arms over Madrid's radio:

> Citizens of Madrid! Each of you has here on this soil something that is ash; something that is soul. It cannot be! It shall not be that impious intruders trample the sacred tombs of our dead! The mercenaries shall not enter as heralds of dishonour into our homes! It cannot be! It shall not be that the sombre birds of intolerance beat their black wings over the human conscience. It cannot be! It shall not be that the Fatherland torn, broken, entreat like a beggar before the throne of the tyrant. It cannot be! It shall not be! Today we fight. Tomorrow we conquer. And on the pages of history, Man will engrave an immense heart. This is Madrid! It fought for Spain, for Humanity, for Justice, and with the mantle of its blood sheltered all the men of the world. Madrid! Madrid![1]

Madrid workers, mobilized by their unions, moved toward the front dressed in leather jackets and peaked caps. Many were unarmed and went into battle knowing that they would have to acquire their weapons from those who had been killed.

As desperate as this hastily assembled citizens' army was, it was not without hope. On the morning of 6 November there was a hint of things to come. German Junker bombers appeared as usual, accompanied by a squadron of Italian Fiat fighter planes, committed to bombing and strafing the defenceless civilian population. The air-raid sirens were still sounding over the city when suddenly overhead appeared a group of planes bearing the red emblem of the Republican Air Force. Hidalgo de Cisneros, commander of the air force, captured the moment in his memoirs:

> What the people of Madrid saw that wonderful morning can never be forgotten . . . Forgetting the danger, they poured out from their shelters into the streets. These people had lived in fear, suffering day after day, unable to

defend themselves and their city from the enemy's heavy bombings. Now they were watching with indescribable delight the first air battle over their previously defenceless city. The people of Madrid watched as the Republican pilots, in a show of acrobatics and manoeuvres, shot down nine enemy planes, one after another, while the others fled in disgrace, pursued by the Republican fighters.

With tears in their eyes the residents of Madrid cheered the Republican aviation. I was particularly struck by the fact that there was even greater enthusiasm and delight in the cheers for the Soviet planes. I was sure that we had kept the arrival of Soviet planes a secret.[2]

This challenge to fascist air supremacy was swiftly followed by new developments on the ground. Early on Sunday, 8 November, the citizens of Madrid awoke to the sound of marching and singing. However, it was not fascists who had broken through the city's defences, as many feared; rather the noise announced the arrival of the first of the international volunteers, singing "The International."

There were the three battalions which formed the 11th International Brigade: the Edgar André, which was German; the Commune de Paris, which was French and Belgian; and the Dombrowski, which was made up of Polish volunteers. They were accompanied through the streets of Madrid and down the Gran Via by two squadrons of French cavalry.

By the evening of the same day, the Dombrowski Battalion was in line at Villaverde, the machine gun company of the Edgar André was in position in the Hall of Philosophy and Letters in University City, and the Commune de Paris Battalion was in the Casa de Campo, where the fiercest fighting raged. Here Franco's African army repeatedly charged a line which would not budge, with every move to outflank the republican forces being successfully countered. The arrival of the 11th International Brigade shattered the fascist attack on Madrid, denying Franco the quick victory he so desperately wanted.

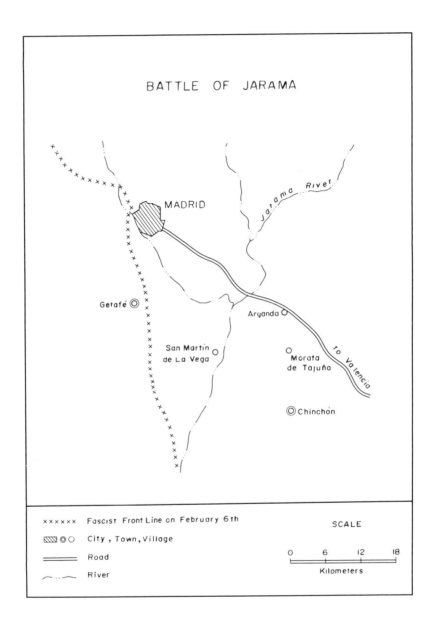

BATTLE OF JARAMA

MADRID

Jarama River

Getafé ◎

Aryanda ○

San Martin ○
de La Vega

Morata ○
de Tajuña

to Valencia

◎ Chinchón

×××××× Fascist Front Line on February 6th

▨◎○ City, Town, Village

══ Road

⌇ River

SCALE

0   6   12   18

Kilometers

36

The successful defence of Madrid caused both sides to review their situation. War Minister Largo Caballero, prompted by the voluntary spirit so evident in the defence of the capital, created a new republican army based on the civilian population. A central, unified command structure was agreed upon, and the practice of attaching political commissars to regular army units was introduced.

For Franco, the defeat at Madrid had been a devastating blow. His well-armed, professional army had been forced back by what, to him, was a civilian rabble. For the sake of his personal prestige and that of his cause, a successful counterattack was imperative. He therefore made plans to outflank the capital by attacking in the Jarama River valley to the east, cutting the Madrid-Valencia highway, and isolating the capital from the Mediterranean coast. Here the Canadians, now arriving in Spain in increasing numbers, would receive their baptism of fire as part of the 15th International Brigade.

The main fascist attack began on 6 February 1937 at La Marañosa, where the two republican battalions fought until they were exterminated. The rebel forces advanced to Gozquez de Arriba, but the republican lines held, preventing a further advance on San Martin de la Vega. The fascist push had placed the main road between Valencia and Madrid within artillery range, and they prepared for their next attack.

By 8 February it was evident to the republican command that the main blow would be directed at them across the Jarama River, so General Miaja sent reserves to reinforce the regular republican army under General Pozas. The 11th and 12th International Brigades were ordered to the front, while the newly formed 15th International Brigade was ordered to prepare for action. Facing them was General Varela's fascist army, composed of combat veterans from the Africa corps, antitank artillery units, cavalry squadrons, artillery, and two heavy machine gun battalions made up exclusively of German soldiers disguised as members of the Spanish Foreign Legion.

Captain Tom Wintringham, commander of the British at Jarama, dubbed them "the blond Moors."

Troop movements began on the night of 10 February, with the first attack aimed at seizing the bridge at La Marañosa. Moorish troops crept through the woods and surprised the André Marty Battalion, cutting the throats of seventy men sleeping in the trenches flanking the bridge. The bridge had been so poorly mined that when the charges were set off by remote control, they merely lifted it into the air; when it settled it acted like a pontoon. By 10:00 A.M. the Moorish cavalry had overrun the French internationals and established a bridgehead across the Jarama.

The fascist advance was slowed by the remainder of the André Marty Battalion and the Dombrowski and Garibaldi Battalions. General Lukacs, commander of the 12th International Brigade, regrouped the Poles and took over the gap left by the French. The Poles were finally reinforced by Spanish *carabineros* and Soviet tanks, and the line before Arganda held. By 12 February, heavy casualties had forced a halt to the fascist attack.

General Varela then shifted the direction of his attack, on 13 February, towards Morata de Tajuña, which was defended by Lister's 11th Brigade and Gal's 15th Brigade. The newly formed 15th Brigade consisted of 600 British, 800 French and Belgians, 800 men of various Balkan nationalities, and 550 Americans; randomly mixed with the British and Americans were Canadians, Irish, Finns and Cubans. The international soldiers were deployed in the hills in front of Morata, with the British taking up and defending for seven hours a position dubbed "suicide hill." To the south of the British there was a dangerously vulnerable, unmanned, three-mile gap in the republican lines. Firing and skirmishing continued throughout the night.

On 14 February began what became known in Spanish as *El dia Triste del Jarama* (the day of the sorrow of Jarama). Lister's brigades were forced back by the fascists and the 180 men of the British Battalion were forced to retreat towards

Morata. The next day the Jarama sector was placed under the direct command of the Madrid military *junta*, with General Miaja and Colonel Rojo going to the battlefield to direct operations in person.

The republican forces, regrouped and reorganized, began counterattacking, and threatened the entire fascist front; only a massive intervention by the Condor Legion bombers prevented a fascist collapse. The battle finally settled into fixed lines in the Jarama valley. This ended the republican command's efforts to drive the fascists back across the Jarama River. Fifty thousand men had died in three weeks, and now trenches and fortifications were turning the sector into a fortified belt defending Madrid.

Frank Ryan describes how the republican forces turned defeat into victory:

> On the road from Chinchón to Madrid, the road along which we had marched to the attack three days before, were now scattered all who survived—a few hundred Britons, Irish and Spaniards. Dispirited by heavy casualties, by defeat, by lack of food, worn out by three days of grueling fighting, our men appeared to have reached the end of their resistance . . . And now, there was no line, nothing between the Madrid road and the fascists but disorganized groups of weary, war-wracked men . . . As I walked along the road to see how many men we had, I found myself deciding that we should go back up the line of the road to San Martín de la Vega and take the Moors on their left flank.
>
> I found my eyes straying always to the hills we had vacated. I hitched a rifle to my shoulder. They stumbled to their feet. No time for barrack-square drill. One line of four. "Fall in behind us." A few were still on the grass beside the road, adjusting helmets and rifles. "Hurry up!" came the cry from the ranks. Up the road towards the Cook House I saw Jock Cunningham assembling another crowd. We hurried up, joined forces. Together we two marched at the head . . . The crowd behind us was marching silently. The thoughts in their minds could not be inspiring ones. I remembered a trick of the old days

when we were holding banned demonstrations. I jerked my head back: "Sing up ye sons o' guns."

Quaveringly at first, then more lustily, then in one resounding chant the song rose from the ranks. Bent backs straightened; tired legs thumped sturdily; what had been a routed rabble marched to battle again as proudly as they had done three days before. And the valley resounded to their singing:

> "Then comrades, come rally,
> And the last fight let us face;
> The International
> Unites the human race"

On we marched, back up the road, nearer and nearer to the front. Stragglers still in retreat down the slopes stopped in amazement, changed direction and ran to join us; men lying exhausted on the roadside jumped up, cheered, and joined the ranks. I looked back. Beneath the forest of upraised fists, what a strange band! Unshaven, unkempt; blood-stained, grimy. But, full of fight again, *and marching on the road back.*

Beside the road stood our Brigade Commander, General Gal. We had quitted; he had stood his ground. Was it that, or fear of his reprimands, that made us give three cheers for him? Briefly, tersely, he spoke to us.

We had one and a half hours of daylight in which to recapture our lost positions. "That gap on the right?" A Spanish Battalion was coming with us to occupy it. Again the "International" arose. It was being sung in French, too. Our column had swelled in size during the halt; a group of Franco-Belge had joined us. We passed the Spanish Battalion. They had caught the infection; they were singing too as they deployed to the right . . .

As the olive trees loom in sight, we deploy to the left. At last, we are on the ridge, the ridge which we must never again desert. For, while we hold that ridge, the Madrid-Valencia road is free.

Bullets whistle through the air, or smack into the ground, or find a human target. Cries. Shouts. But, always the

40

louder, interminable singing. Flat on the ground, we fire into the groves. There are no sections, no companies even. But the individuals jump ahead, and set an example that is readily followed—too readily, for sometimes they block our fire. In the thick of the battle we organize ourselves with a certain amount of success into sections.

The Spanish problem is quickly solved: "Manuel! What's the Spanish for Forward?" "*Adelante!*" yells Manuel, and waves the Spanish lads on. "*Abajo!*" And down they flop to give covering fire. A burly French lieutenant runs over to ask me for grenades . . . shouting "*En Avant!*" Ahead of us are little cones of blue-red flame. Now we know where the Moorish and German machine-gunners are. Oh, for a few grenades! As we hug the earth we call to one another to direct group-fire on those cones.

Flat on our bellies we push forward. Inch by inch. Darkness falls like a blanket . . . Advancing! All the time advancing. As I crawl forward, I suddenly realise with savage joy, that it is *we* who are advancing, *they* who are being pushed back. And then, in actual disappointment: "The bastards won't wait for our bayonets!"

We are in the olive groves. Firing ceases. We are on our feet, feeling for one another in the inky blackness. I stumble against a soft bundle. I bend down. His spiked bayonet scrapes my hand. He is one of ours. His face is cold. He has been dead for hours. So we are back where we were at midday.

. . . the men who had been broken and routed a few hours before settled down for the night on the ground they had reconquered. They had dashed fascist hopes, smashed fascist plans. Thenceforward, for more than four months, they were to fight, and many of them to die, in these olive groves. But never again were the fascists to rout them. They were to hold that line, and save Madrid; fighting in the dauntless spirit of the great rally of that afternoon, fighting too, in the spirit of those reckless roars of laughter that night in the Wood of Death."[3]

The Lincoln Battalion, commanded by Robert Merriman, and including Cubans, Mexicans, Puerto Ricans, American Indians, Black Americans, and a Canadian section, had reached the Jarama front on 15 February and dug in behind the British. Parts of the 11th and 15th Brigades, commanded by General Gal, took part in an attack against Pingarrón. The American battalion tried to advance through a triple line of machine-gun fire but suffered 50 percent casualties—two hundred men—and the attack ended.

On 16 February the Lincoln Battalion marched from Villanueva de la Jara to Albacete, was outfitted, and was in Morata by evening. On the following day, the Lincolns moved up to a hill which overlooked the lines of both sides. The troops dug in and remained there under heavy fire for five days.

The republican army was preparing an attack and the Lincolns were consequently moved closer to the front lines on 21 February. Two days later they went into action. On 27 February they attacked the heavily fortified hills stretching before the Jarama valley on the east side of the river. They advanced for about six hundred metres and dug in, but were unable to hold the position and withdrew to trenches previously held by the Dimitrov. Here they received reinforcements, some of whom had been sent to the front with no preliminary training. It was in this engagement that Elias Aviezer from Montréal was killed. He was one of the first Canadian casualties.

By March 1937 it became clear that neither side was any longer strong enough to mount an effective offensive. Both sides settled into an uneasy stalemate.

Alex McDade of Glasgow wrote "There's a Valley in Spain" (sung to the tune of "Red River Valley") to commemorate the battles around Jarama. Several renditions of the song were popular with the 15th Brigade, including the following:

There's a valley in Spain called Jarama,
That's a place that we all know so well,
For 'tis there that we wasted our manhood,
And most of our old age as well.[4]

McDade was killed in the battle of Brunete.

On 5 April a company of the Lincoln Battalion fought to support the Garibaldi Battalion, which was attempting to push back a fascist salient. A French-Canadian, Roger Bilodeau of Montréal, received a special commendation for bravery in this action:

> It was during the battle on April 5th that a young French-Canadian stood up to the fighting traditions of his people. In the attack that day the Battalion found itself in a position where the men could advance no further against the fascist machine guns. Most of them were not able to return till dark. Roger Bilodeau of Montreal, Section leader . . . went over the top with the Battalion, and following orders dug in. It so happened that he was close to the trenches when the attack was halted and decided he would take a chance on making his way back. This he succeeded in doing without getting hit. On his arrival in the trench he heard that there was a comrade seriously wounded in No-Mans land taking cover behind one of the many olive trees in that area. It was still light and this area was in full view of the fascist machine gunners. During the attack one of our tanks had become wedged in a sector of the trench and couldn't move . . . [It was] in flames, lighting up the area through which one would have to make his way in order to reach this comrade. Bilodeau and an American comrade considered that if they waited until dark they would be silhouetted against the light of the fire. The light of day and the light of the flames were equal risks; in the field was a bleeding comrade whose chance of life depended on immediate rescue. They dashed out and brought the comrade to safety. Bilodeau was cited for this act of bravery; he was presented with a watch by the brigade Commander and given ten days leave.[5]

The stalemate on the Jarama front persuaded the republican command to try to wrest control of the western approaches to Madrid from the fascists, who had been installed since November 1936 in the hills and ridges known as the Heights of Romanillos. The republican strategy was twofold. First, it was to force Franco to divert troops from the north where the Asturian forces faced almost certain defeat. Second, the republicans hoped to cut off the fascist salient which reached into the suburbs of Madrid, thus reducing the threat to the city. The 15th and 13th (Dombrowski) International Brigades and the 18th Corps were deployed in this campaign, which became known as the Brunete offensive.

On 5 July the 15th Brigade arrived at Valdemorillo on the Madrid-Corunna highway. Ten divisions were deployed in the olive groves near the town and at midnight the entire army began to move south. At dawn on 6 July 1937 the battalions were deployed on the ridges west and north of the battlefield.

Initially the 15th Brigade was ordered to bypass the village of Villanueva de la Cañada, which was to be taken by Spanish republican troops, and seize the heights beyond which overlooked the Romanillos. The Spanish troops were thrown back, however, and the 15th Brigade moved to their support. Villanueva de la Cañada was vigorously defended, and the 15th Brigade at first failed to make any headway. The British Battalion was ordered to circle the village and cut the Brunete road, and then move towards the church. Jack Roberts describes a scene in which the fascists tried to escape by using the villagers as cover:

> It was dusk of the first day when our Battalion had advanced to within about three hundred metres of Villanueva de la Cañada. Some were lying down in the ditch beside the road; five of us were taking cover behind the dung-heap on the right. Suddenly someone shouted: "Don't fire, there are children coming from the village."

> We looked down the road and saw about twenty-five people, men, women and children. In front was a little girl

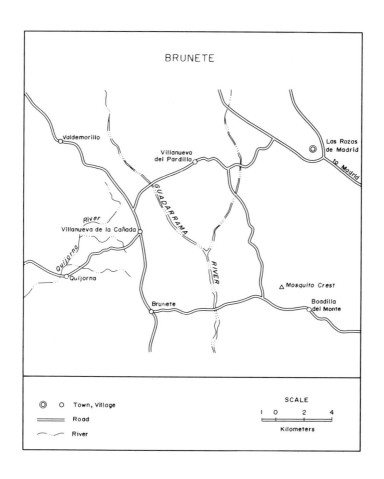

BRUNETE

Valdemorillo

Villanueva
del Pardillo

Las Rozas
de Madrid

To Madrid

GUADARRAMA

River
Villanueva de la Cañada

Quijorna

Quijorna

RIVER

△ Mosquito Crest

Brunete

Boadilla
del Monte

SCALE

◎ ○ Town, Village

Road

River

1 0 2 4

Kilometers

45

of about ten years of age. Behind her came an elderly woman, a boy of fourteen or so, a few old men. The remainder were young men. As they approached they shouted: "*Camaradas! Camaradas!*"

Believing them to be refugees, we answered them and called them forward. Some of us were now standing, some walking to meet and welcome them.

Pat Murphy of Cardiff, was the nearest to them. He approached them, telling them to lay down their arms if they had any. For answer a revolver blazed. Then the fascists who had been driving this group of old men, women and children as cover for them, started throwing hand-grenades in our midst. For a few minutes pandemonium reigned . . .

The crash of grenades, the barking of guns, and the shrieks of the women and children are still in my ears. But in ten minutes it was all over; the last of the fascists lay dead. Then, forward we charged and stormed the village.[6]

Bill Brennan recorded the engagement in more detail:

On the night of July 5th, the Lincoln, Washington and English Battalions were in a reserve position on the Brunete front, approximately ten kilometers behind the lines from where they were to start the attack on the morrow. Their position in reserve was along the banks of the Aulencia River . . . The Battalions took [their] place and moved up with the rest of the troops, to a point from where they were to . . . attack. The next morning, July 6th, they were informed that the signal for the attack would be the firing of artillery. The Spanish and International Brigades and the cavalry advanced in perfect military order. Our troops knew that unless the enemy were very well fortified and had sufficient troops, victory was assured.

The higher command had planned to take Villa Nueva de la Cañada by 11 o'clock that morning, and while the town was in a state of siege, to . . . attack the next line of resistance. As the Battalions approached Villa Nueva de la Cañada, they were met with withering rifle and machine gun fire as well as a deadly barrage of artillery . . .

46

A great number of our tanks had completely surrounded the town shelling the enemy positions. They were met with a stiff enemy resistance, which resulted in the wrecking of two [tanks] and setting them afire . . .

That morning the Lincoln had been brought up into position. Company One commanded by Bill [Holliwell] took a position on the left hand side of the main highway running into Villa Nueva de la Cañada. The position proved to be unsatisfactory, and they moved again, across to the right hand side of the highway waiting there for further orders. The men were tired out after the long march from the Aulencia River and the twenty kilometer march from Torrelodones the day before. During the march from Aulencia many of the men were forced to drop their packs and blankets due to the extreme heat. On arriving at the ridge from where the attack began, the men were out of water. Paddy O'Neil leader of the Canadian section sent one of the men to collect the canteens and go for water for the section. The nearest water supply was at least a half a kilometer away, and the section went into action before the water carrier returned.

The terrain over which the section had to attack afforded very little cover. John Oscar Bloom the 24 year old red-headed boy from Edmonton, who dashed over the ridge into the attack shouting "Come on Mackenzie Papineau" was killed instantly. Paddy O'Neil was wounded but did not want to leave the section, so he dashed forward again receiving another wound which was fatal. There were other casualties, Scotty Kane, Bryce Coleman, Joe Armitage, all killed in the advance. The advance of the section was halted. They had been lying under the hot July, sun in the open field without water all day. The water carrier had been unable to reach them. They stayed in their positions until dark, and then the wounded were brought in. By that time troops had taken Villa Nueva de la Cañada and Brunete.

They assembled next morning and checked over their numbers. The casualties were five dead and six wounded in the section. Tom Traynor took over command, and they joined the company in the Battalion which marched around the outskirts of [Villanueva de la Cañada] towards Brunete . . .

The story of the heroic battle of our troops on the 6th would be incomplete without mentioning the excellent work of the Lincoln Battalion Doctor. Doc Aaron Magid, the 35 year old Winnipeger, who left his profession back in Canada and came to Spain, certainly won the admiration of the members of the Battalion that day.[7]

Lee Burke, another Canadian fighting in this engagement, described his experiences:

We bid farewell to Albares for what was to be a journey around the north west side of Madrid near El Escorial, with stopovers. This was when Miller, Cowan and Burke lost their place in the infantry. This is where the Canadians lost two of the forty at least. The three of us were put in the Lincoln machine-gun company (called Tom Mooney). We were the crew for Ray Steele and Ruby Ryant's machine gun, and they were teaching us about machine guns on every stop over.

Our machine guns were on a crest before the town of Villa Nueva de la Cañada giving cover fire to our infantry. I remember I saw this wounded vet trying to make his way back. I recognized him. It was Moffat, one of the 40 from Calgary. I ran toward him to give him a hand when Ray Steele hollered at me to get the hell back. I ran back and Ray told me "They could have killed both of you." I guess that was Lesson One.

When we did take the town it was with mixed feelings. We learned the cost to do so. The 40 or less Canadians took a beating. Paddy O'Neil was killed. John Oscar Bloom was also killed beside *El Gran Hombre* (the big man) Bryce Coleman, Scotty Kane of Toronto and Joe Armitage.[8]

THE BATTLE AT MOSQUITO CREST

After the battle for Villanueva de la Cañada was over the brigade advanced towards the Guadarrama River, crossing it at several points on the morning of 8 July. The men then moved towards the Mosquito Crest, the dominant point on the

Heights of Romanillos. The fascist troops offered little resistance, abandoning food and materiel as they retreated to the Heights. However, they commanded enough artillery and aircraft to keep the republican forces almost immobile.

Caught and killed in the crossfire at Mosquito Crest were two Canadians, John Deck and Nicholas Harbocin. Bill Brennan described the heavy fighting which occurred:

> They moved out on the road leading to the Guadarrama River. The Battalion commander, Oliver Law, called for volunteers for a scouting party to be led by the chief of scouts, John Deck. For a few minutes nobody responded to the call. They had been through a nerve-wracking experience the day before and they knew the work of the scouting party.
>
> Then Nicholas "Nick" Harbocin and another Canadian stepped out, and a few more followed. The scouting party received their instructions and set off. The main body moved along the road following the instructions of the head scout. They marched for an hour, passing a cavalry unit stationed on the side of the road, and made their way into an olive grove overlooking the positions of the enemy.
>
> They did not know the exact location of the enemy. It was necessary to send two men up to investigate a white house situated on a high point overlooking a deep dry river valley. This house might have been in the hands of the enemy. On the other hand, it was suspected of being the brigade headquarters.
>
> The enemy position was finally located and the battalion was brought to a position in front of the Guadarrama River under cover of a thick growth of bushes. There they crouched with rifles in hand ready to make the charge. The Canadian section was to lead off the infantry.
>
> The tanks rolled up and the signal came. They charged up alongside the tanks with the most blood-curdling yells, across the river and up the hill towards the fascist trenches, John Deck in the lead. They were to be the second line of attack, but most of them found themselves in the first line.

After the fascist trenches had been occupied by our troops, John Deck, Nick Harbocin and three other Canadians had advanced too far ahead and lost their battalion. They decided to try and make their way back to their unit on the basis of information obtained from one of the Spanish soldiers.

They began to cut through a valley which was actually No-Man's-Land in front of Mosquito Ridge. They made slow progress through this valley under the cover of willows alongside a small creek. They then headed up the side of a hill which they thought was giving them cover from the enemy.

But they were completely exposed to the enemy who waited 'till they were half way up the hill and then opened up with machine gun fire. They made a dash for the sparse cover that the hillside provided and, under the guidance of John Deck, they were able to gather their strength for a dash up the hillside and over to safety.

Deck ordered one man at a time to take short spurts up the hill to avoid being hit by enemy fire. This method helped to save the lives of the men.

John Deck was the last man to make his way over the ridge to the battalion.

On the morning of the 7th the Washington Battalion was told to march until they reached a bridge, to cross it, and continue marching until they contacted the enemy.

The next morning the tanks went into action crossing the Guadarrama River and, because of the enemy's weak position, they were easily routed. The Battalion waded across the river and gave chase. Although the fascists had no time to entrench themselves along the river, they had strongly entrenched positions on Mosquito Ridge from which they were able to hold off the advance.

On July 9th there was a concentrated attack made on Mosquito Ridge. The attack failed . . .

The Lincoln and Washington Battalions held the further-most point of the salient that had been driven into the fascist lines, the most difficult and demoralizing position to hold for they were constantly under fire from three directions . . .

After our troops had taken the fascist trenches above the Guadarrama River they continued advancing . . . The battalion command decided to take to the road for they could make better time. They marched along this road in route formation for about two kilometres and walked right into fascist advance positions . . . The battalion had to take cover and occupied a position on the side of the road facing Mosquito Ridge . . .

Fortification work began immediately. The Dimitrov Battalion on the left began to drive the fascists out of the olive grove and established their own positions . . .

The next day, July 9th [sic], the Lincoln was ordered to prepare to attack and took their positions on the brow of the ridge. The battalion commander, Oliver Law, ordered the battalion forward. Over the ridge they went, down the side of the hill and alongside of the olive grove that had been the main position of the enemy the day before.

John Deck was dashing forward at the head of the men, waving his rifle, when he was hit and instantly killed.

The battalion commander was killed and a few of the officers were wounded.

The Canadian section again got far in advance of the rest of the battalion to a small olive grove in a little valley facing the enemy lines. They lost contact with the battalion and were under heavy enemy fire. The light machine gun and riflemen ran out of ammunition.

Tom Traynor, still in command of the section, undertook the hazardous task of making his way back and contacting the battalion.

This he succeeded in doing. He was ordered to take over command of Company One as the commander had been wounded, and he was instructed to see that every man retreated to his former position.

Traynor had to make his way forward to the isolated section to give them orders to retreat. In retreating the section had to leave its position one man at a time up to the olive grove held by the fascists the day before. The spaces between the rows of trees were enfiladed with enemy machine gun fire and it was in this grove that the brave young lad from Windsor, Nick Harbocin, was killed.

Bob Traynor was wounded, calmly reported to the commander, and made his own way back to the first aid post.

The Canadian section was put under the charge of Bill Brennan who had arrived at the Brunete front from Officers Training School on July 6th. The section was reinforced with five Canadians from the OTS who had succeeded in locating the battalion after the attack on the 9th.[9]

The fighting around Mosquito Ridge had been intense, and casualties high, forcing a reorganization of the American battalions:

July 13 found us back in reserve behind the river under continuous enemy shelling. Next day we were joined by the George Washington Battalion and we were combined under the new name of Lincoln-Washington Battalion.

Heavy casualties had taken their toll. Our battalions of 300 and 500 men respectively now comprised a total of about 350 men in a single battalion.[10]

VILLANUEVA DEL PARDILLO

On the evening of 16 July the Lincoln-Washington Battalion moved towards Villanueva del Pardillo, where a fascist breakthrough was expected, arriving on the morning of 17 July. The men took up reserve positions half a kilometre behind the lines, where they were shelled and bombarded by enemy planes; one man was killed and five wounded. The battalion was then ordered to the front, and took up its position in the front lines under heavy artillery fire. Bill Brennan was there:

A group of the enemy had managed to advance to within 40 metres of the trenches and were waving white handkerchiefs with their arms in the air. It was the opinion of the Spanish that these men wanted to surrender and they sent out their commander to talk with the leader of the enemy group, who was Moorish.

They had advanced a small distance without their arms, having left them behind in a small gulley in No-Man's-Land. It was later discovered that in the gulley they had placed a number of their troops with machine guns.

The leader of the Moors then asked the captain to tell his men to give up, that conditions were wonderful on their side. It became clear that they were working another of their many ruses. The captain gave a negative reply. They were permitted to retire and pick up their rifles while our troops withheld their fire.

The fascists now realized that their ruse had petered out and they opened fire from their hidden guns in the gulley. That group of Moors was wiped out as our machine gunners had the range the whole time they were attempting to talk the men into surrendering.[11]

On 19 July the battalion was ordered back to its old camp along the Guadarrama River, the Canadian section scouting the way back from Villanueva del Pardillo. No sooner had they arrived the next morning than the men were ordered to the front, where fascist forces had reached the river. The battalion moved out and pushed the enemy back about one kilometre from the river. Jenei Gabor, one of three Hungarian-Canadians, was killed here by machine gun fire on 22 July. On 24 July the battalion was ordered to occupy a position which had been deserted by a company of the 16th Brigade.

COUNTEROFFENSIVE AT BRUNETE

Franco's forces now began a counteroffensive in the Brunete sector, with small groups of Moors attacking positions held by the Canadian section of the Lincoln-Washington Battalion. The Canadians, thinly spread over an area previously held by an entire company, quickly ran out of ammunition and were ordered to retreat, narrowly avoiding encirclement.

In order to avoid being cut off several brigades, including the 15th, were ordered to retire on 24 July. That morning the Third Company, commanded by Alick Miller, was ordered to take up a position in a large olive grove which was under artillery fire. Bill Brennan, the section leader, was wounded there and was replaced by Charlie Parker. The position was a death trap and the battalion was ordered out at 3:00 A.M. on 26 July.

The fighting at Brunete marked a turning point in the war, for it relieved the pressure on Madrid, and prolonged the life of the Spanish republic. A contemporary account analyzed the importance of the battle:

> When on July 6th the Republican army swept down the road to Villanueva de la Cañada and Brunete, the initiative on the vital Madrid front passed into the hands of the government forces.
>
> The Brunete offensive was an important step in the evolution of the Republican army. At Madrid and Jarama, in previous months, it had been on the defensive. At Guadalajara it achieved a victorious counter-offensive. At Brunete, taking the initiative, it passed over to the offensive. At Madrid it was fighting with Battalions, at Jarama with Brigades, at Guadalajara with Divisions, at Brunete with Army Corps . . .
>
> On July 18th the fascists launched a counter-offensive. After six days of unceasing effort, they achieved their only success: on the evening of July 24th, they recaptured the town of Brunete.
>
> For some hours the position of the whole Republican line was endangered, as the fall of Brunete cut the Republican line of communication with their base. But, in a brilliant counter-charge, the Republican troops took the town—or rather its ruins—and held it long enough to allow the lines to be rectified. For three more days the fascists pressed hard, but the Republican troops held fast to their gains.

The fascist counter-attack finally petered out on July 26th.[12]

Although the battle which raged around Brunete was a stalemate in military terms, it was an imporant moral victory for the beleaguered Spanish government. Written off in the early days of the generals' revolt, the government and people of Spain had resisted desperately, and at Brunete fought to a standstill a professional army that had expected to sweep all opposition from its path. Encouraged, the republican side fought on, and had it not been for the massive intervention of Germany and Italy on the fascist side, the Spanish conflict would probably have had a different outcome.

FORMATION OF THE "MAC-PAP"

The International Brigades were called out after the engagement at Brunete and sent to rest in the villages in which they had previously been stationed. The medical services of the brigades were put at the disposal of the villagers, and Dr. Magid, a Canadian from Winnipeg, officiated at the delivery of twins.

Although the rest period provided a break from the horrors of war, there was no time for idleness. Reinforcements were brought up to compensate for the heavy losses which had been incurred, and there was talk of reorganizing the brigades, including the formation of a new battalion in the 15th Brigade.

Hitherto there had not been enough Canadian volunteers to warrant the formation of a "named" battalion, and at Jarama the Canadians had fought as part of the Lincoln Battalion. In April they were joined by a forty-man unit and formed into a separate section of the Lincolns. By the time that the fighting at Brunete had ended, however, there were over five hundred Canadian volunteers in Spain, and they began to consider the formation of their own unit. It was felt, among other things, that the formation of a distinctly Canadian battalion would help to increase support for republican Spain in Canada.

It is not known who first proposed that a new Canadian battalion be formed, and named after the leaders of the 1837 rebellions in Upper and Lower Canada. However, a group of Canadian volunteers met in April 1937 (the centenary of the Canadian rebellions) to discuss the issue in an organized manner. Bill Brennan was there and recalls what transpired:

> In Madrigueras there was a battalion composed of two companies of Americans, English and Canadians, together with a company of Germans and a company of French and Italians. It was in this training camp that the name for the Canadian battalion was first raised. Bob Kerr, Ed Cecil-Smith, Joe Kelly, Wally Dent, Ed Yardas and numerous other Canadians decided to call a meeting of their fellow countrymen in the camp and discuss the idea of having a Canadian company in the battalion.
>
> That night they were gathered in the barracks of Number Three Company. All in attendance decided that such a step should be taken and voiced their opinions on a suitable name for the company. After a much heated discussion they unanimously agreed that the company should be named after Mackenzie and Papineau. They then elected Bob Kerr as the delegate to approach the battalion command raising the suggestion of the meeting. The proposal was made to the chief of the base [Albacete] who stated that it would be considered.
>
> At the same meeting the boys voted to send a cable to the Committee to Aid Spanish Democracy informing them of their new proposal to the chief of the base. They also sent the following appeal to Prime Minister Mackenzie King of the Dominion Parliament:
>
> "We implore you from the depths of our hearts to do everything possible to help Spanish democracy. In so doing you are serving your own interests. We are here for the duration until fascism is defeated."[13]

Mackenzie King did not reply. Nor, for the moment, did the 15th Brigade act upon the recommendation of the Canadian volunteers. Resentment in the ranks began to grow, particularly when the Americans, who now had two battalions in the field, expressed the wish to form a third, with a view to establishing an all-American brigade. The Canadians began to feel that they would once again be treated as "leftovers" or as Americans by another name.

The issue was a political one and it was eventually resolved at that level. In June 1937 William Kashtan and A.A. MacLeod were sent to Spain to arrange the return of Dr. Norman Bethune to Canada. They were instructed to inform the brigade command at Albacete that an agreement had been reached to form a Canadian battalion. MacLeod subsequently travelled to Tarazona where he addressed a mass meeting of Canadian volunteers. Ron Liversedge, who was in the audience, recalls the speech:

> MacLeod spoke to the massed personnel of the base for two hours. He gave a history of the founding of Canada, brought in the American revolution, the war of 1812, the defeat of the American attempted invasion of Canada, and, finally, the revolt of the early Canadians against the British Family Compact led by Mackenzie and Papineau. When MacLeod asked for an endorsation for a Mac-Pap battalion, he got it one hundred percent.[14]

The Americans, who now knew they would not form a third battalion, accepted the decision with good grace. Joe Dallet, an American political commissar, spoke for them all when he wrote to his wife:

> The problem was that the Canadians have done wonderful work for Spain. Canadians have fought splendidly in many battalions here but always their national origin and national traditions have been swamped in the publicity splurges for the Lincoln Battalion, etc., for up to now they have never had a battalion of their own . . . The Canadian movement has something in Spain to rally around . . . The Americans took it fine and voted unanimously for it. The Canadian comrades, who are a fine lot, are blissfully happy at having won their objective.[15]

The Mackenzie-Papineau Battalion was not exclusively Canadian, and its first commanding officers were Americans. However, it soon assumed something of the character of the Canadian mosaic: there was a section composed almost entirely of Ukrainian-Canadians in Company Two; Finnish-Canadians from Fort William and Port Arthur were the majority in the Machine Gun Company; and Company Three had a section made up predominantly of loggers from British Columbia. One of them wrote home proudly:

> We know that the loggers and lumber workers of Canada are doing their share here in the ranks of the anti-fascist fighters and we hope that those at home will do the same in the way of moral and financial support.[16]

Training had been a problem since the inception of the International Brigades, and in some cases had been sacrificed altogether in order to send reinforcements to the front. However, the Canadians were determined not to repeat the mistakes of the past, and insisted on a thorough training period which lasted up to four months, the longest for any battalion in the 15th Brigade. For the Mac-Pap it became a matter of some pride, as Stepan Ishchuk wrote in a letter home: "The majority of the men in the Mackenzie-Papineau are considered to be better prepared (the entire battalion is considered to be the best) because after a lengthy training [period] only . . . are they being sent to the front."

Training focussed on the use of rifles, bayonets, light and heavy machine guns, light mortars, and hand grenades. Military discipline also had to be taught, sometimes a difficult task considering the youth and exuberance of the volunteers. Of equal importance were the politics of the war, for the international volunteers were not conscripts. They were in Spain fighting for a cause and it was essential that everyone understand the broader political issues for which the war was being fought.

There were problems to be overcome, however, among them the desperate shortage of qualified officers, and few of the Canadian volunteers appeared willing to take officer training. Joe Schoen describes a typical situation:

> Tiny Anderson, Bill Matthews [Matvenko] and I were chosen to go to officer's school. None of us wanted to, but Joe Dallet explained that there was a severe shortage of

officers, especially lower rank, and were we not there to do what was best for the Spanish people? I thought that men who had already seen action should have been trained as officers. But this was not to be. Tiny absolutely refused. Bill and I had specialized in sniping so after our regular course, we continued training snipers. Our instructors were Russian and the base commanders were German. Bill Matthews did the interpreting in Ukrainian and I did the German interpreting.[17]

The quality and quantity of food also left a great deal to be desired. Bread was the basic issue and on some days there was nothing else to eat. At other times meals were supplemented by a stew or slurry made of rice or chickpeas, onions and a bit of olive oil, with perhaps some meat of dubious ancestry. At the training base at Tarazona there was bread and ersatz coffee for breakfast, with a supper of rice fried in olive oil, *bacalao* (salt fish) and chickpeas. Occasionally mule or burro meat, spiced to make it palatable, substituted for fish. Inevitably there was grumbling about the food, but some men, like Orton Wade of Winnipeg declared it was the only fare they had ever had which had a beneficial effect on stomach ulcers. There was usually peasant wine with which to wash down the food, but most of the potable water was at risk. Dysentery and a number of unknown fevers were endemic.

It was under these conditions, then, beneath a hot summer sky, that the members of the new Mackenzie-Papineau Battalion prepared for a more dangerous ordeal— the Aragon Front.

NOTES
1. Quoted in Robert Colodny, *The Struggle for Madrid* (New York: Paine-Whitman Publishers, 1958), 66.
2. Quoted in *Fighting Side by Side with Spanish Patriots Against Fascism* (Moscow: Novosti Press Agency Publishing House, 1986), 72.
3. Ryan, ed., *The Book of the XV International Brigade*, 58-61.
4. Quoted in Alexander, *British Volunteers for Liberty*, 106.
5. Brennan, unpublished account, NAC, M6 30 E-173 Vol. 1.
6. Quoted in Ryan, ed., *The Book of the XV International Brigade*, 141.
7. Brennan, unpublished account.
8. Lee Burke of Toronto, written account to the author.
9. Brennan, unpublished account.

10. Jules Paivo, personal account written for the Historical Commission in September 1939.
11. Brennan, unpublished account.
12. Ryan, ed., *The Book of the XV International Brigade*, 129-30.
13. Brennan, unpublished account.
14. Liversedge, "Memoir of the Spanish Civil War."
15. Joe Dallet, *Letters From Spain* (Toronto: New Era Publishers, 1938), 52-53.
16. C. Goguen, letter printed in *The B.C. Lumber Worker* (July 1938).
17. Joe Schoen, letter to the author, no date.

Four

The Battles in the Aragon

On 23 August 1937 the republican government launched the fourth offensive of the summer, this time on the Zaragoza front. The battle was fought over a great range of barren hills and wide, desert-like valleys. The dominant high spots, and strategic towns like Huesca, Quinto, Belchite and Fuentes de Ebro, were all held by the fascist forces, with Zaragoza lying to the north. The objective of the republican army was to eliminate these outposts and strike directly at Zaragoza.

Six republican divisions, composed of seventeen Spanish and four International Brigades, attacked from Azaila near Hijar, along a line running from Zuera (north of Zaragoza) to Belchite. The strategy was to have an armoured column sweep through Zuera and move on Zaragoza while Modesto's Fifth Corps, including the 11th and 15th Brigades, would attack around Quinto and Belchite and take the high ground between these towns and Zaragoza, bypassing Quinto and Belchite. These two strongholds were attacked almost immediately by the 15th Brigade.

THE CAPTURE OF QUINTO

Quinto, located in a small dip in the plain, was dominated by Purburell Hill one kilometre to the southeast. The hill, which had been well fortified by German engineers, was one of two elevations. They were divided by a main road but connected by two communicating trenches which ran under it. Company One of the Lincoln-Washington Battalion tried to the force the cemetery but failed and shifted its attack to the southeast. Here Alick Miller, the Canadian commander of Company One, was wounded in the head.

Quinto was shelled by about ten French 75s and American 105 howitzers, while eight Soviet tanks spearheaded the armour and infantry attack, breaking through the barbed wire in the afternoon. Maurice Constant was on the brigade staff and recalled the battle:

> . . . in the fighting at Quinto . . . we had to cross an open space and get down into a ditch, run across the road, get back into the ditch, crawl along it and run across the road again before we got behind the Fabrica.
>
> There were three of us. There was Merriman, some other fellow I can't remember, and me. Now, the fellow who was first was the lucky one because the sniper in the tower would have his first clue that people were coming.
>
> Merriman made a dash across the road, got into the ditch, and that was fine. Then the next guy. By this time the sniper was waiting for him. He shot and missed. The guy got into the ditch, crawled along it and, although the sniper was waiting for him to emerge, he got out behind the Fabrica before the sniper could get him.
>
> Then it was my turn. I knew the sniper was waiting for me. I dashed across the road and got into the ditch. I heard the snap of a bullet. Obviously he had missed me. By this time you are hot and panicky.
>
> I was crawling along the bloody ditch which was only two feet deep, you could just get your behind out of sight and that was about all you could do. There was a body lying in the ditch. I had to crawl over him and, of course, this exposed me. I got over him and to the other side and again there was a snap of a bullet.
>
> I thought, "Thank God! He didn't get me." It was only after I got out on the road and in the Fabrica that someone said, "You know, Constant, you're bleeding. He got you." I asked him where and he said, "He got you in the head" because my face was covered with blood.
>
> It turned out he got me through the lobe of the ear. He was aiming at where he thought I was and he just happened to get through a little bit of earth.[1]

The British Battalion was ordered to seize Purburell Hill. It had been thought, mistakenly, that the fascists would have evacuated the hill when their defences had been breached. Assuming this, the British attacked using only rifles and hand grenades, with little artillery support, only to be stopped by withering machine-gun fire from the fascist lines. Paddy O'Daire took command of the battalion and kept the troops in place until they could withdraw under the cover of darkness. Hugh McGregor, another Canadian who was attached to the British Battalion, described the battle:

> Quinto was surrounded from behind by the Lister Brigade with our brigade attacking directly on the town and having the task of taking the town itself. It was taken at six p.m.
>
> The English were ordered to take Purburell Hill which commanded the main highway. Merriman led them to the position from which the attack was to begin.
>
> Lieutenant-Colonel Copic also addressed the men, stating, "There are only thirteen men on that hill. Go ahead and attack and take the hill."
>
> The battalion prepared to attack in the following formation. The Spanish company was to move up the communication trench on the right. The English company moved up the communications trench on the left, and the American company moved directly on the hill.
>
> They went over the top at three o'clock in the afternoon. Battalion commander Pat Daley was wounded in the stomach. Tommy Lyons, Canadian section leader, was wounded in the head leading his section over the top. Alcide Bigras, a young French Canadian, was killed.
>
> The fire was so intense the battalion could not advance further. The men held the ground they had already advanced over, taking whatever cover offered and waited until dark. It was hot weather, very hard on the wounded who could not be hauled in.
>
> When dark came the troops moved back into the trenches they had left and slept there until four in the morning. During the night 12 fascist deserters headed by a sergeant came over to our lines.

The English Battalion moved to the right flank for the whole brigade was to be used that morning in the attack. Our batteries began an artillery barrage about seven in the morning, making direct hits on the fascist trenches.

The fascist troops, thinking that the fascist planes were ours, ran out and waved a white flag and then ran back when they discovered the planes were theirs.[2]

Bill Brennan has reconstructed the final assault on the hill from interviews with men who fought there:

The final charge up Purburell Hill took another five hours. The attack was led by the British Battalion supported by the Lincoln and 24th Battalions. The fascists hoisted a white flag but, when the brigaders moved ahead, they came under fire.

The adjutant called for three volunteers to meet the surrendering soldiers. Three men volunteered: Lucien [Louis] Tellier, Nels Madsen and a young Finnish lad from the machine-gun section. The Finnish lad and Tellier stayed each side of the road to give cover fire and Madsen and Tellier then crossed the road with Madsen in the lead.

As Madsen neared the foot of the hill he noticed a wounded fascist soldier dragging himself in their direction. Madsen ran to help him and discovered that the soldier was wounded in the legs. Madsen bandaged him.

Madsen's actions helped to convince the fascists who were watching what was going on, and they began to stream out of their trenches in tens and fifteens. Tellier took their rifles while Madsen searched them for small weapons.[3]

On the opposite side of the hill, where the rest of the British were fighting, the battle was progressing along similar lines. Louis Tellier wrote the following account to his brother:

The fascists on the ridge were out of water and called for volunteers to get some. A sergeant and his section volunteered and set out during the night. They didn't bother about the water, however, but came right over to us. The sergeant stated he had been trying to get away.

His men, under separate questioning, confirmed this. Too, they told how he had been carrying on anti-fascist agitation for a long while. This same sergeant brought some sketches of the fortifications on the ridge which aided us in taking it.

But the real significant fact is this: during all the time that this sergeant was carrying out his anti-fascist agitation not one of his men betrayed him to the fascist high officials! They, too, haven't much sympathy for the cause of the rebels.

Remember Jack Lawson [of Vancouver]? He is with our brigade in the anti-tank battery. He was up on a hill not far from me. His crew got wounded so he kept his gun going alone, carrying his own shells, loading, sighting and shooting: a one-man gun crew. The French artillery boys blasted the fascists to hell and the machine gunners got plenty.[4]

The retreating fascist troops were pursued into Quinto by tanks, which succeeded in destroying the strong defence posts. The British reached the cemetery on the town's outskirts at nightfall. The next morning three battalions of the 15th Brigade, including the Lincoln-Washington, were ordered to mop up the fascist resistance. As usual, the church was the stronghold of the fascist defence. Steve Nelson was with one group which moved along both sides of a street past the church, breaking down the doors of all the houses and tossing grenades inside. The Dimitrov and the Lincoln-Washington finally succeeded in surrounding the church, taking seventy-five prisoners. The Spanish battalion moved in that night and finished cleaning up the town. It had taken three days of heavy street fighting to capture Quinto, and casualties were heavy, particularly amongst the officers.

THE TAKING OF BELCHITE

The republican attack now swung towards Belchite, the rail and road junction for Zaragoza. Belchite was well fortified with pill boxes and trenches, which were protected by iron stakes and prongs fixed into the ground. The battle for the

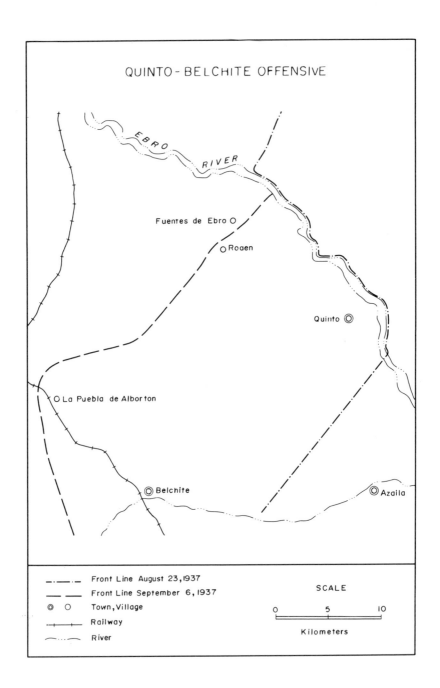

QUINTO-BELCHITE OFFENSIVE

EBRO RIVER

Fuentes de Ebro O

O Roaen

Quinto ◎

O La Puebla de Alborton

◎ Belchite

◎ Azaila

Front Line August 23,1937
Front Line September 6, 1937
◎   O   Town, Village
Railway
River

SCALE

0   5   10

Kilometers

66

town began on 1 September 1937, and was to continue for six days.

The Spanish 32nd Brigade was the first to attempt to storm Belchite, but was repulsed. Then, after the fascists had been driven from the heights which extended from the southeast to the west, the 15th Brigade launched a number of attacks from several different directions. The principal fascist resistance in the town was centred on the factory and the Church of St. Augustin, and these locations were the scene of heavy fighting.

On 1 September the Lincoln-Washington Battalion was dug in about three hundred feet from the church, while the Dimitrov gained a foothold by capturing a one-storey factory about fifty yards from it. However, the initial attacks on the church were unsuccessful. When it was shelled, the fascists evacuated it, only to move back in as soon as the shelling stopped. Scouts were sent in to evaluate the situation and succeeded in capturing a fascist soldier, who disclosed the location of a stronghold outside the church. A new plan of attack was drawn up, calling for a simultaneous, three-pronged assault on the church's entrances. First, an artillery and tank attack was to drive the fascists out. Then, while the church was being shelled, storming parties were to move as close as possible. Finally, the shelling was to stop at a predetermined time, whereupon the men would make a final dash into the church.

The attack was launched as planned, but the left flank ran into heavy machine-gun fire and was unable to advance. On the right a dozen men, led by Dave Engels, left the trenches located forty yards from the church and charged across a gully which ran the length of the church wall. As they were moving through the rear entrance the fascists were coming in the front door. A hand grenade fight ensued and the fascists were forced to retreat. Several men then positioned them-selves at the open front door and held on despite heavy firing from fascists stationed in neighbouring houses. Machine guns and sand bags were brought up, and a barricade was built at the front door, enabling the Lincoln-Washington to stabilize the situation. The church fell in the afternoon.

The bitter, house-to-house fighting in Belchite was complicated by the system of underground tunnels which the fascists had dug. These permitted them to escape from a building as it was being captured and concentrate in new places in the town. Casualties were heavy, and once again Canadians were among those who died. Sergeant Jack Hoshooley, who was attached to a machine-gun company, described the death of his friend Jacob Locke of Guelph-Kitchener:

> On September 3, 1937, Jacob was killed in action at the head of his section in an attack. He was hit in the stomach by three bullets and died instantly. Jacob died as he lived, fighting for the cause of the working-class of the world.[5]

Lieutenant Pete Neilsen, the adjutant of Company One in the Lincoln-Washington, witnessed the death of his friend Jim Wolf of Vancouver:

> War seemed to completely stun Jim up until the attack on Quinto. There he appeared to have made up his mind to fight in the front ranks at every opportunity. During the attack on Belchite he was fatally wounded. He got it in the courtyard of the Belchite church when our unit was engaged in the first assault for possession of this stronghold. A hand grenade exploded near his face smashing one side of the jaw and neck, also penetrating the opposite shoulder.
>
> He could not speak to me. But if it is permitted to repeat what his eyes said alone with the complaint of physical agony it would be: I lived and I die for a better life for my class and I have no regrets.
>
> He could not smoke so he gave me his cigarettes.[6]

Neilsen went on to describe vividly the awful beauty which sometimes accompanies war:

> My experience in Spain most likely to forever live in my memory was the last night in Belchite before the city fell.

The night was beautiful with starlight. Just before dark we built a barricade to get position and to cut off one of the last streets held by the fascists.

Using the protection of the sand bags, about 12 or 18 of us went up an alley past their position, and there we lived through the night. A few of our numbers gained entrance to a large building facing the fascist-held positions. I was furnished with three tired men, one Spanish and two Americans, and told to guard one end of the alley. My guards were so tired that they only awoke when grenades were thrown up the alley in the early hours of the morning.

I was standing with my back to a doorway stroking the muzzle of a starved burro, when suddenly the strains of beautiful music floated over the city for some minutes. Then a speech, then rifle and machine gun fire, and grenades. More music and speeches, followed by a short silence and then a terrific bombardment at the barricades by hand grenades, followed immediately by fascists thundering over them and down the street.

Our comrades in the alley on the other side of the barricades retreated fast and our little group was cut off.

But it was only the fascist brigade officers trying to make a getaway, not an attack.

The whole night was like a fantastic drama: weird, beautiful, dangerous and delightful, because we knew victory was ours.[7]

Fred Kostyk of Winnipeg, who was commended for bravery in action, recounted his role in the battle of Belchite:

It proved a desperate struggle. This was not just another battle or another town. Belchite happened to be the left flank of the advance to Sargossa. It was strongly fortified and they had bragged that even Napoleon could not reduce it during the Napoleonic Wars in Spain. Most of the movements were at night. When the time came to make the final attack, we launched it from the gate and church entrance. Everytime that we attacked and directed our fire from artillery and machine guns, they were able to retreat into their tunnels and as soon as we tried to attack they

69

would reappear and stop us. The snipers especially took a heavy toll. In the end, the decision was made that the only solution was to "overrun" the position by a concentrated dash of all of us. We rushed them and that was the mortal blow, they were trapped. I was one of those who led that final rush and I received a citation for bravery from Col. Copic. Belchite fell a total ruin . . .[8]

FUENTOS DE EBRO: A MAJOR DEFEAT

On 4 September 1937 the Mackenzie-Papineau Battalion, which had not yet seen action, was ordered to stand by. A parade was held in the town plaza of Tarazona, where the battalion was addressed by commissars, generals and other officers. Two days later trucks transported the battalion to the railway station at Albacete. The men were then taken by train to the Aragon front, disembarking at Azaila to join the 15th Brigade, which was poised to attack Fuentes de Ebro. It was here that the Mackenzie-Papineau Battalion was to have its baptism of fire.

The front ran from Fuentes de Ebro to Mediana and to the west it curved back towards Puebla de Albortón. The fortifications at Fuentes de Ebro were an excellent example of anti-tank defence. Fuentes de Ebro was defended by the 150th Division, reinforced by Moors, Spanish Foreign Legion troops and a mobile column stationed in nearby Zaragoza.

The original plan called for a surprise attack at dawn of 13 October, but this proved impossible due to the massive traffic jam which developed as troops moved to the front. The Mackenzie-Papineau Battalion was delayed for three hours, and had to march over the crest of a hill and cut through barbed wire in order to reach their trenches. All the while the enemy maintained a steady fire, inflicting many casualties. The Canadian trenches faced an open plain which ran into a ravine, with the town approximately seven hundred metres away. On the other side of the ravine were strong fascist fortifications which had been built by German engineers.

The confusion which had arisen as the troops moved to the front, as well as the inexperience of certain officers, resulted

70

in heavy casualties. Ron Liversedge described the ensuing debacle:

It was around the last of September that we were withdrawn from the peaceful front of Huesca and piled on the camions for our ride to the Aragon down to Lerida and then southwest to Azaila behind Caspe where we joined the 15th which was encamped in olive groves along the Caspe road.

The men of the Brigade were not yet recovered from the hell of Belchite. It was becoming more difficult to face the overwhelming superiority in arms which the fascists were building up. I was saddened to hear that two of my close friends from Vancouver had died in the attack on the church, Jim Wolf and Charlie Walthers.

The men were in poor physical shape and in a sullen mood, knowing that the Aragon phase of the war was by no means over. As always, when out of the line, the boys complained, cursing the staff, the lack of food, and wondering when the people back home were going to move and force their governments to lift the blockade . . .

It could not be stated that the Fuentes action was ill-conceived, but I am quite sure that it was the most ill-directed action on our part in the whole Spanish war. There was talk after the action of sabotage but of that I know nothing.

We received our orders before leaving Quinto. The 15th Brigade was given the job of making a frontal attack on the town. We would leave the trucks just short of Fuentes de Ebro and take over the trenches in front of the town before daybreak, relieving the Catalonian troops that had been holding the line there.

At twelve noon our aviation would come over and bomb the fascist lines about the town. Immediately following the bombing our tanks would come up and over our trenches and we would go over the top and advance behind the tanks and take the town.

Our journey to Fuentes was behind schedule as the road seemed to be clogged with traffic. There was some confusion and it was daylight as we started to file into the series of very narrow, very dirty, and not overly deep trenches leading off from each side of the road.

I think that more than three-quarters of the Brigade were off the road and sidling along the narrow trenches to their positions when the fascists opened up. There was no warming up but, in a split second, dozens of machine guns started a terrific crescendo of firing, and we received our first casualties among the men who were still on the road.

As soon as we were in our positions we were ordered to open fire on the fascist lines to try and give cover for our men still on the highway to get into the trenches.

The layout was formidable. We were on a plain gradually sloping up to the town almost a mile away. The town was perched on a high ridge, probably two hundred feet, and in front of the town was a deep arroya. All it needed was water in the arroya to make it a very large mediaeval fortress—and we had almost a mile of open plain to cross to get there.

Without time to get acquainted with the whole scene we had to open fire on the fascists and, in a short time, some of our men were firing on the Lincoln Battalion who were away over to our right.

At noon, right on the dot, our aviation zoomed in from behind us and the fascist anti-aircraft guns frantically went into action. There were about fifty planes, light bombers. They swerved to the right, came round in a half circle and strung out in a line and came in for the run over the fascist lines. I think that was the most Republican planes I ever saw in the air at one time all through the war.

Our planes were heading back and the anti-aircraft fire was dying down. The fascist lines were hidden in a dense cloud of bomb smoke and settling dust. We were ready to jump off and waited for the tanks. And we waited for the tanks for one-and-a- half hours.

The fascists repaired their lines and, at one-thirty, we heard the tanks roaring towards us from behind. They were coming at a good lick, seventy-five of them. [According to General Walter (Karol Swierczewski) there were forty-three tanks. See Academy of Sciences of the USSR, *International Solidarity With the Spanish Republic 1936-1939* (Moscow: Progress Publishers, 1975), 96.]

They roared over the top of our trenches nearly crushing one of our men who jumped onto the parapet and was pulled back in.

We were amazed to see twelve men of the 24th Battalion [Spanish] riding on top of each tank. It was said afterwards that somebody on the brigade staff had seen this stunt on a film. There were very few of the 24th who came back.

We scrambled out of the trenches to follow behind the tanks, the Mac-Pap, the Lincoln on our right and the British on their right—the whole brigade in a long line across the plain.

The tanks spread out in a line and started for the town at about forty miles an hour and, at the same time, the fascists opened up with hundreds of machine guns and mortars and artillery. Of course, we could not keep up with the tanks and, immediately, we ran into a murderous fire and the men started to drop all around. In less than fifteen minutes our company strength was reduced by half. There was no cover.

Our company commander went down. Just to my right Joe Dallet, the Battalion Commissar, walking along smoking his curved pipe, a little smile on his face, was hit. I heard the bullet smack into him. He gave a little grunt and I knew he was dead before he hit the ground.

Three of the ammunition carriers in my machine gun squad went down. To the right and a little ahead I saw Milt Hernden, a Negro, and his pal Smitty of the second company go down. One of our company stretcher bearers, Schatz from Toronto, crawled over to see if he could help and, as he rolled Hernden over, Schatz got one through the shoulder.

We advanced slowly and wherever there was a little hummock in the land I would set up my machine gun and rattle off a few pans, firing into the trenches below the town.

There was not much direction being given. Most of our officers were killed or wounded.

Ahead of us we saw the tanks grinding to a halt close to the ravine in front of the town, twenty-five of them on fire and we could see the tank men jumping out of the burning tanks, being shot as they jumped out. [According to General Walter, eighteen tanks were lost in the battle. See Academy of Sciences of the USSR, *International Solidarity*, 97.] We could also see what men were left of the 24th trying to hide behind the burning tanks.[9]

Bill Kardash of Winnipeg, who commanded the tank attack, later wrote an account of his role in the engagement:

A runner brought instructions from the colonel in command of the regiment. My company was to break through the fascist lines, destroy the machine-gun and anti-tank gun nests, fire along the fascist trenches and thus enable the Republican army to advance. "Any questions?" asked the captain. "None," someone replied. "To your tanks, and start upon my signal," were his last words. Five to ten infantry men were placed on top of every tank.

Two other companies moved up, one on each flank. Clouds of dust rose as our tanks advanced at a high speed. The heat inside the tank was terrific. The sound of machine-gun bullets hitting the tank resembled hail on a tin roof.

I was observing the territory ahead, trying to locate the machine gun nest. The driver slowed down, shouting "There is a deep ravine in front of us." "Can the tank make it?" I asked, "if so, go ahead." The tank climbed the hill and over the top, crossing the fascist trenches. An incendiary bomb set fire to our tank, but it was able to advance some thirty-five yards into the rear of the fascist lines.

The motor stopped. Smoke and flames came into the turret where my assistant and I sat. The driver attempted to re-start the motor, but in vain. Some fascists stood up in the trenches watching the burning tank. The first shell

I fired landed right in their trench. I continued firing at the their trenches.

Meanwhile, the fire spread into the tank, and the danger of explosion both of our gasoline and ammunition was becoming great. To stay inside meant certain death; to jump out into the open behind the fascist lines in broad daylight was almost as dangerous . . .

The driver and my assistant jumped out. That was the last I saw of either of them. I kept on firing. When my gun jammed, I switched over to the machine-gun. The heat was becoming unbearable. Revolver in hand, I jumped out.

Five hand grenades exploded at my feet. A bullet went through my leg. I fell some five yards away from the fascist trenches. I did not see much hope for myself. I kept on firing my pistol until I had one bullet left. There was only one thing I knew—the fascists would not get me alive. I raised the pistol to my head and was about to fire the last shot when I saw one of our tanks speeding towards me. I waved my hand and it immediately came to me.

With a final effort, I crawled to the tank. My right hand was hit by shrapnel from another hand grenade. I climbed on to the tank which quickly sped to the Sanitary Service point.[10]

The tanks destroyed the barbed wire entanglements and crushed some enemy bunkers but had little room to manoeuvre in the narrow streets of Fuentes de Ebro, and the fascists held their lines.

With the failure of the tank attack the advance of the republican forces was everywhere arrested, and the troops were forced to seek what cover they could. Liversedge describes the later stages of the battle:

Our advance was slowed down to a crawl and men were trying to dig in wherever they could find a hump or hollow in the ground. The ground in the Aragon is hard and a dinner plate is a poor shovel, but machine-gun fire is a good persuader.

Towards evening the remnants of our company being driven to the left by the heavy machine-gun fire came on to some broken up ground and part of an old trench which we took over. From here on the rim of the ravine we saw the hopelessness of our task.

The ravine was much wider and deeper than we had thought and the town on the other rim much higher. Even with heavy air and artillery cover, which we didn't have, it would have been impossible to take Fuentes de Ebro in a frontal attack.

Two of our men started to try to cross the ravine, but were hit before they had gone a hundred yards. Lane was shot through the nose and Molyneaux through the arm. Both were able to crawl back.

Jim Menzies, from Vancouver, a sergeant, took charge and ordered us to stay where we were, and then sent someone back to try to contact battalion headquarters. At dark we got word to work our way a few hundred yards back onto the plain and as the firing started to abate a little we made our way back.

An attempt was being made to regroup. There were Mac-Pap and Lincoln mixed up with the few survivors from the 24th.

Stretcher bearers were busy getting the wounded back. There was no water and no food had come up yet.

The Mac-Pap Second Company had also suffered heavy casualties and both the company commander, Joe Dougher and his second-in-command, Bob Thompson, were badly wounded. Whitehead [a British volunteer] had taken over our company and he came over and told me to take my gun and Omar Lazure from Montreal, my loader, with a few pans of ammunition and go with some tank engineers who were going to try to repair some of the tanks and to get them back.

The four we went with were Austrians and they were carrying tools and gas cans. We came to a tank and Lazure and I went a little way in front and lay down with the gun ready. The fascists were firing intermittently, but seemed to be ranging over us.

By now it was dark. The tank men were making a hell of a lot of noise. Then Lazure and I heard men across the ravine coming towards us. They were Moors and not very careful about concealing themselves. I told Lazure to go back and tell the tank men that a patrol of Moors was headed our way.

The tank men said they could not fix the tank anyhow and were now getting out of the tank and would whistle when they were ready to go. Before they whistled I had to open fire as the Moors were now coming up our slope. We scattered the patrol but our firing had started fire from all over the fascist lines.

It was an hour before we got back and, by this time, the Brigade was waiting for the Spanish sappers to come and dig trenches.

The sappers came marching silently across the plain and, after a brief conversation with some of our officers, started to dig. These men were prisoners who had been released to aid in the war. They left before dawn. They always worked under fire and they always had casualties.

That night the sappers drew lots of fire. The trenches they had dug were by no means ideal. They were narrow and not deep enough. But the diggers would be back the next night. In the meantime, the men would try and deepen them and fix up firing positions.

Six of us who now constituted Number One Company's light machine-gun squad were taken to the left end of the line and, to our horror, told to occupy two little strips of trench over the rim of the inside slope of the ravine, directly across and below the fascist lines. Worse yet, the two strips of trench were only two feet deep.

The only way we could occupy that bit of trench was by laying flat with our heads at opposite ends and one of us with our legs on top of the others. That was the beginning of the longest day in my life.

> With the coming of daylight and the sun promising a sizzler, the fascist fire grew heavier. During the night they had brought up more artillery and some heavy batteries were shelling our rear, and our aviation was all over the sky and bombing targets in our rear.
>
> The sweet, acrid, sickly stench of human death was thick on the atmosphere. It doesn't take long in hot weather.
>
> Dusk came at last and from above Whitehead called down, "Are you alive down there?"[11]

The 15th Brigade suffered over four hundred casualties, and the knowledge that the republican forces had been defeated made these losses even harder to bear. However, many of the surviving veterans concur with Ron Liversedge that under the circumstances Fuentes de Ebro could not have been captured. A special meeting of officers and commissars was convened at which Crescenciano Bilbao, the Vice Commissar-General and Chief of the War Commissariat of the Army of the East, attempted to discover why Fuentes de Ebro had not been taken. Those who attended the meeting later reported that it had been stormy, and that deep differences of opinion had surfaced.

On 25 October the 15th Brigade was relieved by a Spanish brigade and withdrew to Quinto to recover from its losses. Ed Cecil-Smith, then a lieutenant and second-in-command of the Mackenzie-Papineau Battalion, was promoted to the rank of captain. Bob Thompson, the American commander of the Mac-Pap, fell ill shortly thereafter and was succeeded by Cecil-Smith, who thus became the first Canadian to command a battalion in Spain.

REORGANIZATION AND TRAINING

On 23 September 1937 the Defence Ministry published the Decree on the Status and Organization of the International Brigades, formally incorporating the foreign volunteers into the Spanish republican army, and subjecting them to the same training, organization and regulations as regular Spanish soldiers. Uniforms and equipment were standardized, although the international volunteers were permitted to wear a special insignia on the right side of their shirts or jackets. The brigades were to be mixed and were to include Spanish volunteers. As well, 50 percent of the vacancies for non-commissioned officers, officers and commanders were to be filled by Spaniards. The base of the International Brigades remained at Albacete, but the decree stipulated that only personnel with a minimum of three months of front line experience could be appointed to the Albacete base head-quarters.

In the ensuing reorganization, discipline and proper training were emphasized, for it was recognized that enthusiasm alone was not sufficient to win battles. Particular attention was paid to the training of officers, for the lack of a competent officer corps was blamed for unnecessary republican losses, such as those which had occurred at Fuentes de Ebro. The importance of discipline was paramount, for the nature of the Spanish conflict was such that the men in the International Brigades were frequently forced to fight seemingly hopeless holding actions in the face of superior enemy forces. In an undisciplined army, the effect of such a situation could be devasting. Lee Burke astutely described the predicament he and others faced:

> We never did have the forces, planes, artillery, tanks to continue the offensive. Our offensives were only to distract and throw off balance the attacks the fascists were planning. We could only attack by surprise, take so much territory, prisoners, guns—and then try to hold on against their counter-attacks, never having the forces necessary to continue ahead for any great length.
>
> After stopping their counter-attacks, we had to hold on and wait for the democracies to help us fight their first battles. We waited! But kept on dying and fighting.[12]

The Mackenzie-Papineau Battalion was stationed at Pezuela de las Torres, an old castle on the Madrid highway, and was joined by a detachment of Finns from the 11th Brigade. Two months of intensive training followed. Then, on the last day of the year, the call came for them to move out once again.

On 15 December 1937 two republican armies, numbering 100,000 men, attacked Teruel in order to divert Franco's attention from the Guadalajara front. Teruel, located at an altitude of 3,050 feet, was a strategic objective, blocking as it did a main road from the northwest to Valencia and the sea. The Spanish loyalists took Teruel and advanced to the west of the town, establishing a new front running from Rubiales in the south to Concud in the north. This offensive took the fascist command by surprise, and the loss of the town was a serious blow to Franco's plan to bring the war to speedy conclusion. His reaction was swift and furious and, with an overwhelming superiority in arms and artillery, the fascists quickly retook Teruel. The International Brigades were ordered to prevent the Fascists from breaching the front.

On the morning of 31 December the 15th Brigade left Mas de las Matas, moving by truck along dangerous, icy mountain roads to the Teruel battle zone. The Mac-Pap was ordered on the same day to move north to Argente, a flat, saucer-like plain located to the west of the republican lines. Here, some forty kilometres north of Teruel, the battalions of the 15th Brigade met and deployed into adjacent villages, establishing a line against possible fascist assaults directed eastward at the Teruel-Rudilla highway.

The Mac-Pap marched to the open, snow-covered fields and was told to dig in. The temperature was -18°C and many of the men suffered from frostbite. At night they took refuge in the village, which had been almost completely abandoned, and returned to the battlefield in the morning. After suffering under these harsh conditions for ten days, the battalion was moved to Cuevas Labradas, where it was to support the Spanish forces.

When the Mac-Pap moved into the line the exact location of the enemy was unknown. Ed Cecil-Smith, Niilo Makela (the

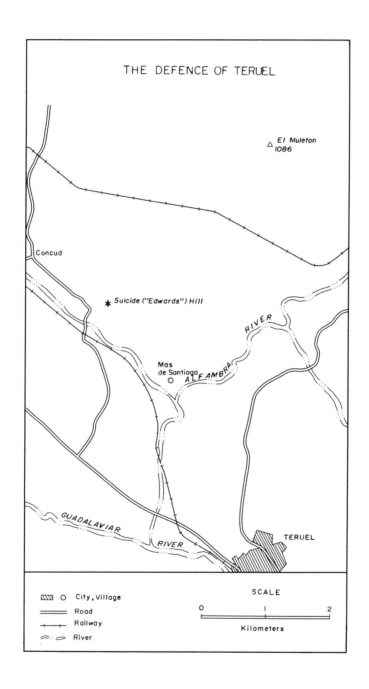

THE DEFENCE OF TERUEL

△ El Muleton
1086

Concud

✳ Suicide ("Edwards") Hill

Mas
de Santiago
O   ALFAMBRA RIVER

GUADALAVIAR

RIVER

TERUEL

SCALE

▨ O City, Village
───   Road
┼─┼   Railway
≈≈≈   River

0   1   2

Kilometers

81

commander of Number One Company) and Harry Patterson went out on reconnaissance in no-man's-land, where they came under machine-gun fire. Another patrol of three, including Yorky Burton and Clyde Taylor, was captured, and fascist prisoners taken the next night reported that the men had been questioned and executed.

The 15th Brigade was then moved to the tip of the fascist spearhead on the outskirts of Teruel, called "the post of honour" by Copic, the brigade's commanding officer. The Mac-Pap passed between El Muleton and Santa Barbara, crossed the Alfambra River and took up positions on the eastern length of La Muela, straddling the railway line and the gorge of a stream.

Fred Mattersdorfer, a volunteer from British Columbia, and Maurice Constant were with the scouting parties which preceded the main advance. They had a close brush with death, as Constant recalls:

> You came around this bend and emerged in full view and then you were out of sight of the artillery. There was a line up of about 15 trucks waiting to make the run.
>
> One would make the run, get through, and then another one. As soon as he started a run, the shells would start to come. One truck was already rolled over and in the valley on its side.
>
> Then our truck's turn. The scouts in the back were nervous and my second in command was beside me in the middle and I was on the outside.
>
> As soon as he started shells started to come and sure the driver lost his nerve and turned the truck off the road into the mountainside. Now we were sitting ducks. All the scouts in the back jumped off and took to the ditch.
>
> I leaned forward. The fire extinguisher is on the passenger side. No sooner was I out than there were explosions all over the place. When we got back into the truck and got moving again, there was a huge hole in the fire extinguisher and in the back of the truck cabin. When I leaned

forward to open the door, the artillery shell hit where my head had been.[13]

Once Number One Company had reached the front, Niilo Makela deployed his troops along a seventy-foot cliff edge with their backs to the valley. The fascist trenches were approximately fifty metres away. On a hill at Celades the Mac-Pap replaced the Spanish 129th, whose troops were half frozen. There were dugouts but no machine-gun nests; these had to be built under artillery fire. The no-man's-land lying between was filled with frozen bodies. Number Two Company, composed of Spaniards and commanded by Ricardo Díaz, was positioned to the right of Number One Company, but on the valley floor. Number Three Company was deployed east in an arc, flanked by the Spanish Marineros, and occupied three small hills between La Muela and El Muleton. The machine-gun company, commanded by Jack Thomas, was dispersed among the rifle companies. Nels Madsen set up his machine gun in a shoe factory west of the city, supporting Makela's men.

The Lincoln-Washington Battalion took up positions among the shattered buildings on the outskirts of Teruel and the British deployed along a thousand-metre line running across the top of Santa Barbara, overlooking the valley. The 24th Battalion (Spanish) took up positions along the northern slope of the same range of hills.

Maurice Constant had his brigade observation post up on the Santa Barbara with the British, and had a clear view for miles behind the enemy lines. Constant and Mattersdorfer, who seemed to lead charmed lives, had another close brush with death:

> They were aware that we were there and, regularly, the German artillery would throw something at four o'clock sharp. It was ten minutes of shelling begun so punctually you could set your watch by it, so five minutes before it began we took positions behind the brow of a hill and waited until the dust settled and then moved back.

It was risky business. One day I was there with Fred Mattersdorfer, squatting in one of the back trenches while the shelling was taking place. There was an explosion. Everything went black. When the dust cleared the rifles in front of us were twisted and the wooden stocks were full of holes. Not one of us had a scratch on him.

The only explanation we had is that the shells must have hit the back trench wall against which we were leaning and the blast was directed against the front wall. It seemed unbelievable.[14]

Exposed to enemy fire and the fury of the elements, the 15th Brigade waited for the enemy assault they knew must come. The cold was so intense that even the food they received was frozen, having been hauled for seven miles across a windswept, snow-filled wasteland. Only the fiery Spanish cognac made life bearable.

On 17 January General Aranda's Galicia corps, supported by six hundred artillery pieces, attacked along a front extending from Celades to Teruel. The Thaelmann bore the brunt of the attack on El Muleton while the Mackenzie-Papineau Battalion was threatened by the First Navarres Division. The latter were beaten off because the British antitank battery atop Santa Barbara was able to fire into the fascist trenches over the heads of the Mac-Pap. The Thaelmann meanwhile held firm throughout the afternoon and Aranda's forces fell back, only to shift their attack to the Spanish Marineros and a knoll being held by a squad of Canadians commanded by Lionel Edwards. Canadian snipers led by Leonard Levenson and Jack Penrod helped to hold off the enemy. Bill Matthews described the scene:

The battalion sniper, Swederski, a miner from Sudbury, came to our positions and wanted to shoot at the fascists. We had been firing at the fascists and we plugged some of the loop holes in the parapet so that no light would show through so as to prevent the fascists from picking us out.

Swederski pulled the rag out and stuck his rifle out and got a bullet through the head. He did not know what hit

SPAIN'S FIGHT FOR DEMOCRACY

The Ambassadors of

THE SPANISH GOVERNMENT

Senora Isabella de Palencia
● Spanish Ambassadress-Elect To Sweden

Hon. Marcelino Domingo
● Leader Of The Left Republican Party and Former Minister Of Education

Rev. Father Luis Sarasola
● Catholic Priest, Author, and Scholar

Who Are Now Touring Canada Will Tell of the

STRUGGLE OF THEIR PEOPLE AGAINST FASCISM

IN REGINA AT THE STADIUM
(Which will be Heated)

TUESDAY NOVEMBER 3rd. 8. P.M.

Auspices Regina Committee to Aid Spanish Democracy

Collection to Help Finance Canadian Hospital Unit in Spain

Above: *Edgar Williamson, the first Canadian volunteer to go to Spain.*
Facing page, top: *First anniversary of the formation of the 15th International Brigade, Massey Hall, Toronto, 1938.*
Facing page, bottom: *Edward Cecil-Smith (centre), commanding officer, Mackenzie-Papineau Battalion, flanked by Dr. Julius Hene (left), and Hamish Fraser (right). François Touchette Collection.*

Above, top left: *Gunnar Ebb, a Finn who succeeded Niilo Makela as commanding officer of the Machine Gun Company, Mackenzie-Papineau Battalion.*
Above, top right: *Jules Paivio, photographed in Spain in 1938.*
Above, bottom left: *Lieutenant Joe Schoen, Starbuck, Manitoba. The photograph was taken in Spain in 1937.*
Above, bottom right: *William C. Beeching, scout with the Lincoln Battalion.*
Facing page: *A memorial plaque, constructed and erected in the field at Jarama, 1937.*

TO OUR FALLEN
COMRADES
OUR VICTORY
IS YOUR
VENGEANCE

JUNE 1937

Facing page, top: *Canadians from the Lincoln-Washington Battalion, Jarama, June 1937. François Touchette Collection.* Facing page, bottom: *Republican troops moving up to the front.* Above: *A group of "Lincolns" including volunteers from Great Britain, Ireland, France, Germany, Estonia, Finland, Denmark, Greece, the U.S.S.R., Poland and Canada. The sign in the left rear says "Tim Buck Blvd."*

Facing page, top: *The Canadian Blood Transfusion Unit, with (left to right) Hazen Sise, Dr. Norman Bethune, and Henning Sorensen. François Touchette Collection.*
Facing page, bottom left: *Dr. Norman Bethune. François Touchette Collection.*
Facing page, bottom right: *Florence Pike, R.N.*
This page, top: *Jim Dobson and Bill Matthews at the Teruel front, January 1938.*
This page, bottom: *Ukrainian Section One of Company One, Mackenzie-Papineau Battalion, at Kilometer 19, February 1938.*

Above: *Mackenzie-Papineau Machine Gun Company. Commanding officer Niilo Makela is second from the right.*
Facing page, bottom left: *Sketch of Teruel by Ed Komodowski, January 1, 1938.*
This page, lower right: *Bill Matthews and Butch Goldstein, Barcelona, 1938.*

Facing page, top: *Fred Mattersdorfer (with guitar) and comrades en route to Madrid by train for a rest after the battle of Sierra de los Baños, 1938.*
Facing page, bottom: *The Mackenzie-Papineau Battalion on parade through the streets of Marsa, July 1, 1938.*
This page, top: *A group of western Mac-Paps before crossing the Ebro, July 23, 1938.*
This page, bottom: *First Section of Company Two, crossing the Ebro, 1938. Bill Matthews is facing the camera.*

Facing page, top: *Bombing victims, Barcelona.*
Facing page, bottom: *Alec Forbes and Walter Hellund on their return to Canada. National Archives of Canada, C 67453.*
Above: *Return of the veterans, Union Station, Toronto, 1939. National Archives of Canada, C 74968.*

Reconstructed memorial to the volunteers of the International Brigades. This monument replaced one destroyed by Franco in 1939.

him. Nick Falkowski dragged his body out and we notified the battalion.

Our battalion Commissar, Sol Wellman, came from headquarters and we buried Swederski.[15]

Despite the fact that they had suffered heavy casualties at the hands of the Marineros and the Mac-Pap, the fascists attempted to circle behind the Canadian positions and penetrate to the city's outskirts. Two squadrons of Moorish cavalry cleared El Muleton and rushed the Mac-Pap headquarters, which were located in a railroad tunnel, only to be driven back by Cecil-Smith and the battalion staff.

On 18 January El Muleton was retaken by the fascists, and the Thaelmann was forced to retreat to the British positions on Santa Barbara. The following day the fascists again attempted an attack through the valley. The three small hills, occupied by the Marineros and approximately forty of Edwards's Number Three Company, were mercilessly pounded by fascist artillery; the shelling literally ripped off the tops of the hills. Lionel Edwards described the engagement:

> I was in command of that advanced post on the Mackenzie-Papineau's right flank. We had started with thirty men and four machine guns. The fascists blasted hell out of us with heavy artillery and, in between barrages, sent their troops over to attack. But their men were too scared to get anywhere. We could see them sneaking up with their officers threatening them with revolvers. We'd let them get into short range and murder them.
>
> But after two days steady artillery fire all our machine-guns had been blown up by direct hits and there were just four of us still holding the position. All the rest were dead or wounded.[16]

Ed Komodowsky, who referred to the elevation as "Suicide Hill," gives this account of the fighting:

> Morning came with a bright sunshine and we prepared for another day on Suicide Hill. It was frosty but clear and it was a pleasure to watch another sunrise. In the front

lines, especially on a "hot" front, it is more so than ever in anyone's life. It may always be the last one and you are conscious of that fact all the time. However, a much grimmer sight was our lot that morning. We looked to see what it was that the fascists had been doing all the night before, if we could, and there, facing us was a battery of four cannon, pointing directly at our position. They had nothing to worry about. We had nothing to hit them with. They had set them up during the night and even now they were scurrying around putting up the finishing touches. There might have been more pieces further towards the overpass but these four we could not miss seeing. They were getting ready for us.

They had finally discovered our vulnerable point and by setting this battery on our left, they were going to deliver to us an artillery cross-fire.

These were rapid firing, high velocity, German artillery pieces, of the four inch caliber type, which they were trying out during the Civil War in Spain. Soon they would make their move . . .

We were surrounded by fascists and we estimated that we were in the midst of at least 1500 troops. This was a very conservative estimate, for we did not even include those in the long trench. It was more like over 2,000. They thought the road to Teruel was wide open . . . the situation on our position was becoming more and more serious as the fascists stepped up their offensive. The artillery from Concud was pounding our trenches on the hill and as the fascists continued to increase their machine gun posts we came under severe fire. Worst of all, the bullets were hitting both sides of our parapets on the trenches. Our time was getting short. We would have to make a move soon.

Our stretcher bearers both got wounded, O'Shea and Bill Tough. Bill got it in the leg and he lost it eventually. I didn't smoke, so I contributed my smokes to him when they came around to collect for him. A Cuban, Jimenez, was one of the officers in the mini trenches. [Pat] Melville was one of my friends also, Joe Schoenberg was the adjutent [sic] to our C.O., Lionel Edwards.

As the situation began to worsen and in fact was becoming desperate, Edwards sent me for reinforcements to Battalion H.Q.s. That meant running the gauntlet of the machine gun fire from the hill to the bridge. I set out . . .

I was supposed to make a strong plea at H.Q.s for reinforcements and impress on our command that the situation was desperate and rapidly becoming impossible. They had to give us aid or else give the order to abandon the position. So they scuttled around looking for reinforcements, whoever they could spare. They finally came up with one of the H.Q. clerks who had never been out of the cave that I know of. They gave him a rifle and told me . . . "here are some reinforcements right now and if we can get anybody else, we will send them down too" . . . I looked at them but I was only a messenger and said nothing. This poor fellow followed me and as soon as we got into the open he began to bend down as much as possible. I said to him . . . "there is nothing going to hit you here, save your back to when we come to the danger zone". . . but he wouldn't believe me. I don't blame him. He did not know what an inferno he was heading for and to me, it seemed kind of ridiculous to send him. What could he do, if he ever got there. We needed a couple of hundred men, not a clerk who was petrified with fear even before he got close to the hill. He began to crawl along the ground when we came to the bridge. I told him that from here we will have to make a dash in spurts to coincide with the firing of the machine guns. As soon as you saw the bullets veering off, spring and run and drop down as the return fire approached again. Also watch the trajectory of the bullets as they hit the embankment so that you can judge how far down to lower yourself. That's what I did but what happened to him, I don't know. I didn't see him again. I told Edwards what had transpired and he just grimaced. He knew it was all over.

The firing from the fascist machine guns was becoming so severe that nobody could lift their head above the trench for any length of time. The fascist artillery from Concud kept increasing and slowly the whole trench system began to disintegrate on the hill, there was no longer anybody to rebuild them or even to man them.

Now came the finale . . .

The time was a little past noon. I came back to my position
. . . I had about a hundred [rounds of ammunition] and
the rifle . . . In the final second, I had to part with it, I
threw it away into the creek, I took the last look of Suicide
Hill and took off. My choice was the creek for I knew the
trail very well. I jumped into the icy creek for it was frozen
on both sides of the banks and only a narrow channel in
the center of the creek was free of ice. That was my escape
route. I dived over the foot bridge and keeping my head
below the river bank, to escape the bullets, I raced towards
Battalion H.Q.s. In places the water was only ankle deep,
other places it was above my waist and I had to keep my
face only inches above water, till I came to the bend in the
trail and was out of danger and out of range of the bullets.
Now this is not the way Hollywood would have done it, or
John Wayne or Alan Ladd, etc., but then we were not in
the Never Never Land of Fantasy of Hollywood or
Disneyland, but in the "down to earth" bloody trenches
and fields of Spain.

When I came to Battalion H.Q.s, I told them that the saga
of Suicide Hill was over. However, it had accomplished its
role. The stand on the hill broke the arrogant plans of the
fascists to sweep to Teruel that day.[17]

During the battle for the knolls held by Edwards and his
men, the British rushed three companies to shore up the
defence. The Major Attlee Company was caught in poor
trenches and hit hard with artillery. They moved into a nearby
blockhouse but in doing so exposed Edwards's flank.

On 22 January a new line was thrown up by Edwards and
the British which held against the attacks of the enemy.
However, forty young Spaniards in Company Two were told
that they were surrounded. They broke and ran, leaving their
trenches and going over to the fascist side. Niilo Makela,
seeing them run, ordered his company to fire on them.

Andy Haas was with the British Battalion in Dusty Miller's
company at the start of the Mac-Pap operations in the Teruel
area. He states that the British were stationed on a cliff and a

trench led to the huge underground dugout that formed the Mac-Pap headquarters. When the Spanish troops changed sides, Haas says, a unit was formed

as fast as they could and shoved into the breach to try to stop the fascist advance. Our officer was an American. We halted the retreat, braced them up and proceeded further down to see what the situation was there. The officer asked for a volunteer to contact the English Battalion for information and to inform them where we were and where the line was now after the retreat, we had made a tentative new line. Nobody volunteered, so destiny pointed to me and I was elected. The message I was supposed to give, orally, was that they should hang on by all means as our information was that there were tanks coming to help the situation out.

I had to go back the way I came in and by following the directions given to me, I found myself in the same spot where we had stopped the marineros. When I got there, I saw they were retreating again. So I tried to hold them back all by myself. I had become a whole army, real John Wayne stuff. I took a stand, raised my rifle pointing it at the men and hollered at them to stop or I will shoot. As I pointed my gun at each one of them, they would fall down and stay that way. It quieted down for awhile and the marineros cooled down and stopped their retreat. I counted how many men I had stopped and it was 13.

Soon another bunch of retreatees came down and here I was alone again to stop them, I became puzzled what I should do, whether to remain here trying to halt the retreat, knowing that eventually they will rush me, when just as if in answer to my thoughts, an American officer came down the hill. I hollered to him to give me a hand with these Spanish retreatants.

He said, "let them go" . . . he further stated it was an ordered retreat, so I went with them.[18]

On 3 February the 15th Brigade was withdrawn from Teruel and marched southeast to an assembly point at Kilometre 19 (Puerto de Escandón), where it was ordered to rest for forty-eight hours. Casualties had been very high. Ed

Cecil-Smith reported that over eight hundred volunteers went into action on 31 December; only two hundred survived.

It was perhaps this terrible reality that prompted General Walter to meet with the brigade staff and remind the volunteers that they had made a considerable and crucial contribution to the battle. It was of some comfort to the Canadian survivors to learn that the Mac-Pap had been cited for its superior performance by General Juan Modesto, the commander of the Fifth Army Corps. He promoted Ed Cecil-Smith to the rank of major, Díaz and Edwards were made lieutenants, Niilo Makela was promoted to battalion staff, and Sol Wellman was given a citation.

The 15th Brigade was ordered to Valencia where the men were to rest and receive new equipment. En route, however, word was received that the fascists had mounted a massive counterattack from the north, through the Celades region, and the volunteers were recalled to the front, at the town of Segura de los Baños, seventy-five kilometres north of Teruel.

The Mackenzie-Papineau and the Lincoln-Washington were instructed, respectively, to take the strategically important fortified hills of Atalaya and Pedigrossa. On 16 February, in bitter cold and sleet, the two battalions moved off under the guidance of local peasants. It took the Mac-Pap five hours to get into position and to cut its way through the barbed wire entanglements that encircled the lower slopes of Atalaya. Frank Rogers, the commissar of the Mac-Pap, described what followed:

> Scattered into small groups we penetrated the enemy lines. The hills were controlled by a small group of soldiers, who were very well positioned behind barricades and in deep trenches. On each hill was [sic] six machine guns and two mortars. But what made this attack truly difficult was the terrain.
>
> In order to capture these hills we had to walk or run across an open field, which was inside the enemy's machine gun and mortar range. If we managed to get actually by the

hills we would remain ideal targets for the snipers and machine gunners.

The Canadians arrived in front of the other hill an hour before sunrise. They sent men to all the paths leading away from the hill and built shallow trenches to protect them from the machine gun fire and they were ready before sunrise to present their demands to the fascists to either surrender or fight.

When the first rays of the sun came from behind us, the Canadians opened fire all together, which woke up the men who were asleep on the hill. It must have sounded to the enemy as if the end of the world had come, because according to their information, not a single Loyalist was supposed to be within a four mile distance. The enemy surrendered with his weapons at six o'clock that morning and we were able to send 80 prisoners with guards to the rear lines.[19]

Joe Schoen of Winnipeg, who was also in the assault, narrowly escaped being wounded, thanks to a gift from his sister:

When I was about half-way up the hill one of the grenades exploded close beside me and knocked me off my feet. My right leg went numb and I could not get up for a couple of minutes.

Jim Tate, our first aid man, looked at my leg. But there was no sign of a wound. A week or so later I knew what happened. I had received a dozen white hankies from my sister and I had stuck the unopened parcel into the right pocket of my great coat before the attack. When I opened the package they were holed by a piece of hand grenade. The shrapnel was stuck in the cloth of the coat.[20]

The attack on Atalaya was a complete surprise to the enemy, and the Mac-Pap casualties were light. Ben (Butch) Goldstein was wounded and James Cochrane of Windsor was killed.

Bill Matthews described this engagement and a subsequent assault:

The barbed wire was cut by Frank Bobby [Tony Costello], Jim Tate, Butch Goldstein and one other. I think all the wire cutters were wounded. Frank Bobby was wounded in the foot.

We captured the hill within minutes, with prisoners. In the morning the Americans attacked the hill next to ours and we had a good view of the action from our positions. But they had a difficult time as the fascists were waiting for this second attack and the Lincoln-Washington suffered heavy casualties. But they took the hill within an hour or so. Now there was a third hill, and the Mac-Pap was given the honour.

It was a heavily wooded area and you couldn't see anything. A whole battalion could have been 100 yards away and not be seen.

Company Two commander, Alick Miller, was wounded and we were now under command of an American, I have forgotten the name [it was Nahanchuk].

We were told the 11th Brigade was on our right. We couldn't see it. We were told that at such-and-such a time there would be a heavy barrage from our anti-tank guns against the hill. On going into the woods we came across a section of men. No one spoke. No one from our group asked who they were. I surmised they must be a group from the 11th. They happened to be a fascist patrol and they notified the hill that we were going to attack it . . .

The fascists were waiting for us. The hill came alive. We were pinned down, some wounded and some killed. After we gathered up the wounded and left our dead, we quietly left.[21]

James Lompik of Edmonton, who was serving with the Dimitrov Battalion of the 11th Brigade, fought in a different sector of the front:

We stopped for a rest for four hours, changed our foot cloths, got a full supply of cartridges and grenades, received a day's ration of food and got some sleep.

On February 16, 1938, at two a.m. we stood to, and at three a.m. we attacked. Over rocks and hills and by five in the morning we surprised the fascists from the rear and, in heavy hand-to-hand fighting for an hour we captured all the fascists. The trenches were ours, but at a high cost in lives, mostly of Jewish and Hungarian companies.[22]

On 19 February 1938 the 15th Brigade was moved into reserve around Calades and then once again moved past Teruel to Kilometre 19, since the fascists were in the process of retaking Teruel.

THE RETREATS

Franco could not be content with the temporary stalemate which had developed on the Teruel front, for time was not on his side. International opposition to fascism was growing, and he had to regain the military initiative before the western powers bowed to internal pressure and intervened on the republican side. He thus planned an offensive designed to drive the republican forces to the natural barrier created by the Ebro River. The fascist armies would then break through to the Mediterranean, dividing and subjugating republican Spain.

Franco massed four Spanish and one Italian Army corps, two divisions of reserves, twelve companies of German tanks, thirty German antitank companies and twenty-five German fighter and bomber squadrons—a modern, motorized force of over 150,000 men. Facing it were the 11th and 15th Brigades and the 35th Division of the republican Fifth Army, numbering at most 35,000 men, with at best sixty planes and sixty tanks.

The fascist onslaught began with a tremendous artillery barrage across the entire front. During the first two hours the entire fascist bombing fleet made three flights along with hundreds of fighter planes which strafed the troops and dropped light bombs. The overwhelming superiority of the fascists' firepower and their mastery of the skies sufficed within a few hours to breach the republican lines, in spite of desperate and heroic resistance.

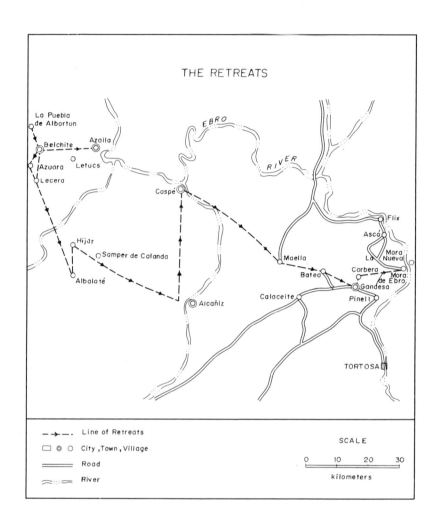

THE RETREATS

La Puebla de Alborton
Azaila
Belchite
Letucs
Azuara
Lecera
EBRO
RIVER
Caspé
Flix
Asco
Hijar
Samper de Calanda
Maella
Mora Nueva
La
Corbera
Mora de Ebro
Albalaté
Batea
Gandesa
Alcañiz
Calaceite
Pinell
TORTOSA

Line of Retreats
City, Town, Village
Road
River

SCALE
0   10   20   30
kilometers

Most of the international volunteers referred to the ensuing rout of the republican armies as "The Retreats." A retreat is the most difficult experience which an army can face, for it is punishing, demoralizing and unrelenting. Those who survived the retreat of the republican forces from March to April 1938 emphasize the disorder, the terror of being captured by the Moors or the fanatical Requetés, and the agony of not knowing what had become of friends and comrades.

Franco's forces manoeuvred around the flank and rear of the retreating republican army, cutting off its paths of retreat and forestalling efforts to capture advantageous positions from which it could have made a stand. The republican forces were in utter confusion, for the central command posts were scattered and disorganized, and contradictory orders were issued from various sectors of what remained of the front. Some of the men lost hope and ran in panic, some surrendered, some fought to the death. There were instances of arbitrary trials and firing squads. Everywhere there was chaos.

On 8 March the 15th Brigade, which was stationed in frontline reserve, received intelligence that something was wrong at the front. The information indicated the possibility that an offensive was being mounted by the enemy, although it appears that no general warning about such an offensive had been issued by the higher echelons. The information received included a report that an entire battalion of the brigade in the front line had deserted to the enemy.

About midafternoon on 8 March the chief of operations, Maurice Constant, accompanied by two others, was ordered to the front to ascertain the situation. On their way the three met fleeing deserters who told them that the front had just collapsed. Moving closer, they confirmed that a kilometre or more of the front was under concentrated artillery fire and aerial bombardment, and that troops were leaving the sector in disorder.

When the brigade command was informed of the actual situation it issued an order to have the brigade move up to the front. Constant's scouts returned to the battle area and observed that a heavy concentration of enemy troops, artillery and armour was taking place. The republican lines had been breached and the troops were in retreat.

The Retreats were carried out in two phases, the first from 9-28 March, and the second from 1 April. Many written accounts of them survive, but one of the most compelling is the following undated military report by Ed Cecil-Smith:

> When given the order to move Battalion 60 [Mackenzie-Papineau] to Letux from Hijar, about March 6th, I was informed that a strong enemy push was expected to develop in the next few days, coming from the west and attempting to come between Alberton and Belchite, then swinging south.
>
> Brigade 95 [Marineros] was to counter-attack, catching the fascist column in the right flank as it moved east, and the 15th Brigade was to be held in reserve in the towns of Letux, Belchite and Lecera.
>
> The enemy attack began on the morning of March 9th in the vicinity of Fuentetodos. By about ten a.m. our patrol on the Letux-Fuentetodos road reported bodies of men retreating towards Letux. Most of these were from Brigade 153. Early in the afternoon troops were retreating along the Azuara-Letux road and were stopped by our patrols about two kilometres from the latter town. These were from the 24th Division, 153 and 95 Brigades, and from attached artillery units.
>
> In almost all cases the highest ranking officers with the men were *sargentos*. The exception was an artillery unit which marched with two lieutenants, a quartermaster and one 2nd lieutenant-subaltern, carrying with them the breech blocks of their guns.
>
> Under the reported circumstances, I was called to brigade headquarters in the afternoon and ordered to move the battalion into position north of Azuara.

First, orders were to the effect that our forces from the brigade at Azuara would consist of Battalions 59 and 60, one anti-tank gun and a company of engineers, with attached transmission services, etc.

Verbal operation orders were to the effect that the enemy had taken large sections of first and second line trenches and had isolated about two battalions of the 95 Brigade on two positions each side of the Fuentetodos-Azuara road; that tanks had been seen within three kilometres of Azuara, to the rear of the above-mentioned heights and that upward of 100 *camions* had been observed moving down the highway towards Azuara and about six kilometres distant.

Battalions 59 and 60 were to move north from Azuara in the darkness, contact the enemy, counterattack him and drive him back and form a line connecting the two heights held by the 95th Brigade.

In the meantime, one company of our battalion [Company One] had been placed in position in unoccupied trenches about two kilometres north-west of Letux, when it became obvious to us that no organized line existed between Letux and the rapidly advancing enemy. Their position (approximately) was later taken up by the brigade machine-gun company, although this company took position a little behind those previously held by Company One.

One section of Company Three had also been sent for the afternoon to discover what the situation was to the west of Azuara. When recalled, they reported that our troops still held heights around Herrera. although the line to the north of that seemed to have folded up.

Later, orders from brigade were to the effect that battalion 60 would advance north from Azuara and build a line from two to three kilometres from the town, while battalion 59 occupied a position south west of the town on the other side of the river.

Just as positions were being taken up, the battalion commander was called to headquarters of Brigade 95, where Major Merriman informed him that the orders had come through to the effect that Battalion 59, the anti-tank gun and the engineers were ordered to move at once to Belchite and that undoubtedly orders to move battalion 60 would come through soon.

Meanwhile runners were sent to call in Company One, which was then about six kilometres to our right and the battalion was ordered, on instructions from Major Merriman, to rest until telephonic orders came from the brigade.

At about four a.m., Captain Kamy called from brigade to say that the expected orders had not come and that positions should be taken up.

So positions were chosen and the battalion began to dig in about five a.m. in a semicircle about 1.5 kilometres from town.

No further communications were possible with brigade as early in the morning the telephone central of division moved out without warning our transmissionists.

Before seven a.m. the enemy *avions* made their appearance and within a half hour artillery fire was opened on our positions and on those of the remaining forces on our right flank. A company or so of the 95 Brigade also still held an advanced position on a hill near the road, 200 metres ahead of the line.

The enemy attack lasted without slackening. In fact it intensified almost continually until nightfall, after seven p.m.

All day forces were leaving the line to our right—no *enlace* [runner] was ever made to our left, although we sent out at least three kilometres in that direction. When we stopped troops passing through Azuara and crossing the bridge, they made a detour and crossed the river at a ford about one kilometre to our right.

By the middle of the afternoon [about 2:30 p.m.] I was informed by the [lieutenant-colonel] commanding Brigade 95 that he had been ordered to retire his troops across the river to the south of Azuara, and that he would take up positions on the ridge behind the river. He also stated that three entire brigades had retired from our right, thus leaving no troops between us and Belchite, and also that the left flank had retired over the river.

At about the same time engineers belonging to a unit which I am unable to name, attempted to blow the bridge which connected us with the rear positions. Three large explosions took place but, fortunately, the structure was not completely demolished, but enough room was left to cross it.

Only one battalion commander of the 95th remained on the north of the river with us. In consultation with us, he stated that he was willing to stay so long as we did. However, his men were leaving and, although he shot four or five of them, he was unable to stop the retreat. At nightfall, only he and about half-a-dozen of his officers remained. They were placed on our right flank with one of our machine-guns. Our losses this day were ten killed and 29 wounded.

The only communication we had with outside was with our kitchen in Letux. This was contrived by the transmissions who cut in on the civil line at both ends. After nightfall we held a conference of officers where I reported on the situation. I informed the comrades that we had received no orders to retire and all that I knew of the situation.

In view of the fact that the battalion of the 13th Brigade which was promised as coming to our assistance had not shown up, and that the patrol we sent down the Letux road to guide them in did not report (they never did report, although we waited until about two a.m. They must have been taken prisoner), and also because the brigade machine-gun company joined us, not only without machine guns but also without rifles, I ordered that the battalion move back over the river and take up position with the 95th Brigade on the high cliff in the rear.

This decision was also based on the knowledge that the enemy had infiltrated across the river on our left flank, climbed the cliff and just as dusk fell was already firing into the rear of our position with machine-guns. We lost two men from this fire.

About 9:30 a.m., comrade Joe Gibbons phoned our kitchen to say that he had encountered General Walter on the road and that I was to report to divisional headquarters to make a report.

In preparation for moving across the river we collected all the wounded comrades and placed them in a command red truck and with a small guard of brigade scouts and others we took the truck along the Letux highway. We encountered no enemy. Neither did we meet our patrol.

Later, at divisional headquarters, General Walter was not free to speak with me until nearly four a.m. At this time I received orders to move the battalion to a position at kilometre eight on the Belchite-Lecera road to act as a reserve unit.

I decided to move the battalion via Samper de Sals but, not knowing the exact route, we had to go, using the kitchen truck (the kitchen had by now been moved to Lecera) and explore the road.

It was just breaking dawn when I arrived at the battalion position on the heights behind Azuara. Already the enemy artillery was firing and our machine-guns were engaging the enemy who were entering the town.

When we searched for the 95th Brigade to inform them of our order to move out, we discovered that they had entirely disappeared during the night. The result was that one of our machine-guns and its crew, as well as about eight other comrades, were cut off from the rest of the battalion by the enemy.

Leaving a small detail to try to contact them, I ordered the remainder of the battalion to leave for Lecera. Wounded were again evacuated in the truck we had brought. Our armoury truck sent out the night before carrying a number of trench mortars and machine-guns left behind by the 24th Division never got through and must have fallen into the hands of the enemy.

Expecting that the fascists would open fire on us with shrapnel from the several batteries of 75s which they were using against us, I ordered the troops to move in open march of approach formation.

The fact that enemy aviation did not show up for several hours, and that enemy infantry must have mistaken us for their own troops, we were not fired on until we reached Samper.

Just before reaching Samper, about five kilometres from Azuara, we passed positions already occupied by enemy troops, but continued without engaging them as our mission was to arrive at a certain point at the earliest possible moment. We arrived in Lecera about noon and reported to brigade headquarters for further orders, but it was evident that considerable changes had already taken place in our front since the night before.

About two p.m. we received our first orders to the effect that the division was moving down the Albacete road a few kilometres and that we should place the battalion across the left flank of the line of march, protecting the troops from an attack from the north.

Within fifteen minutes we received three different orders. The last of these was that we should march along a road about 500 metres north of the highway, take up a position near a village called Picon, or something of the sort, and at once contact brigade on the main road.

Just as the battalion was about to move off, divisional officers arrived with different orders again. Take up positions on the south side of the road and to the north, protecting both ˙sides for a distance of about two kilometres from town. This we did.

Enemy forces then advanced on Lecera from the south. We engaged several of his tanks and fired on infantry which had occupied a rise to the south of town. While we were actually engaging in this fight, about 150 metres south of the highway a captain from division staff arrived with orders to take up position across a *barranco* running in a north easterly direction about three kilometres from where we were.

When I pointed out that we were already fighting off an enemy attack from the south, he insisted that the tanks were ours and that the infantry was the 13th Brigade. This latter information we knew to be wrong as the 13th were on high ground about a kilometre to our left flank. The staff captain would consider no variation of his orders, and produced a map which indicated that various units of the divisions were in position in a circle around the town. These included battalions we had seen move off in the Albacete direction several hours previously.

Following orders, we withdrew our forces from their positions. Two companies and several machine-guns went up the *barranco*. One company remained in reserve and the other company stayed close to the highway for contingencies. As we were moving across, the fascists attacked the town from the south, undoubtedly assisted by the fact that they no longer faced the fire from our battalion.

Some time later I was approached by a Mexican captain who introduced himself as the commanding officer of three battalions of the 13th Brigade in the vicinity. The captain stated that he wished to counter-attack Lecera and wished us to act as his reserve.

I explained to the comrade what my mission was as given me by the division, but agreed that I could protect his right flank and also use one company as a reserve for him. The counter-attack failed.

About 10:30 at night we learned from *teniente* James Ruskin of brigade transmissions that the British Battalion was still in position north of Lecera. At once we sent a patrol of about seven men to contact this battalion and inform them of the fall of Lecera, suggesting a route for their withdrawal.

Orders for our withdrawal to [Albalate] arrived about 11:00 p.m. Our patrol found that the British Battalion had already left. We marched down the road some distance behind the 13th Brigade battalions, supplying rear and flank guards for the column.

(March 11th).

Our losses for the day were not very great. The heaviest loss was the machine gunners at Azuara who were either captured or killed. About eight or nine a.m. we arrived at our positions [1.5] kilometres north of Albalate, where the brigade was supposed to reorganize. While we were eating lunch the machine-gun and mortar company of the 11th army corps who were supposed to protect Albalate from the south, passed through our lines very rapidly, stating that the town had been captured by the fascists.

We had heard no shots fired, but I sent runners to the companies to prepare for orders.

Just at this time comrade Nikolai came through camp and gave me verbal orders to take the battalion via Hijar to Alcañiz. We formed on the highway and commenced to march. The battalion staff marched with our Third Company, then under the command of Captain Brage.

A panic developed on the highway. Tanks, trucks, ambulances and our cavalry tore through the infantry. Drivers and occupants leaned out and shouted to the soldiers that the fascists were on their heels. The infantry was thrown into confusion and many of the units lost their cohesion. We lost contact with one of the companies of the battalion as other units crowded between us.

A mounted courier came up with orders to go first to Alcañiz and then to Caspe. Just outside of Hijar enemy cavalry units cut the rear of our column off, mounting machine guns on the highway. In order to lighten our machine-gunners for the long march, the company commander had ordered them to place their guns on a truck which he thought belonged to the brigade. I later learned from a comrade in the Rakosi Battalion that the truck was theirs. Many of us were then forced to cross the river and make our way overland towards Alcañiz. Owing to the fact that our forces were from now on split and in several places at the same time, it is impossible to state what the casualties were.

During the night of March 12th, part of our battalion patroled Hijar keeping the fascists from getting across the river. Later we formed a line (a few) kilometres east of Hijar on a ridge. These positions we held all day not taking a great deal of part in the action of the day. During the late afternoon a patrol from Company Three reported having seen enemy forces occuping the town of Samper de Calandas [*sic*].

At night we learned that we were to move again towards Alcañiz as a flanking attack was expected. However, the brigades did not move off until nearly daylight. Again we supplied the rear guard. In the course of this march again the various units became mixed together. Not only did various battalions of one brigade mix in, but the same was true of the various brigades. No orders were given as to where we were actually going. Just orders to march towards Alcañiz. Owing to the fact that my battalion was split into two, with the rearguard company to the back, I utilized the ambulance as a means to control the troops.

The enemy cut up from Andorra and cut the road just west of Alcañiz. From what I have heard since, the brigade staff was in a position to know this fairly early, but they failed to notify our battalion of the fact. As a result, one company was left off and marched away with another brigade (the 12th I think) as this brigade seemed to be moving in an orderly manner. As for our ambulance, the failure to notify the troops in the rear resulted in our driving right into the enemy positions where they straddled the road.

Several machine-guns and a tank gun opened fire on us from point-blank range, about 50 metres when they started up, but we saw them before they opened fire and had swung rapidly onto a cart road running to the left. This led behind a large *fabrica* and we were able to escape on foot. The ambulance had to be abandoned because a small lake completely surrounded us on three sides, the fourth being towards the enemy. We escaped on foot still under fire from the machine guns and tank cannon. A *practicante* [first-aid man] was killed, and I became separated from the doctor, Lieutenant Dagar. He went into Alcaniz that evening and found the place full of Moorish and Requeté troops.

This was on March 14th. Those who were near the front of the brigade column, many of them were later picked up by truck and taken to Caspe. Those of us at the rear, however, made over the mountains for Maella. Next morning, on orders from the local *commandancia* which insisted that Caspe was taken and was evacuating Maella, we moved back to Batea where we set up a camp. By next day, upward of 200 men of the brigade were collected there. On the morning of March 15th, there passed through camp several ambulances making for a battle reported in the vicinity of Escuarton. Leaving Captain Brage in charge of the camp I rode north on an ambulance.

In Caspe that part of the battalion there was occupying the cemetery hill to the left of the town, in an effort to counterattack the enemy's advance on to a hill overlooking point.

We held this point against enemy infantry and tanks until evening. At this time the hill was held by such forces as the 15th Brigade had in Caspe, that is, besides about [1.5] companies of Mac-Pap, also smaller units from the Lincoln-Washington and British, each under their own commanders.

I do not recollect precisely at what time and in what terms the orders came for us all to retire. My memory is that it came from Major Merriman. We then, as dusk fell, took positions between town and the cemetery, about 500 metres from the cross roads occupied by brigade headquarters.

These, and other positions in the vicinity, we held for several hours. Then, in the early morning, under orders from comrade Doran who then assumed command of the brigade, we mounted a night attack against the cemetery. The Lincoln-Washington were elsewhere. Only a bare handful of British were able to take part, and three companies of the 14th Brigade supposed to assist us, refused to move because "their captain-adjutant had gone back to town", about a kilometre to the rear.

So, with the aid of fire from our tanks which was very effective, although it wounded several of our men, we took the hill. It was fortified by the enemy while he held it. Three heavy flat machine-guns were taken, fifty or sixty rifles, more than 30 prisoners, ten mules and other supplies, including a range finder.

This attack was made with little more than a hundred men with two light machine-guns and no hand grenades. It naturally took a long time, nearly three hours, to take the hill since the Rakosi Battalion, which we were told would make a flanking movement, never showed up, and we made only a frontal attack.

That men who had been through so much during the previous few days still had the determination and energy to do this was a great credit to the men of the Mackenzie-Papineau Battalion.

Possibly because of the failure of other units to move as planned in the night attack, the enemy, during this time, was able to advance rapidly on both our flanks, taking positions on the right in the railroad station and church steeple, and other houses in that part of town. On our left, they placed machine-guns in the olive groves and had either a light tank or an armoured car on a cart road, hidden partly by the olives.

Just as dawn broke, the British patrol reported that they had been driven out of a little red *casa* [house] on the railroad track which protected our long line of communication back to Caspe. I sent a runner back to brigade but, owing to the distance, it took a great deal of time for an answer to arrive.

When it did, it merely repeated the information I had previously sent in with respect to our situation. Meantime the companies of the 14th Brigade, which we had placed to guard the roads and flanks, were seen to be retiring, whether under orders or not I do not know. But, in half an hour, they had completely moved away. As the enemy fire from our rear was growing stronger, I sent a runner to brigade asking for assistance in the destruction of these enemy positions, either by gun fire or assault. Otherwise, with men tired and somewhat upset, I felt we could not hold our position.

Fortunately we had sent in our prisoners, captured guns and mules to town just before daybreak.

As the runner was so long in returning, we were not sure that he had gotten through the very heavy machine-gun and rifle fire covering the open field between us and town. Therefore, I ordered certain sections to cover the retreat of the remainder and informed the British of my decision, advising Captain Wild to leave with us, which he did. No officer had been named as in command of either the attack or holding of the hill, except Comrade Chapeyev and, as he never showed up, I assumed the responsibility, seeing we were so far from the brigade and from the rest of our troops.

Crossing the railroad cut, the river, and open fields under machine-gun fire cost us a number of lives and resulted in considerable disorganization of the units.

Just as we reached the lines of the 12th Brigade, a full kilometre behind our previous positions, I met the runner returning with orders to hold the hill. By that time I had lost control of the men and was not able to regain it again as, of course, comrade Wild and I were among the last of those retiring.

This was the last actual action the battalion was in, although during the day and night of March 16th we held various positions on the road between Caspe and Maella and were strafed and bombed by enemy planes.

On March 17th, about four a.m., we received orders to move back to a point between Maella and Batea, where the brigade was reorganized.

Without referring to reports previously made to the brigade at that time, I cannot state the number of dead, wounded or missing. These were compiled at Batea and were not finished until I left for Valls (hospital) a few days later.

Our records were lost in the subsequent action.

But I do recollect that, on March 20th, we had gathered together just over 250 from the old battalion, besides new recruits who came up. Also that we had turned in two machine-guns and a Dektyarov [Soviet machine gun] and 135 rifles.[23]

As the Mackenzie-Papineau Battalion moved to Azuara during the night, the Lincoln-Washington fell to on the road and marched northwest to the front. After five or six kilometres they came to a series of hills which dominated the area. The battalion left the main road near the base of a hill and crossed a bit of a small rise. When they were almost around the hill, the men came under intense small arms fire.

The command was given to retreat back over the lowest range of hills and to dig in. Although the retreating troops gave covering fire, the casualties were heavy. Indeed, it was initially rumoured that the Lincoln-Washington had been virtually wiped out in the engagement. The battalion established a position on an unfortified ridge and began firing, even though the battalion command had no idea where the enemy was.

Jim Foley, the commander of the battalion scouts, sent a three-man patrol to scout out possible enemy positions; in charge of the patrol was Bill Beeching, a Canadian volunteer attached to the Lincoln-Washington Battalion. At the same time Foley led some of his scouts into a nearby monastery, which was located on a promontory, hoping to gain an accurate picture of the front. They were no sooner in the monastery than they came under intensive and continuous air attack; the building was strafed incessantly and they were forced to leave.

Beeching's patrol had encountered no enemy positions within an arc of several kilometres, and on the way back met a patrol from the British Battalion. Almost immediately they came under heavy artillery fire, and concluded that there were not likely to be any enemy troops in the area. Both patrols returned to their respective battalions to report, but by this time the front held by the Lincoln-Washington appeared to be exploding. Having lost a man, Beeching and the remaining American volunteer were ordered to bring up some ammunition. Under constant heavy fire, both from planes and artillery, they slowly made their way towards the ammunition dump, which was located by a first-aid post. Several armoured cars were stationed there, and the drivers agreed to take the scouts with the ammunition up to the Lincoln-Washington position. However, as they approached the front they met the retreating battalion, which withdrew to Belchite, establishing positions east of the town near the St. Augustin church.

Beeching rode on a truck carrying Frank Rogers and a few other soldiers who had been wounded by the exploding artillery shell which had killed Dave Reiss and Eric de Witt Parker, the commanders of the Lincoln-Washington. The driver drove his small truck through Belchite, which was under heavy artillery fire. The streets were filled with rubble and buildings were crumbling all around, enveloping everything in great clouds of smoke and dust. To Beeching, it seemed miraculous when the truck eventually reached a position near the *fabrica*.

Beeching and a member of the British Battalion were posted to guard the *fabrica* because it contained some supplies which were to be moved out. However, they were forgotten in the retreat. The British guard disappeared and Beeching, now alone, was considering his options in the ominous silence when a small truck carrying some officers drove up. They told him to get in the truck since they were going to "try to get out."

The experiences of the British Battalion differed little from those of the Canadian and American units, except in detail. The British had been ordered to move approximately 3.5 kilometres north towards Mediana, where they came under a surprise attack as they took up what they had thought to be reserve positions. Finding that the front was deserted, they fell back to Belchite, where confusion was already a problem, as the men of the different battalions were becoming mixed and isolated in small groups.

Of paramount concern to the commanding officers was the need to reestablish some sort of cohesion and morale among the troops. However, in the chaos of the retreat this was not easy. Bill Matthews describes the uncertain situation faced by the exhausted troops:

> We retreated for a day, maybe two, tired, hungry, no sleep. Any villages we came to were deserted and they had been bombed by the fascists. We might get a few nuts or a bit of wine in these deserted villages. We came to a valley and water and trees, and were told to rest. The first of our meals came by truck, the first meal in several days.
>
> Word came that we were to establish a line around this area. Soon word came to get the hell out of there. We went about a kilometre and a troop of fascist cavalry came at us. We were taken completely by surprise. They came at us swinging their swords and were gone just as some of us started to fire.
>
> The next stop was east of Hijar, trying to reorganize and not sure where the units are. Our commander, Ed. Cecil-Smith, adjutant Wheeler and commissar Sol Wellman were not around and no one knew where they were. Niilo Makela takes over. Fascist observation planes are active in our area.
>
> General Walter, division commander, shows up and is trying to find out where the fascist troops in the area are. So, that night, we go back into Hijar with General Walter. There are no villagers there. It was a very dark night and we went through Hijar and started up a slope. Luckily someone loosened a stone that rolled down, and all along the ridge machine-gun fire broke out. No one in the Mac-Pap patrol was hit. We had found out where the fascists were.[24]

Included in this patrol were Bill Matthews, Tom McDonald, Amedée Grenier, Fred Mattersdorfer and Bill Beeching.

A position was established on the ridges outside of Hijar, and was backed up by a single tank. During the day the Moors

110

tried a cavalry attąck. Mattersdorfer, Beeching and Schuler, an American suffering from jaundice, were in the observation posts on the down slope when the attack began. It was a fiasco for the Moors, but their cavalry remained active.

The fascist aviators boldly flew reconnaissance missions over the republican lines. At times the men below could distinctly see their helmets and goggles. One of the pilots was too persistent, however, and a single shot rang out. Paddy McElligott, a volunteer from British Columbia, became one of the few soldiers to ever shoot down a plane with a rifle.

The position near Hijar became vulnerable and once again the volunteers were forced to withdraw. Bill Beeching and Joe Hecht of New York had just occupied a fox hole which they had dug when the order came to retreat and move towards Alcañiz. However, when the men approached Alcañiz they discovered that it was already in the hands of the fascist forces.

Antiaircraft guns had been brought up to Alcañiz and the front changed so rapidly that sometimes the antiaircraft battery merged with the front lines, firing directly at the fascist troops. Frank Hadesbeck recorded in his diary that the republican armoured train tried to reach Alcañiz but could not, since the fascists had bombed the railway connection between Hijar and Alcañiz.[25]

Fred Mattersdorfer illustrates the confusion and sometimes panic which occurred:

> While walking on the way to Alcañiz artillery shells were coming from east and west. We were in the middle, about five of us.
>
> Mike Kubenic who was with me ran north. I hollered at him to go south, and I chased him for a couple of hundred yards until I lost him. So I had to turn back south myself. It was the last anyone heard of him. He was one of my best pals.[26]

Such scenes could be replayed dozens of times with men vanishing, selling their lives in a brief fight with the enemy, unseen and alone.

Bill Beeching was in an isolated group which made its way to a deserted farm. While searching the area for food they were startled by the sound of cavalry approaching and were forced into the only available refuge—a root cellar. This was exceedingly dangerous, since a suspicious enemy need only toss a grenade into the open door and everything would be over. To Beeching, who was the lookout, it seemed that each of the twenty or more Moorish cavalrymen studied the cellar before passing on. The men left the farm as soon as the cavalry had gone, only to have another harrowing experience in an abandoned shed above a village. Two Dimitrov scouts advised them that it was not safe, and to post guards if they intended to remain. This they did, but guards and men alike fell into an exhausted sleep. Bill Beeching, sleeping near the door, was roughly awakened by one of the Dimitrov scouts, who held a hand over Beeching's mouth to keep him from crying out. All of the men were awakened in the same manner, and led to the Dimitrov outpost higher up the mountain. Looking back they saw the torches of a fascist patrol surrounding their hut.

Alcañiz had fallen before the republican troops reached it, and the retreat began once again. Bill Beeching was with a group of Americans when one of them, Danny Shannon, said that he had retreated far enough. He stated that he had not come to Spain to run away from the fascists, and refused to back up any more. Shannon could not be dissuaded, and asking his fellows for tobacco and ammunition, he built himself a small stone parapet facing back the way he had come. Reluctantly, his comrades moved on. Ten minutes later they heard the sound of intense small-arms fire, then utter silence. The retreat continued.

THE BATTLE FOR CASPE

The Mackenzie-Papineau Battalion was amongst the retreating republican forces when a stand was made at Caspe. Bill Matthews was there:

112

We headed further east towards Caspe and we were told that we were to form a line there. We got to Caspe and began reorganizing. Edward Cecil-Smith was with us, but not Wellman or Wheeler . . .

We took up positions west of Caspe in an olive grove and among some almond trees. There were other trees and shrubs growing there and we could not see too far. We heard the rumble of tanks coming along the road but could see nothing. I was standing out in the open trying to locate any movement. Then, suddenly, there was a burst of machine-gun fire. Bullets were hitting at my feet. I got to hell out of there.

Then rifle and machine-gun fire broke all along our front. The tanks were to the right of us and moving to our rear. We were told to move back.[27]

Niilo Makela, a trusted and respected commander who had repeatedly distinguished himself both for courage and leadership, was killed in action at Caspe. Paddy McElligott, who was himself cited for bravery in the battle for Caspe, had accompanied Makela to the top of an earth-covered water reservoir in order to spy on the enemy. In McElligott's words:

Suddenly Makela gave a grunt and seemed to lean over. I asked him: "Are you all right? Have you been hit?" Makela answered, "It's nothing. I'm alright" and then said "let's go." We turned and walked down the hill, I to my men and he to his command.

I looked over and saw him being helped and knew he must have been wounded. That's the kind of commander he was. He would never give in. He had great control over himself.[28]

Makela was helped to a first-aid post and then put on a hospital train. Doctors operated but were unable to save him. A memorial for Makela was held in a small town, where a street was named after him and a plaque was erected in his honour.[29]

A constant problem plaguing the republican forces during the battle for Caspe was insufficient knowledge of the location of the fascist forces. In one operation, Red Walsh of Vancouver, the commissar of Company Two, dispatched patrols to the flanks. The patrols were led by Scotty Ross and the Canadian adjutant, Geoffrey Allstop. Ross made it back, but Allstop's patrol disappeared. In this grim manner the command discovered the whereabouts of the enemy. Frank Thirkettle describes a typical incident:

> We arrived in Caspe to find it in our hands. We marched into position. My section went ahead as scouts, Red Walsh our political commissar accompanying us. Suddenly a bullet struck between Llewellyn and I. We had contacted the fascists![30]

Bill Matthews remembers that it was sometimes very difficult to tell friend from foe:

> That evening our company was on patrol east of Caspe and we came across another patrol. Who were they, Republican or fascist? The other patrol was very cautious as well. Both were ready to fire on one another. To our relief it was some of the 11th brigaders, the Thaelmann.[31]

The battle of Caspe was to be the last engagement in which Maurice Constant fought, as he described:

> Caspe was the end of it for me. By the time we were dug in, the enemy used methods to attack us. We were often surrounded. We would put together about 17 or 25 men, hold a position on a ridge, and then we would get it again.
>
> I was told to hold a position on a ridge just outside of Caspe. It was a sort of a stony ridge across the road. As usual, they came and strafed and bombed us. During one of the strafings, I got it. I was taken out by one of my scouts and brought back to the rear to where the walking-wounded station was.
>
> Standing there was Copic who, apparently, had heard from Division Headquarters and came up. He saw me and said, "Constant! What happened to you?"—and he commandeered an ambulance to put me in. There was a big line up, but I got put in. When I was taken out of the

ambulance I was wet with blood. The guy above me had been bleeding and was dead.[32]

Ed Cecil-Smith and the Mackenzie-Papineau Battalion set out from Caspe bound for the positions occupied by the 12th Brigade. En route, however, the men were caught in the fields by a raking machine-gun fire. Thirkettle describes the action:

Suddenly to our left rounding the hill barely 30 yards away, a large body of the enemy appeared. How they managed this I have never been able to discover. Immediately, Captain Dunbar, staff officer, commanded us to fire. Captain Dunbar ordered a slow steady fire-retreat. Dunbar aroused my admiration by his coolness and command of the situation.[33]

On 20 March, when the Mackenzie-Papineau Battalion mustered at Batea only 250 men, half of its original strength, remained. Many of the men had lost their weapons, and the battalion was reduced to two machine guns, a light machine gun, an automatic rifle, and 135 rifles. The Mac-Pap camped four kilometres west of Batea for the rest of the month. Here it was joined by 175 new volunteers, including some from the hospitals and training schools.

The fascists increased their pressure on the republican forces after 22 March, with a new drive towards Catalonia. The situation became increasingly desperate for the loyalists and their international allies, and all hospitals, camps and rest-homes were visited by commissars and commanders, calling on those who were able to report to the front. The commitment of the international volunteers remained high, and many of the men returned to battle with wounds that were not fully healed. The Tarazona training base was emptied and brigade headquarters reestablished at Barcelona.

To the ranks of the veterans were added fresh volunteers. These reinforcements were often shaken when they joined their battalions at Batea, as Al Amery recalls:

Our first sight of the men who had recently been in battle was somewhat of a shock. They looked full of life, like wild animals, their fierce eyes gleaming with a kind of battle stare that cut through you.

They looked like wolves in human form. A kind of ferocity lurked in their unwashed bodies and ragged clothes as I had never seen before. And, whether they sprawled on the ground, leaned against an olive tree, stood still, or walked, they never looked relaxed. Thin, haggard and drawn, they always seemed on the verge of bursting into action.

I was amazed at their description of bloody details and the horrors and miseries of battle. But, as soon as we reached the trenches, I could never see them again from the same point of view.[34]

While the 15th Brigade rested and reorganized, fascist troops were converging on the city of Gandesa, which would be the scene of the next major battle.

THE FIRST BATTLE OF GANDESA

On 31 March the 15th Brigade marched to a point west of Gandesa at the crossroads where the Gandesa-Calaceite highway is intersected by the road from Batea. The Lincoln-Washington Battalion marched north towards Batea, while the Mackenzie-Papineau and British battalions went west. In the Gandesa area twenty republican brigades faced over 200,000 well-armed fascist troops.

The British were in the vanguard in the move towards Gandesa, and clashed with the fascist forces advancing on the city. In a skirmish with tanks along the road Wally Tapsell, the British commissar, was killed while Frank Ryan was taken prisoner and Malcolm Dunbar was wounded.

The Mac-Pap was situated along a road a few kilometres away. Jimmy Higgins, a volunteer from Saskatoon, describes the fighting:

On the afternoon of March 31st (1938) orders were received to march. The fascists had blasted their way

116

through the flank and there was a danger of that whole part of the country being cut off if they reached the cross roads.

Machine-gun squads were separated from the companies and sent ahead with orders to stop empty trucks and take them as close to the front as possible.

Our squad was made up of me as a gunner, Ray Henderson and his brother, Stanley, Claude Nash, Tommy Roberts, Tom Blackburn, under the leadership of Amedée Grenier.

With the help of a Spanish officer we were able to get a truck after marching for five or six miles. We finally reached the crossroads. Turning right towards the west we made our way slowly along the torn road filled with bomb holes, burnt trucks and dead bodies. Trucks were still burning and by their light our driver managed to navigate quite a distance before the truck slid into a bomb crater and turned on its side.

From then on we met hundreds of women and children trekking back to our rear. The villages they had lived in were smouldering ahead of us. This meeting with women and children fleeing from the terror of the invader was a sight that overshadows all others. I stopped to take a bloody, battered, dead little body from a woman and, until this day, I do not believe that the poor woman knew her baby was dead. It seemed as though she was walking in her sleep.

Scouts ahead sent back word that the fascists had been contacted. We began to spread out and find positions for our guns.

April 1, 1938.

Fascist planes came over to observe our positions. The fascists opened up with a heavy artillery barrage.

We had no flanks. The enemy got well behind us and when they attacked we were pretty nearly surrounded. We fought, going back slowly, taking a stand in small groups wherever we could find cover. The light machine-guns stayed until last in order to cover the retreat of the others and then came back when the riflemen were giving enough cover to fire.

Tommy Blackburn lost our group and was captured.

At this time only 13 of us were left of the company, and our gun was ordered to cover their retreat. Ray Henderson, his brother Stanley, and I, were left to carry out this order.

We were signalled to go back after awhile. Ray went first. Stanley and I had just picked up the gun when he was shot through the head. He was killed instantly, and I shouted to Ray to come back and help me with the ammunition.

Ray came back and helped me to roll his brother off the ammunition box and then, making sure that Stanley was dead, we made tracks out of that place. We got safely to where Tommy Roberts, Claude Nash and Amedée Grenier were, and were met by Captain Brage, who again ordered us into a position to fire on the advancing enemy.[35]

The squad found out it was encircled, but Brage saw a chance to get the men out. They travelled five hundred yards through a heavy growth of woods, and came under crossfire at the bottleneck, but got through and rejoined the Mackenzie-Papineau Battalion, which by then numbered only eighty men.

The Mac-Pap began its retreat towards the Ebro River. In a letter to Canada, Pat O'Hara of British Columbia wrote:

I guess you read about our last action. It looked like all hell had cut loose on that hill at Gandesa. Planes, artillery, tanks, anti-tank guns, machine-guns and Christ knows what were there at us, and still we held off for a day-and-a-half against all odds. Then came the order to retreat. At the time I was sergeant of a patrol [2.5] kilometres behind the fascist lines trying to contact the 11th Brigade, but the 11th had other positions the day before.

How we got out is a marvel. Never lost a man.[36]

NOTES

1. Maurice Constant, taped interview with the author.
2. Quoted in Brennan, unpublished account.
3. Adapted from Brennan, unpublished account.
4. Printed in *BC Lumber Worker*, 6 October 1938.
5. J. Hoshooley, written account to author.
6. Cited in Brennan, unpublished account.
7. Ibid.
8. Taken from E. Komodowski, *With the Mackenzie-Papineau Battalion in Spain* (Winnipeg: the author, n.d.), 60.
9. Adapted from Liversedge, "Memoir of the Spanish Civil War."
10. W. Kardash, "Tank Attack at Fuentes del Ebro," *The Marxist Quarterly* 18 (Summer 1986): 48-49.
11. Adapted from Liversedge, "Memoir of the Spanish Civil War."
12. Lee Burke, written account to author.
13. Constant, interview.
14. Ibid.
15. William Matthews, written account to author.
16. Interview with Lionel Edwards, *The Volunteer for Liberty* 11, no. 33 (6 October 1938).
17. Komodowski, *With the Mackenzie-Papineau Battalion*, 39-53.
18. A. Haas, in ibid., 16-17.
19. Taken from "Our Sons in Spain." Selected translations by Varpu Lindstrom-Best from Meidän Poikame Espanjassa, edited by K.E. Heikkinen (unpublished manuscript), 25-26.
20. Schoen, written account.
21. Matthews, written account.
22. J. Lompik, written account to author.
23. This is the longest military report written by Cecil-Smith to have been found by the author. Although it is undated, it appears to have been written shortly after The Retreats.
24. Matthews, written account.
25. Saskatchewan Archives Board, Fred Hadasbeck, Diary.
26. Mattersdorfer, written account to author.
27. Matthews, written account.
28. J.P. McElligott, written account to author.
29. McElligott claims that the memorial plaque was erected in the first town the troops were in after crossing the Ebro during The Retreats. This would likely be Mora de Ebro.
30. Frank Thirkettle, written account to author.
31. Matthews, written account.
32. Constant, interview.
33. Thirkettle, written account.
34. Al Amery, written account to author.
35. H.J. Higgins, written account sent to the Historical Commission of the Mackenzie-Papineau Battalion, 21 March 1939.
36. O'Hara's letter is in the possession of the author.

Five

Crossing the Ebro

The spring of 1938 was a bleak one for the republican cause in Spain. The confusion and casualties incurred in The Retreats were aggravated by the knowledge that Franco's forces were succeeding in their breakthrough to the Mediterranean, dividing Spain and forcing the republican army across the Ebro River. Even the crossing of the river had an ominous symbolism, as Amedée Grenier would later recall:

> Orders came during the afternoon [1 April] that everyone was to try to make it to the Ebro. We were to start after darkness, to leave our lines in an orderly way making the least noise possible. I walked across the Ebro at midnight. The bridges, road and railroad were blown early in the morning . . . I was still carrying my light machine-gun when I crossed the river. I gave my machine-gun to a unit of the Dombrowski. Later, when Díaz rejoined us, he asked me if I still had it. I said I had a certificate showing that I had delivered it to the Dombrowskis. Díaz laughingly said, "You cannot fire at the enemy with a certificate."[1]

Nor, he might have added, could a civilian army win a civil war when the government it was trying to uphold was rife with political division and defeatism. Tragically, this was the case in Spain in the spring of 1938. The military superiority of Franco's forces, supported as they were by Germany and Italy, contrasted sharply with the continued diplomatic isolation of the republic, and persuaded many republican leaders that their cause was doomed.

Two prominent socialists, Largo Caballero and Indalicio Prieto, became rallying points for members of the Cortes who had concluded, after the defeat at Teruel, that the republic could not win. Against them, Prime Minister Juan Negrín rallied the republican loyalists. He assumed the defence portfolio and formed a National Union government. The new cabinet included representatives from both of the major trade unions, five members from the republican parties, including one from the Catalan *Esquerra*, four Socialists, and one member each from the Basque Nationalist and Communist parties.

On 1 May 1938 Negrín issued a thirteen-point program which outlined the war aims of the government. The commitment to defeat fascism was reaffirmed, and the prime minister called for an end to foreign intervention in Spanish affairs. At issue, the program proclaimed, was the defence and preservation of a democratic republic, with universal civil rights, freedom of conscience and religion. The government promised to respect regional autonomy without prejudicing national unity, to respect all property legally acquired, and to embark upon a policy of national reconciliation following the defeat of the fascists.

TRAINING FOR A NEW ASSAULT

The high ideals outlined in the government's thirteen-point program reminded many of the international volunteers of the reasons for which they had initially come to Spain, and helped to restore morale in their ranks. The prospects of the republican government were not promising, but with a grim determination the International Brigades set about consolidating, training and reorganizing their forces, as Bill Matthews remembers:

> When we got over the Ebro to the east side we dug trenches, improved fortifications, deloused ourselves and got clean clothing, ate regular meals and were issued with new equipment. Replacements began to come in.

> Company Two headquarters was in a *hacienda* with a large wine cellar and sacks of nuts. Lee Burke was our telephone operator and he issued a bulletin board containing daily news.

> Debates raged. Each time the League of Nations met there were rumours that the French border would be opened,

that food, clothing, medical and army supplies would be coming, that squadrons of planes and divisions of French troops were at the border to aid the Republican government—that aid would be coming at any moment, that world opinion would force the League of Nations to aid the Republic.

Debates and newspapers were for aid to Spanish democracy. Spain will be the death of fascism! History was being made in Spain. I was so proud of being a part of it.

We were finally withdrawn from our positions on the Ebro on May 15, 1938, and stationed outside of the village of Marsa.

Here we went into training manoeuvres, practised crossing the river, celebrated July 1st with a sports day—football, rifle shooting competitions, extra rations.[2]

The temporary respite in the volunteers' lives after crossing the Ebro, however, brought its own set of problems, among them the loneliness and longing for home which are common to all soldiers. This sense of isolation made the men highly critical of the Spanish postal system for they suspected, rightly or wrongly, that mail and parcels from home were being lost or withheld. The volunteers read stories in Canadian papers about shipments of parcels to Spain, but these often failed to arrive. Parcels that did get to Spain were taken to Albacete where they were examined. Since many volunteers received nothing from home, the contents of these packages were divided and apportioned out, regardless of ownership.

Letters from home, being perhaps less tempting targets, arrived with somewhat more regularity. Sam Huhtala remembers the excitement created by the mailman's call of "Cartas! Cartas!":

This was the Spanish mailman's cry every morning when he made his rounds that June, 1938, when the Mac-Pap were encamped in a narrow valley some distance east of the Ebro River for rest and some retraining.

In the morning, after the boys had rolled up their blankets under the nut bushes and washed their faces hurriedly in the cold water of an irrigation channel, they lined up for their morning coffee with red-wine-dipped toast. Then they wiped the night dew from their rifles and machine guns, which was followed by an idle period before roll call. It was at this period when the mailman arrived. More and more furtive glances were cast down the road on the opposite hillside where he would come with his little van.

When the van stopped opposite the camp site, he would throw a bag over his shoulder and coming down the little incline and over an old bridge he would joyfully call: *cartas!*

The shy and more reserved would stand back, while the eager ones would crowd around as if he was Santa Claus. Sometimes he was when one of the volunteers received a package from home containing smokes, which were usually shared with one's platoon and other friends.

When the mailman pulled from his bag a packet of letters, the boys crowded a little closer. Toes were stepped on, heels were kicked, and the shorter peered over the taller on tip-toe. Letters were passed from hand-to-hand.

Hope and expectancy faded from other faces in the same ratio as the bundle of letters dwindled.

Most of the letters were for the Spaniards in the ranks who made up about half or more of the international brigades. Writing material and stamps were a necessary part of a Spanish soldier's equipment.

The volunteers also received some mail, but not in any comparable volume. When a letter was received it was taken to a quiet little place. It was handled with hesitation. The handwriting or the return address told who it was from. The postmark was noted when the letter was mailed. The censor's stamp was glanced at. Then it was opened carefully and read.[3]

While the troops were in training at Marsa, Valledor replaced Copic as the commander of the 15th International Brigade and John Gates was made brigade commissar. Ed

Cecil-Smith had returned to command the Mackenzie-Papineau Battalion with Frank Rogers as commissar and Sol Rose as battalion adjutant. Companies One through Four were commanded by Lionel Edwards, Henry Mack (who had been commanding officer of the Mac-Pap during Cecil-Smith's convalescence), Pedro Roca and George Carbonell (a Puerto Rican); the machine-gun company was commanded by Gunnar Ebb.[4]

The International Brigades were being prepared at this time for an assault across the Ebro River. Success in this operation was possible, but the closing of the French border had resulted in a scarcity of arms, and the men were told they would have to try to capture enemy weapons whenever possible. The training program also adopted special defensive measures designed to reduce casualties. The men were taught that with strict discipline it was possible to survive artillery barrages, bombings, strafings, and tank assaults. To imbue this sense of discipline the army initiated the *Actavistas* (activist movement), a mass struggle for training designed to achieve a high level of fighting efficiency and combat readiness.

Participation in the movement was optional, but once soldiers had committed themselves to the *Actavistas* they were expected to perform to the best of their abilities. The men took a pledge which, roughly translated, went like this: "To care for the arms as for my life; to be a champion of unity, a worthy representative of the government of national union; to struggle without rest against the pessimists and provocateurs; to be strongest in attack and firmest in defence." Speed, efficiency, and the proper maintenance and preservation of weapons were all goals of the *Actavistas*. Indeed, the men were expected to know their weapons so well that they could take them apart and reassemble them while blindfolded.

ATTACK ACROSS THE EBRO

The *Actavistas* succeeded in building up morale in the troops, but the movement's success also depended on the

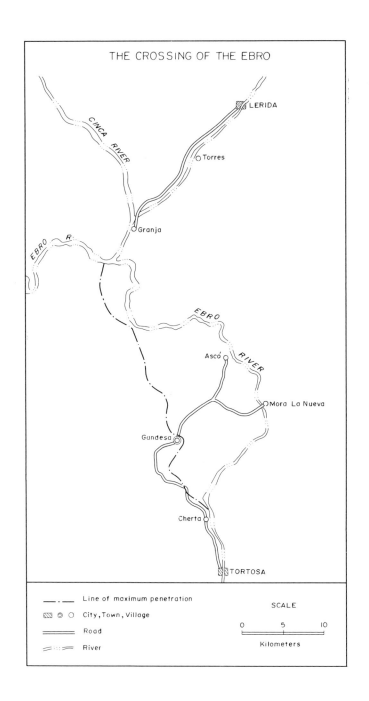

THE CROSSING OF THE EBRO

Line of maximum penetration
City, Town, Village
Road
River

SCALE

0   5   10

Kilometers

125

training and abilities of the commanding officers, commissars and non-commissioned officers. All were to be put to the test in the fierce fighting which followed the assault across the Ebro River on 25 July 1938.

The republican counterattack astonished not only the fascists but the world at large. It was a bold and brilliant stroke which showed that the republic still had the reserves and the will to continue the fight, in spite of the devastating blows it had suffered in the spring. Tactically, the attack was a success, for it forced Franco to halt his offensive against Valencia and to divert his divisions to stem the republican advance. Ultimately, however, although the republican forces established a bridgehead which was to be held for three-and-one-half months, the republic lacked the economic potential which would have enabled it to combine the defensive and offensive strategies in a cohesive action on a wide range of fronts.

Lionel Edwards stated that "we didn't know the battle orders, but it must have been to cross the Ebro and go as far as you bloody well could!" On the way to Ascó, Edwards was badly wounded by the exploding shell which killed Uuno Munnumaki of Port Arthur.

According to Lee Burke, the element of surprise was crucial:

> I don't know how the men were briefed but somebody briefed us the night before we crossed and said we'll have no plane support, or artillery, or tanks. It is a total surprise attack in which we shall take towns, supplies and arms. I thought it was very good. At least you are not waiting for planes and tanks that don't appear. But tanks must have crossed on pontoons and did get into action.[4]

In a letter published in the 13 August 1938 edition of *The BC Logger*, Walter Gawricki wrote:

> Comrades, I want to tell you about our offensive on the Ebro River. No kidding! It was a real offensive! We had very little material, even some of our comrades had no rifles,

but we had a good slogan: "Go and get it from the bloody fascists." So we went. When we crossed the river, believe me, we showed them what we could do. We gave them a big surprise.[5]

Once again, however, there were instances of the poor communications which had continually plagued the republican forces, as Mike Storgoff of Winnipeg recalled:

We thought we'd have a chance. We made it across the Ebro, but we didn't have guns. We had no place to run. Sometimes we didn't know where the enemy was.[6]

But even war has its comic aspects, and Bud Crossley still laughs when he recalls the crossing:

Why in hell didn't they find guys who could row boats? It was a bloody mess sometimes, with us sitting in the middle of the Ebro going round and round.[7]

Fred Kostyk and his boatload of troops, much to their surprise, were treated to a political lecture while crossing the river:

. . . the Gandesa offensive developed and I became a part of it with the Lincoln-Washington Battalion. It began at night and before we could do anything we had to cross the Ebro River. I was in a boat with about six other men and we were rowed across by a Spaniard who was sympathetic to the Republican side and he decided to tell us all about it in the middle of the river. He stopped rowing, stood up, and began to preach to us, to give us a "pep talk," to tell us all about the great part we were about to play in the struggle. Eventually we made it to the other side.[8]

Bill Matthews, whose picture with a boatload crossing the Ebro has appeared in several histories (see photo section), recalls:

July 25, 1938, the Mac-Pap crossed the Ebro. The 11th was ahead. They crossed during the night. There is a picture in the Landis book entitled "Lincolns crossing the Ebro." This same picture is in the book *International Solidarity with the Spanish Republic* printed in the USSR.

The picture is of a boat being pushed by a Canadian named Red Linton of London, Ontario. It is the first group of the Mac-Pap, the first part of Section One, Company Two. Others are Bill Matthews, a Spanish runner named Eduardo and other Spaniards. The person in the wide-brimmed hat is Jimmy Clark, Toronto printer, who worked at Everready Press. The person near the right is Rod (I think that is his first name) MacKenzie of Vancouver who was killed near Gandesa.

This picture was also used by the National Film Board in its production of "Los Canadienses."

Two days previous, during the night, we started to move towards the river on foot. During the early hours of the 25th the 11th Brigade went across. Then, at daylight, the Mac-Pap crossed. The Mac-Pap assembled in a valley on the opposite side of the Ebro.

The fascists opened up with artillery fire and Lionel Edwards and Nick Meyers were hit. The Mac-Pap advanced west until nightfall and bivouaced on each side of a Gandesa road. There was a sound of tank tracks on pavement coming toward us. On the command to halt, this object opened fire and we returned it. It happened to be a former fascist ambulance captured by the 11th Brigade which was bringing back wounded. As a result, all were killed except the soldiers firing from the ambulance.[9]

Joe Schoen describes his impressions of the crossing and the fighting which followed:

The Thaelmann crossed the river first, during the night, and had pretty well taken care of the enemy infantry. We were all supposed to be over the river before daybreak. But it was about 10 a.m. before we got across. Our casualties were not heavy and we made quite an advance into enemy territory. Took a couple of towns that had been by-passed by other troops and were still in enemy hands.

On the second day we started our advance on Gandesa. During this advance Bill Matthews was wounded in the neck, a wound nearly severing his jugular vein. A little while later a company commander, I believe it was Stan Udin [Svens Udden] from Port Arthur, was shot in the

128

mouth. The bullet exited in his neck. As I passed him I could see great gushes of blood coming out of his mouth. I thought he was finished, but had a pleasant surprise. We met in Barcelona after I came out of the hospital.[10]

Bill Matthews describes the early hours of the battle on the other side of the Ebro:

A French-Canadian comrade, Omar Lazure, was killed outright by an artillery shell. He was a little bit ahead of me. We were in a staggered formation. We both hit the dirt when we heard the shell coming. I escaped with minor injuries, mostly sand and gravel splinters in my nose and left ear.

We advanced about twenty miles that first day. There was no food except what we found along the way. We also found a lot of clothing and military equipment that had been discarded by the enemy in their flight.

After a few days pontoon bridges were built so that light trucks and an ambulance could cross, usually at night. Later some artillery and tanks came across.

Sergeant Mike Dyrow was sergeant of a platoon, very able man. He was put in charge of the men building bridges across the Ebro. He was killed on the Ebro during one of the bombing attacks.[11]

Oleksa Sheveliuk describes the difficulties he and his fellows encountered:

As we were building the pontoon bridges and transporting the soldiers to the other side the fascist planes were bombing us non-stop. The first planes having unloaded a quantity of bombs on us would fly away making room for the next wave of planes loaded with more bombs. Nevertheless, we managed to do our job of transporting the necessary units and materials.[12]

Andy Haas of Winnipeg helped to build a pontoon bridge across the Ebro and then carried food and ammunition across it by hand:

We were watching the bombing of the trucks that were lined up beside the pontoons, waiting to get across, three miles of them. The fascists had a field day with them. We were helpless, no anti-aircraft artillery.

Then the fascists opened up the dam at Lerido. It swept away the pontoons . . . The Ebro is a mighty river. I made a dash for the pontoon and started across. I was the only one though. When I was about half way across and racing towards our bank, the water broke the pontoon from its mooring, but on our side and even tho' I was racing I realized I would never make it across. I had . . . to make up my mind very fast what to do as the wild foaming waters began to swing the pontoon rapidly away from the end . . . So I made up my mind very fast, jumped into the water and fortunately reached our shore.[13]

On 30 August 1938 Ed Cecil-Smith wrote the following account to Beckie Buhay of Toronto:

By now you must be aware that the battalion did its duty well in the present campaign.

Besides supplying the best elements among those who ferried over the various international brigades and others, we were the first battalion in the brigade [the 15th] to cross the Ebro.

Lionel Edwards of Edmonton, Captain of our Number One Company, among others, was wounded while we attacked and captured Ascó, the first town taken on the right bank of the Ebro.

Our battalion also must be credited with having driven closer than any other to the key town of Gandesa. Unfortunately we were on low-lying ground by that time and the difficulty which battalions on our right and left encountered in the hills made it necessary for us to withdraw to positions which were not dominated by enemy fortified in the hills.

None of this can be thought to indicate that the other battalions of our brigade, or other brigades of our division, or other divisions even, did not do just as well. Perhaps we were just lucky in being given certain assignments.

You remember I wrote you several months ago about Lieutenant Copernico and his bravery which saved his company during the retreat at the end of March. You recollect that he walked out and engaged the fascist officers in a discussion and allowed himself to be taken prisoner.

I am now able to give a sequel to it. Comrade Copernico remained a prisoner for a couple of weeks and then, along with others of our boys, managed to escape. For eighteen days they made their way behind the fascist lines, finally breaking through and rejoining the loyalist troops in the Levant.

He is now incorporated in that part of the international brigades which still remain in central Spain. We learned about his thrilling escape in a very mundane way. He wrote enquiring about his back pay! This, I think, is quite in keeping with his heroism. He, himself, didn't think he was being a hero at all.

ESTABLISHING A BRIDGEHEAD

The Mackenzie-Papineau Battalion came under heavy fire from mortars and bombers at dawn on 25 July. Companies One and Two, reinforced by heavy machine guns and the headquarters section moved on Ascó, while Companies Three and Four, with the balance of the machine guns, moved on Flix. Both towns were taken, offering only light resistance. A company of fascist cavalry and a battalion of infantry gave up at Flix, while the garrison at Ascó killed its commanding officer and surrendered. Brigade scout Fred Mattersdorfer recalls:

> When we crossed the Ebro and were near Corbera, I was on patrol with three other scouts and came across Lieutenant Cooper and two Spaniards with 200 or more prisoners, seven Moors among them. The Moors had wanted to kill Cooper and his group. One of the Spaniards was a commissar and he told the fascists we owned all the territory for miles around. But we actually didn't have any soldiers back there at all. The fascists got scared and came with Cooper, bringing two machine guns with them, all their rifles and ammunition. We had to go about five miles

more to brigade headquarters. There we told them to put up the rifles and machine guns on a pile.[14]

Six men from the Mac-Pap were left to patrol in Flix, and the rest turned south to join the other companies, which were moving towards Corbera. By late afternoon all the Canadian forces were united and were advancing rapidly under heavy enemy air bombardment. The fleeing fascist troops abandoned everything in their haste to escape.

Just after sunset, the men heard the sounds of heavy equipment moving across their front. They got off the road but discovered that the noise was being made by the 13th Brigade, which was driving captured artillery and tractors. Patrols from the 13th Brigade helped the Canadians move into Corbera at dawn. They moved through the town to a coulee on the western approaches where they were issued shoes, blankets, sardines and octopus which had been taken from the fascist supply depot. The remaining supplies were then distributed among those of Corbera's citizens who had stayed in the town.

The fascists heavily bombed Corbera on the afternoon of the second day. The Mac-Pap and the British Battalion were by now deployed outside the town, on the fringes of the target of the air raid. Here an act of gallantry took place which would still be remembered forty years later, in both Spain and Canada. Jimmy Higgins describes what occurred:

> I recall an incident of saving a young boy. I was in one of the towns [Corbera], close to the Ebro River. I had been sent into the town to see if anything could be done to help out in the wake of a bombing. A first aid place had been set up in the winery. We looked for victims of the bombing attack although most of the people had left town.

> A plane came over and made a direct hit on the [water] storage tank. José noticed somebody being swept down the stream that had been flooded by the damaged tank. Taking off my coat and telling José to hang onto three hand grenades and make sure the machine-gun was

guarded, I went into the river and manged to catch up to a boy of about 12 years of age.

Within a few minutes I had pulled him in close to the bank and, as the boy could not walk because of the damage to his legs, I carried him to the winery. While I was carrying the boy I was trying to tell him who I was. In what Spanish I could muster, I told him I was a Canadian and that my name was Jim. Anyway, I doubted the lad would survive.[15]

The boy, whose name was Manuel Alvarez, did survive. When, months later, he learned from his father that the "foreign volunteers" had left Spain, he vowed to find the "tall soldier" who had saved his life. It was a vow he kept forty years later, when he found and was reunited with Jimmy Higgins in Peterborough, Ontario.[16]

THE SECOND BATTLE OF GANDESA

The Mac-Pap was ordered to move on Gandesa. Two kilometres from Corbera it encountered heavy fascist fire from the hills surrounding the town. In the distance, the sound of fascist vehicles approaching Gandesa from the opposite side could be clearly heard above the din of rifle and machine-gun fire.

Bill Matthews was one of the first casualties in the assault:

As we advanced, we came under heavy fire. I was hit in the neck and shoulder. I was taken to the rear, waited for a truck at Corbera which took us, late in the evening, to the field hospital. At this time, there was [sic] not many vehicles crossing the River Ebro as the fascist planes were bombing all the pontoon bridges.

Dr. Magid, a wonderful comrade and doctor, was at the field hospital. In the morning we crossed the Ebro and went to a hospital in the side of a mountain. In the evening, we boarded a train and headed north.

There were white uniformed waiters on the train and in the dining car. I was dirty and bloody, and was now being waited on by spotlessly clean, polite waiters. I do not recall what was on the menu but surely I must have enjoyed it.

133

I was sent to the hospital at Mataro, a converted monastery. I was there for two or three weeks, and was sent to another, and was asked if I was OK for duty. When I said I was I was sent to Barcelona, stayed in a hotel room on the Ramblas with Lieutenant Joe Kelly of Vancouver. That was the most frustrating part of my life in Spain. In two or three weeks, I got word to report to my battalion at Sierra Cavalls [as] company commander. The company personnel numbered about 160 or 170. Later on it was reduced to 90. I still dream about our losses.[17]

For four days, with only rifles and machine guns, the international volunteers repeatedly attacked positions that were well-defended with a wide range of weapons and air support. The British, poorly armed, attacked up the slopes of Hill 481, known as the Pimple, and the Canadians continued to assault Gandesa. Each time they were repulsed.

The training the men had received prior to recrossing the Ebro served them well. Although fighting a better-equipped enemy, the volunteers were able to continue the battle, in spite of heavy losses and in less than ideal conditions.

The hills were really small, rocky mountains. Men were hit and wounded by stone fragments as often as by bullets and shrapnel. It was impossible to dig trenches in this rocky terrain, and the men had to pile up rocks as parapets and to use rock piles as shelters. It was also difficult to bury the dead, whose bodies soon littered the hillsides and coulees. In the July heat the battle- ground was quickly permeated with the terrible stench of unburied and rotting bodies. C. Arden Nash of British Columbia was there:

We crossed the Ebro on July 25. We lost a few men but saw little more until we reached Hill 481 near Gandesa. We lost many good men here, among them my good friend "Moon" Keenan. One man who had most of his hand shot away panicked. I jumped on him and wrestled him to the ground so we could calm him down and bandage his wound.

I no sooner finished with him than I had to do it all over again with another man. That night I helped bury many

134

good men in shallow graves and ditches. The next day I came across a hand sticking out of the ground as though pointing at the bombers and fighters in the sky.

We were moved down to the bottom of the hill where we were to make an attack on Gandesa, but we didn't get far before we were pinned down by intense fire. But the wounded needed help, so I went to the assistance of one man who panicked. However, I was able to get him behind a large olive tree and sat on him until he calmed down and I could talk to him.

The bullets were clipping the edge of the trees and missed us by inches. I couldn't carry him, so I told him to crawl back through a grape field to the road where he would be safe behind the bank. He made it OK, but I decided to run. The first time I got up to go my knees were too weak to hold me. I made it back through heavy fire. I should have crawled. For this I got a citation, but I am sure there were many more deserving men.[18]

Several Canadians were killed in the battle which raged around Gandesa. Arvi Myllikangas of Toronto and a Finn named Manninen in Larry Cane's squad were killed by artillery fire. As well, Robert Gordon of Timmins, John Wandzilak of Winnipeg, John Polichek and George Keenan of Vancouver, and Arthur Johnson and Jack Steele of Toronto all died. It had been Jack Steele's second stint of service. He had fought earlier at Jarama, had returned to Canada on a speaking tour, and had volunteered once again to fight in Spain.

The fighting was so fierce that almost all of the international volunteers were wounded, like Frank Thirkettle:

Suddenly I felt a terrific blow on my left arm that turned me completely around and down. A bullet had broken my arm. For a few minutes I laid still to take stock of my bearings. Observing that a few yards away I could get under cover, I got to my feet and attempted to run. Barely had I taken a few steps and Whang, I was hit through the upper part of the leg and down I go. It was terribly hot and I became terribly thirsty. Reaching around for my water bottle, I had just finished the little drop that was left in it, when it went flying through the air and the fascists commenced target practice on me, hitting me again in the other leg.

After a while [Alexander] Forbes [of Saskatchewan] dashed over to help me. While trying to get my wounds to stop bleeding the fascists fired at us. So I told Forbes to leave. He tried to get the stretcher bearers to take me out. Towards darkness the stretcher bearers arrived and carried me to the dressing station.

After my wounds were dressed I was placed in an open truck and taken to the river, crossed the river on a row boat, and then by ambulance to a dressing station, then by train to Barcelona.[19]

After ten days of fighting the 15th Brigade had not taken the Pimple, nor had it managed to secure a hold in Gandesa. After a further ten days the 15th Brigade was taken out into reserve along the Corbera-Mora de Ebro road, about three kilometres west of the river, where it camped in an olive grove for eight days.

THE LAST DAYS IN THE LINE

On 15 August the 15th Brigade was ordered to Sierra de Pandols, where the Mac-Pap was about to enter into its last and most difficult engagement. The entire area was barren, the jack pine and mountain scrub that had once covered the rock having been blown and burnt off by bombs and shells. The dead bodies of republicans and fascists alike lay in stinking, worm-infested, fly-ridden piles. It was impossible to dig in, and gun positions were prepared by painstakingly filling sandbags with rocks and chips. There was no water and the only route into and out of position was a precarious mountain trail up the face of a cliff that dropped into a frightening ravine. In the words of a contemporary issue of the *Volunteer for Liberty*, "All we did in the Pandols was to endure and hold."

The Mackenzie-Papineau Battalion was in position on Hill 609, the Lincoln-Washington was on Hill 666 to the right of the Canadians, and the British Battalion was in immediate reserve. The Mac-Pap faced a large, saucer-shaped valley, carpeted with the dead. Ordered to attack the heights on the other side, the battalion crossed the valley, but was driven back by grenades thrown down from the heights above. To this special kind of hell was added an artillery and mortar barrage that continued for over seven hours. It wiped out half of the Mackenzie-Papineau Battalion.

It was here that Ivor "Tiny" Anderson, the hero of the *Ciudad de Barcelona*, lost both his legs when hit directly by a mortar shell while charging up a terrace. Arthur Linton attempted to comfort him, but was asked by Anderson to say goodbye to one of his friends for him. Sensing his intention, Linton tried to talk about patching him up, but Tiny retorted: "When we get back home from here, boy, there's no pension, no nothing." He then took his rifle and shot himself.[20]

On 26 August an exhausted, depleted 15th Brigade was moved into reserve several kilometres from the Pandols, to be replaced by the Spanish 43rd Brigade. Several of the volunteers, who had put in fourteen months of service, with at least six months at the front, were now given leave to travel to Paris. Among those from the Mac-Pap who made the trip were two Americans, Joe Gibbons and Karl Cannon. They were joined by Lee Burke and Bill Holliwell, who had served continuously since Jarama. They all took their leave confident that they would return to Spain refreshed. This was not to be.

On 10 September the Mac-Pap returned to the front, forcing a salient which threatened the right flank of the fascist line. The battalion held its new position, then was taken out to reserve under heavy mortar fire along the hills of Sierra de Lavall de la Torre, close to Hill 565. Here they underwent some training and were reinforced, mostly by young Spaniards and ex-fascists.

On 22 September the 15th Brigade returned to its old position in the Sierra de Cabals amidst rumours that Prime Minister Negrín had agreed to the evacuation of all international volunteers. The Mac-Pap now occupied Hills 565 and

561, overlooking the Corbera-Gandesa highway. To its right were the Lincoln-Washington and British battalions.

The fighting was fierce and the death toll continued to mount. Morale was then shaken when it was confirmed that Negrín had indeed agreed to unilaterally withdraw the International Brigades in the vain hope of ending all foreign intervention in the civil war. The men at the front felt betrayed, for all of them knew someone who had been either killed or wounded, and they were not prepared to quit. They had not achieved the purpose for which they had come to Spain, and they felt a deep commitment to the Spanish people.

Bill Matthews was never to forget the last days in the line:

In the evening, the food truck arrived with food but no newspaper, which we got at all evening meals. The men began to ask: why no paper? The fact is that the newspaper was reporting that the international brigades were being withdrawn and the command did not want us to know because we had to relieve troops at the front. No other troops were available to do so. That was the hardest part. In Spain almost two years. We are to be sent home. And now, on the last day, we will be killed. We had the heaviest concentration of artillery fire that I experienced in Spain. Henry Mack and Joe Schoen were wounded and were walking out. I saw them leave. A young Spanish soldier came to me with his light machine gun jammed on account of the dirt. The fascists were attacking. Paddy McElligott was there. That day still bothers me. Company One (which I now commanded) had arrived with 150-160 men. Roll call next day accounted for 97. We had an American sergeant who was second in command of Company One. Afterwards, he said to me: "Bill, we made it!" Then a squadron of planes came over and dropped their bombs right in our midst. The American had his leg and arm blown off, and died. After we left the lines a squadron of fascist planes approached us and dropped their bombs. They landed among us. I hugged the earth, gritted my teeth at the screech of the bombs coming down. The roar and concussion lifted me in the air. A big clump of earth landed smack on my head. I thought to myself: I've had it!

I've had it! After a few seconds I realized that I was still alive. I got up and saw some men trying to put a bandage around a Canadian company's commander's head. He was the commanding officer of Company Three or Four. A chunk of the bomb was sticking out of his head. In a moment he keeled over. We got blown all to hell. It still bothers me.[21]

NOTES
1. Amedée Grenier, written account to author.
2. Matthews, written account.
3. Sam Huhtala, written account to author.
4. Lee Burke, written account.
5. *The BC Logger*, 13 August 1938.
6. Interview with author.
7. Interview with author.
8. Quoted in Komodowski, *With the Mackenzie-Papineau Battalion*, 62.
9. Matthews, written account.
10. Schoen, written account.
11. Matthews, written account.
12. Translated by Peter Krawchuk from *The People's Gazette*, 9 March 1938.
13. Quoted in Komodowski, *With the Mackenzie-Papineau Battalion*, 30-31.
14. Mattersdorfer, written account.
15. H.J. Higgins, written account, found in his personal papers.
16. For a full account of the story, see Manuel Alvarez, *The Tall Soldier* (Toronto: Virgo Press, 1980).
17. Matthews, written account.
18. C. Arden Nash, written account to author.
19. Frank Thirkettle, written account.
20. There are several versions of this story. One has it that Tiny Anderson did not have a rifle and was given one when it became clear that he was determined to take his life. Another version claims that his last words were: "I'm not going back to Hastings Street [Vancouver] to sell shoelaces."
21. Matthews, written account.

Six

A War on Many Fronts

It is customary to associate foreign volunteers fighting in Spain exclusively with the International Brigades. However the volunteers, including Canadians, served the republican cause in a number of capacities: with the partisans, artillery, communications, scouts, medical services, transport, air force and the cavalry.

THE PARTISANS

The *guerrilleros* (partisans) were officially known as the *Servicio de Investigacion Especial Periferica* (Special Periphery Investigative Service), and played an integral role in the republican struggle against Franco. The partisan movement was widespread and spontaneous, usually springing up wherever the republicans were defeated by the fascists and forced to retreat. The movement was particularly strong in León, Galicia, Zamora, Andalusia, Estremadura and Asturia. The partisan strategy of harassment was designed to disrupt fascist attacks on the republican army, and to this end bridges were blown up, troop trains attacked, communications interrupted and patrols assaulted. The effectiveness of the partisans was proven by the fact that Franco was repeatedly forced to reassign troops from the front to defend territory he had believed to be safely conquered.

There were attempts to coordinate the activities of the partisans with those of the republican army. For example, the arrival of Italian troops at the Jarama front was delayed by three days when partisans, including Canadians, blew up a bridge behind enemy lines. As well, prior to the Brunete offensive, the rail link between Madrid and the fascist supply base was cut by partisans. Too often, however, the republican High Command failed to take advantage of the possibilities created by guerrilla warfare.

140

Most of the Canadians who served with the partisans were of Finnish ancestry, coming from the Fort William-Port Arthur region of Ontario (now Thunder Bay). They included Matti Hanni, Reino Keto, U. Kuokka, Irgo Korpi, V. Laaksonen, Utamo Makela, J. Perala, Toivo Saari, and Vaino Veikkola. Two Americans, William Aalto and Frank Rogers, who later served as commissar of the Mackenzie-Papineau Battalion, and Lieutenant Gunnar Ebb of Finland, who would later command the Mac-Pap, also fought with the partisans. Rogers later recalled the cool-headedness which partisan activies behind enemy lines required:

> It wasn't so difficult getting through the enemy lines as the lines weren't continuous in the beginning of the war, and in the mountain areas there were considerable gaps.
>
> Sometimes we dressed as peasants, sometimes as railroad workers and very often we put on the Falangist uniform. Once I nearly burst out laughing when a fascist patroller near a small village saluted me as I passed by in a Falangist officer's uniform with my comrade.[1]

Canadians were associated with dangerous and highly specialized partisan activities. The groundwork was carried out by the local population, while the partisans were expected to bring technical knowledge and military experience to any operation involving the direct engagement of the enemy; all work was done at night. Canadian volunteers recalled that at the beginning of the Spanish conflict the partisans were so effective that the Italian troops refused orders to move at night, for fear of attack. Franco was forced to post bounties— 50,000 *pesetas* for partisans taken alive and 25,000 *pesetas* for partisans delivered dead.

The republican side claimed that between December 1936 and September 1937 partisans blew up 1,256 trains, 91 trucks, 43 cars, 7 bridges, 29 patrol posts, 10 railroads, 2 ammunition depots, 5 water plants, 4 electric power plants, and killed and wounded 10,000-15,000 of the enemy.

Toivo Saari had originally joined the Lincoln Battalion and was then moved to the southern front as a partisan. He later recalled one of the actions there in which he had participated:

> I was located at that time near the city of Granada which belonged to the fascists in southern Spain. We had planned to stop the movement of the military trains to the front and there we had to mine the railroads and blow up the trains.
>
> Quietly we tiptoed to a suitable place where the rail line circled a soft swamp at the height of about six or seven feet and where it was easy to make it fall into the mud.
>
> I was the only one in our group that knew electrical equipment because my five other comrades were Spanish and had not yet had time to be specially trained. Therefore, I had to perform the task.
>
> I arranged my equipment while the others watched with the machine guns just in case.
>
> As we climbed up the mountain we heard the puffing of the train in the darkness of the night. Even the enemy dared not keep the lights on! We followed the train in great excitement. Now it is coming to the target. We waited, our fingers in our ears. Now! The train is right on target. (It didn't explode) I grabbed my hair and pulled it in frustration because, up till now, I had always managed to perform my job well and with success . . . I will go and check even if I have to go alone, I said to the group Captain.
>
> With two other partisans we quietly approached the place where our secret was and I stuck out my hand to remove enough dirt from on top of the mine to cut the electric wiring. But just then an order came in the darkness: "*manos arriba!*" (hands up!)
>
> Instantly we rolled down the embankment while the bullets rained after us.
>
> There it was, then, the malfunctioning of my equipment. While we had been there for the first time, we had a strong guard system, and the fascist patrolmen who had noticed

us were afraid to attack or reveal themselves. But, once we had left they had defused our mines. [Ten policemen were firing at them and Saari did not have the strength to follow his fellow partisans up the hill before he was surrounded. He hid in a field of peas which was inundated with about six inches of water. There he crawled around for about three hours and realized that dawn would break soon.]

What to do? Surrender? No! That would be a shame! And they would shoot me right away in any case. Best to try to break through.

I put a hundred bullets into my machine gun and had another hundred ready in case I needed them. I moved along a large ditch where the water was up to my arm pits. I got to a good position from where I could see several of the guards . . . I opened fire.

I managed to shoot about 150 bullets when my automatic rifle overheated and broke down. I checked for the guards. It was quiet.

I jumped over the road from where there was [sic] only a couple of hundred metres to the mountains that would shelter me from the enemy.

But I was disappointed. Those two comrades that were with me had told the Captain they thought I had been hit and that most likely I was lying cold in the field of peas.

I had to travel alone without any kind of weapon. I went around the fascist patrol and eventually got to the river bed to the place where I knew we kept horses on the other side. I swam quietly across the river and tiptoed towards the barn.

I knocked. No one answered. I opened the door a crack and whispered: anyone here? Our captain jumped up, hugged me for a moment, and said, "All of our comrades are here. Now to the horses. It is dangerous to stay here any longer."

In an instant we were on our horses, galloping along the mountain valleys which took us to our patrol camps where we were given warm coffee.[2]

Canadian veterans of the partisan movement who survived and returned to Canada would thereafter maintain that the outcome of the Spanish civil war might have been different if the partisans had been able to acquire the arms and material necessary to pursue their objectives successfully. These volunteers were convinced that the Spaniards among whom they lived were prepared to risk their lives to defeat the fascists. They were denied the means to do so.

THE ARTILLERY

George Kostoff, a Canadian of Bulgarian origin, served with the artillery in Spain. He and several other Canadians of central European origin, including Istvetan Kiroff, Nicolas Atanasoff, Anton Ivanoff, John Andreef, George Markoff, Gregor Christoff, Norman Vassilov, and two volunteers named Leomo and Lovier, were sent for training at Almansa. Here two predominantly Slavic-speaking units were stationed, one composed of Poles and Czechslovaks, the other a Balkan unit, made up mainly of Bulgarians, Yugoslavians and Romanians; the largely American John Brown Battery was also at Almansa.

In July 1937, after two months of intensive training, the men were transferred first to Madrid, then to the Escorial, and finally to Villanueva de la Cañada, where they took part in the battle for Brunete. After the fighting at Brunete was over, they were moved back to Madrid, and then to the southern front at Peñarroya in Estremadura. The mercury mines near Penoria were a tempting target and the fascists, in particular Italian troops, made concentrated but unsuccessful attacks on them.

In March 1938 the battery was moved to Toledo, and after that battle back to Estremadura to guard the mines once again. Kostoff felt that the sole purpose of his artillery unit was to protect the mines, which the fascists were never able to take.

Kostoff recalled that the relationship between the international volunteers and the Spanish people was a warm one, and told a story which illustrated this:

> I was on leave in a Spanish village. There were, perhaps, 20 or 30 thousand people in it. One day I saw a boy in the street, he was very white. I asked him why he was so pale and he told me that he had fallen and a wound had opened. I asked him to take me to his mother.
>
> I tried to speak to her as well as I could in Spanish. I said it appears that his wound is not healing. She said it was not. I asked her to bring her son to our doctor assuring her that he would look after him.
>
> She did take the boy to our doctor who cleaned the wound and attended to it. The boy got well.
>
> Then, one day, we went on leave to this same village and we saw this Spanish woman with her boy and girl. She asked us to come to her home for dinner. You know, they didn't have any food. She gave us a chocolate bar to eat. In turn we gave them some chocolates we had. We never saw them again as we were moved to another position.[3]

John Malko was one of eleven Canadians attached to Artillery Unit 63A. Malko had fought with the Austrian army in World War I, and had later served as a machine gunner with the Red Army in the Ukraine. On 12 August 1937, after twenty days of training at Almansa, he and his fellows were sent to the Cordoba front, where the republicans were launching an offensive, and were assigned to the 68th Division. Unit 63A was equipped with two heavy howitzers, manufactured in 1887, which fired fifty-five kilogram shells. Fifteen men were assigned to each artillery piece. Malko and his unit remained in position in the Pozoblanco sector for two months, firing an average of 160 shells daily from their antiquated weapons.

Jack Lawson of Vancouver was the first Canadian in the Spanish antitank units. Lawson arrived in Albacete on 18 May 1937 and was immediately assigned to the antitank battery which was then being formed. The men underwent rigorous training until 8 June, when they left for Jarama, arriving two days later. They were attached to the 24th Brigade of the 15th Division and remained at the front for seventeen days. Lawson recalled that their battery knocked out an average of one enemy machine gun daily.

Lawson's battery moved out of Madrid on 30 June and was attached to the 15th Brigade at Torrelodones. On 3 July the battery moved to Guadarrama, on the outskirts of Villanueva de la Cañada, and took up a position on a ridge overlooking the town. The men saw no action here and four days later moved to a position closer to Brunete, overlooking the fascist lines on the opposite side of the river. It was from this point that the republican forces began their offensive on 8 July.

The battery spent what Lawson described as "five bad days" in the battle of Mosquito Ridge at Brunete. It was then moved to a new position along the Guadarrama River, to the right of a large castle which was the control point of the main road cutting through Villanueva de la Cañada and Brunete. After a further withdrawal the battery was stationed at Ambite.

Lawson states that the men discussed the mistakes made at Brunete with their new commander at Ambite, and how the work of the battery could be improved. After a lengthy rest the battery moved to the Aragon front and fought in the battle for Quinto, where it was instructed to capture the heavily fortified church. After this engagement the battery was moved repeatedly and finally took part in the fight for Belchite, where the men fired an average of 1,190 shells daily from their three guns. After Belchite the men in the antitank battery were sent to rest at Azaila.

Frank Hadesbeck of Regina was in the antiaircraft artillery. He attended an antiaircraft school at Manises, a small town outside of Valencia. He volunteered for a German battery because he understood some German. In late January 1938 his unit was sent to Barcelona, which was under heavy aerial bombardment.

Hadesbeck was assigned to a big gun on the Montjuich heights. On 1 February 1938 his battery brought down two fascist bombers. On 7 February the men were ordered to Montalban on the eastern front. There, they brought down a bomber on 9 February and another plane two days later. On 19 February the unit was transferred to the Teruel front and over the next two days helped bring down several enemy planes. One Italian pilot was taken prisoner, and kept crying "*mi Ruso, mi Ruso!*" (I am Russian!). Hadesbeck says that the man was "terribly frightened of being killed. He had been told by the fascists that all pilots were killed before they could get to a commanding officer."[4]

Hadesbeck was a participant in the long nightmare of The Retreats, fighting and falling back continually. However, despite the confusion, the fatigue, and shortages in ammunition and supplies, Hadesbeck's unit was able to bring down at least sixteen enemy bombers between mid-March and the end of June.

The men were also chronically short of food, as the 27 August entry in Hadesbeck's diary records:

> Ted Marsh brought a little fox terrier with him. But this morning it disappeared. Later in the morning Number Three gun crew were frying some meat. Though they said it was rabbit, it didn't have long ears. I know. We never before had to resort to dog for food.[5]

By the end of October Hadesbeck was back with the International Brigades, and on 17 November was sent to a small village about forty kilometres from Valencia named Villanueva de Castellon. Here the men were given one day's ration of food, consisting of a loaf of bread, two sausages and some marmalade. They were finally evacuated by boat to Barcelona.

Ron Liversedge had been stationed behind the lines after being wounded but like many others requested a transfer to the front. In early February 1938 he was assigned to the predominantly American 35th Artillery Battery, and fought throughout the subsequent Retreats, as he relates:

Our battery was in action between Alfambra and Teruel and were lobbing shells over the town into the advancing enemy. I was put to helping carry the shells and cordite charges.

It was quite evident that this was the biggest offensive of the war up to date. The fascists had built up formidable forces. All along the front their big artillery guns were firing continuously, the sky was filled with their aviation and they had lots of tanks.

It was the beginning of the drive which, in less than two months, reached the Mediterranean and cut the Republican territory in two.

Two days after I arrived at the battery the fascists retook Teruel, and the internationals, giving ground inch-by-inch and, as we pulled out our guns, we met the remnants of the MacPaps [sic] being withdrawn behind newly dug positions manned by fresh Spanish troops.

This was the way the Retreat was. The fascists had plenty of reserves and their preponderance in material was so overwhelming that they could afford now to concentrate on one portion of our lines, spend days and millions of dollars in bombs and shells in breaking through, and then rush tanks and men through the breach and push ahead until stopped again.

That our resistance was stubborn can be attested to by the very fact that it took the enemy two months to drive a wedge to the coast, a distance of about 100 kilometres.

Somewhere in the country around Mora we blew the breach out of one gun, injuring some of the gun crew, and the gun was pulled out, hooked up to a truck and sent to the artillery park at Valencia.

All the country around us was one huge eruption, the earth shaking with explosions of shells and bombs, by day the air thick with the fumes of cordite and falling bomb dust and, at night, the sky lit up with the explosions of shells and bombs.

148

Food came up and we ate and drank automatically, hardly knowing or caring what we ate.[6]

After nearly four months of fighting and retreating, Liversedge and the other survivors of the 35th Artillery Battery were assigned to the Dimitrov Brigade, which had been renamed the 129th Brigade. Liversedge continues:

> For us commenced our last and worst phase of the war which lasted for four months. Four months of stubborn retreat without let up against an enemy whose superiority in weapons rated at over ten to one, and in aviation probably at one hundred to one. It was a pitiful sight to see a dozen Republican Chatos going up to meet fifty German bombers and fighter escorts.
>
> We joined the Brigade at a place called Mosqueruela at the end of a long plain between mountains . . . Day-after-day, artillery and bombers concentrated on our lines in the centre of the plain where Spanish Carabineros were holding the line. It was the heaviest bombardment I had witnessed up to that time. Night and day it continued for a week. Daily the sun was obscured by the smoke and dust and, at nights, a red glow lit up the plain. It seemed that nobody could be left alive in that section of the front. Then, from the mountains came the tanks and infantry and troop carriers and the line was broken.
>
> Soon we would have orders to retire and take up new positions in the rear and the process would be repeated. We didn't have the material.
>
> There was a fifteen-mile section of our front in The Levant where we had only one anti-aircraft battery. We retreated slowly across the plain at the same time inflicting heavy casualties on the enemy, but taking terrible punishment ourselves . . . We were sick and tired and hungry and thoroughly exhausted . . . During the retreat we were battered and bombshocked and our nerves became very tight. I saw truck drivers who had been driving for days and nights with ammunition and supplies who would stop on a road and slump over the wheel and sob their hearts out.

The whole army retreated to the Sierra Madres [probably Sierra Alambras] and established a line on the hills.

Here on the 22nd of September the Spanish government announced the decision to withdraw and repatriate all international volunteers. Almost immediately we began to transfer our weapons to the Spanish troops.[7]

COMMUNICATIONS

The role of communications was critical in Spain, and required the use of radio, telephones and runners, skill, knowledge and courage. Lee Burke described the situation:

The "transmissions" [as they were called in Spain] were the signal company of the Brigade. Their function was to keep and service communications to all units of the brigade and throughout the companies in the battalions, as well as to divisional headquarters.

While I always contend that no one faced the exposure and casualties of the infantrymen, it is fair to say that the transmission men repairing the lines during a battle had to go out where the artillery and bombs were breaking them, and he couldn't pick his spot. He had to follow along those lines to the break. Transmission men had their share of casualties.[8]

Although the communications section was composed primarily of Americans, Burke notes that there were also several Canadians, including Len Norris, Len Brown, Bernard Sweeney, Lou Tellier, Howard Bigelow, Carl Perdue, Tom Aucoin, Tom Bailey, Yorky Burton, Joe Gangarossa, Joe Glenn, Wilf Cowan, and a Spanish-born Canadian citizen, Lieutenant Frank Barcena.

Burke was involved in the crossing of the Ebro, and saw considerable action afterwards, as he recalls:

Our group was left at Flix where the pontoon bridges were. Our job was to keep the lines repaired by the river. It was steady work. The fascist planes kept coming over in relays trying to knock out the pontoons. We'd run for cover on the side of the hill behind the town as they bombed. If our timing was good, as they left we'd race back to repair the lines they broke . . .

We went on after that to Gandesa, or almost. All that had to be taken was the hill called The Pimple, which turned out to be the kind we didn't have the remedy for. Time and again, the MacPap and other battalions attacked without planes, artillery or tank support, from our hill across the plain. But the fascists, from high vantage point and backed with heavy fire, proved to be too much.

After a number of attacks a Polish officer came to our hill and was critical of our commander, Gunnar Ebb, for not taking The Pimple. He said we hadn't tried hard enough. Gunnar Ebb picked up a light machine gun and said to the Polish officer: "Come with me. I'll take you with us to attack the hill." The Polish officer left.

I think it was the last attack when I was told to take my phone and another man, a Spaniard, to string wire. It was a short time before the attack and there was no time to do much. We had a telephone and one spool of wire. I was no expert but I looked across to The Pimple and I said "We'll not have enough wire to go that far." However, there was no time. The company started to go. We went further than I thought possible. The company was some distance ahead between us and The Pimple and we were stuck at the end of our wire. All we could do was lie there with the phone, under fire from both The Pimple and the town.

Scotty Chambers with his assistant, Russ Stevens, were the heliograph men. Scotty had a lot of experience in World War I with the signal corp [sic] in the British army in Mesopotamia where Scotty claimed they had made a record in distance signalling with the heliograph.

On one occasion Scotty was given a long, long message to send. A little while and a phone call came, checking up. I told them over the phone that Scotty was still sending. Then a trench mortar zeroed in and knocked out the heliograph.

I asked: "Are you hurt?" "No," Scotty replied, "we're OK. But you can report No Reply!" I phoned headquarters and reported what had happened. That was the last operation

I saw of the heliograph. The long, long message was received by the fascists who probably couldn't wait for the end of it so sent their reply by trench mortar. Scotty was fuming and swearing in his best Scotch accent.

Sierra Pandolls was just big hills of rock, nothing but rock. You'd ruin a diamond drill trying to dig a hole. We were receiving everything from small arms fire to bombings, to artillery. When shells and bombs hit they sprinkled the rocks all over us, too.

Joe Luftig and Louis Stoloff [two Americans] were unbeatable. We all took turns going out to fix the lines. We were all scared but did our job. I can still hear Louie singing at the top of his voice. Between shells you could catch his latest song, "The love bug will bite you if you don't watch out."

I came across Patterson being taken away on a stretcher with one leg shot off. A little further lay Tiny Anderson, with both of his legs off. I saw him for a minute, maybe the longest minute in my life. I could write a book about that minute. It was hopeless for him even if they had a helicopter instead of a stretcher to take him out.

He said: "Shoot me comrade." I couldn't, even if I had a rifle. There was nothing I could do.

I heard a yell and looked around. Joe Luftig was hit. As he left on a stretcher he rose up on his elbow and yelled: "Burkie! Don't send Louie out alone."

I kept my promise. Joe was hardly out of sight when Louie got hit. I was alone with the telephone and the wire. I took the phone to the end of the wire where the other phone was. An infantryman was very close to it so I told him to answer any calls while I went out to fix wire, and to let any sergeant or officer know where the phone was.

And that was the end of Sierra Pandolls. Joe and Louie finished their war, and I was with a group to go on foreign leave which turned out to go back home.[9]

Sergeant Joe Glenn was another Canadian volunteer who was in the communications sector, stationed in Velasques. He describes the difficulties he encountered:

> We really operated on a shoestring. We had no wire. We went to Basquillo and Velasques and some other little town where we ripped out the wires. Their wire was just like the old-fashioned twisted and braided wire we used for lamp cords. We ripped those out, rolled them up on reels. We ran out of friction tape to splice the ends together so we ran up to the hospital there, which was a truck on wheels, and got some surgical tape.
>
> We were short of equipment. We used to go up to that place and rob them of their adhesive tape which they used to tie bandages until they got wise to what we were doing. We ended up just using pieces of paper over the joints and tied it with string. Nobody will ever believe this.
>
> We had a fellow, an American named Domas in our group. We were short on batteries for our phones and he thought of something. He said: "You know when we were kids we used to build huts and forts and things like that and, in the lane back of us, there was a place that bought old car batteries. We found out that if you filled a battery with water and let it sit awhile and then spilled it out you could run a small light bulb with it.
>
> I said that we'd try anything once. So our truck driver took us around all the little towns and garages. We brought back all the old batteries and tried it out. It worked. I don't know why it works. Everybody else would say that we were crazy. But we connected all our base telephones to storage batteries. They were small batteries which could be put into the mobile sets. Those were used at the front.[10]

THE SCOUTS

An organized system of observation is essential in warfare. Ideally, it has to be able to ensure the best possible observation of the terrain and the positions of the enemy. In the Spanish civil war scouts had to be able to assess enemy positions, find the number of artillery pieces and mortars, and where flanks and gaps in the enemy lines were to be found.

They also needed to know the terrain, what cover was available, which parts of the countryside were the most dangerous, and road conditions.

Fred Mattersdorfer was in the brigade scouts, serving under another Canadian, Maurice Constant. Mattersdorfer remembered some of the other Canadians who served with him:

> Among the Canadians who were in the scouts was Martineau from Quebec, O'Leary and Cluny from southern Ontario, Peter Werner from Toronto, Zayjak, Iszczuk and Buchokowsky from Alberta. Buchokowsky was a wrestler and Zayjak was captured by the fascists. Charlie Saunders from Vancouver was a sergeant in the scouts at Teruel.[11]

Mattersdorfer recalled his activities as a scout:

> Maurice Constant was sent up to the front at Belchite to check on the front lines. They were practically deserted so the scouts went in and took over the trenches. There were approximately 20 of us.
>
> Later in the afternoon we got about 30 or 40 new recruits from Tarazona.
>
> We got orders to retreat. The 13th Brigade broke and the fascists had surrounded their position. I was the last to come out as I was on the bottom and had to help Melnychenko from Toronto who was totally exhausted. From that time on I was in the Mac-Pap and didn't get back to the scouts until after The Retreats . . .
>
> At Fuentes de Ebro I had to put flagging out in between the lines so that our own planes would not bomb us. They were fifty feet by one foot. I had to put out four of them. Only one man could do it as it had to be done fast. There were fox holes every hundred feet or so. I changed my timing at each fox hole in order to beat the fascist machine gunner.
>
> One night I went out with four other scouts, crossing the fascist lines. On the way back, we got into the fascist lines,

154

passed them in their own trenches, and went back to their rear until we found a way back to our lines. No one said a word. If the fascists said something we did not answer, just kept walking. If we had answered there would have been a shoot out.

At Caspe I was in the MacPap and was sent on patrol with Captain Gunnar Ebb and Joe Taylor, a Negro from New York. That was right after Niilo Makela was hit. The fascists attacked and we were cut off.

The fascists thought we were giving up. Eight or nine were coming toward us to take us prisoners without firing a shot. I nearly shot Captain Ebb because he didn't say a word until they were less than 100 yards away, and then the three of us opened up.

Then we had to cross the river and we barely made it. On the other side we came to a peasant's house. There were young girls inside. They panicked when they saw Joe Taylor, thinking he was a Moor. They said we could have anything but not to kill them. It took me quite awhile with my limited Spanish to explain that he was an American.[12]

THE MEDICAL SERVICES

The medical services that were manned by international volunteers consisted of 220 doctors, 580 nurses and assistants, 600 stretcher bearers, 23 hospitals, 5,000 hospital beds, 13 surgical groups, 130 ambulances, and 7 surgical wagons. In addition, there was Dr. Norman Bethune's transfusion unit.

Among the popular front-line surgeons was Dr. Aaron Magid, a thirty-five-year-old native of Winnipeg. He won the admiration of the members of the Mackenzie-Papineau Battalion for his selfless devotion to the men and his courageous actions on behalf of the wounded, as Bill Brennan recorded:

He joined the Lincoln Battalion on June 15, 1937, when they were at rest in Albares. There Magid took over his duties from Doctor Pike and found the men in good spirits. While in Albares he carried on the regular duties of doctor as well as trying to improve the sanitary conditions in the camp. From Albares the doctor moved with the Battalion until they arrived at the Guadarrama front when the Brunete offensive commenced. That first day the doctor followed the Battalion until they came into position to attack. He then set out to look for a suitable place to set up a first aid field station.[13]

When he returned from his search Magid found that the Lincoln Battalion had moved and, when he finally located it, discovered its captain, Hourihan, had been badly wounded:

> The doctor did not know how to get the men out as the road was under shell and machine gun fire . . . He managed to reach the first-aid station of the British Battalion where he met Doctor Sollenberg who knew as much as Magid did about a way to the rear. Finally Magid decided to take the route they had used to come into position that morning. As they moved out, Hourihan received a second wound. They trudged through valleys and over a maze of hills carrying Hourihan all the way. It took eight men to get one wounded man back to the waiting ambulances. They managed to carry the worst cases out and moved out more at dark that night. Minor cases were removed in the morning. They were able to bring the ambulances down the main highway at night as the town had been taken by our troops. Richer by a mule he [Magid] had wangled for the carrying of first-aid equipment, he moved up to the battalion which was resting in an olive grove near Brunete.[14]

In addition to Magid, doctors H. Gilasen and Eugene Fogarty, both of Vancouver, served in Spain. Gilasen arrived in Spain in January 1938, while Fogarty served on the staff of the International Hospital at Villanueve de la Jara, near Albacete. Florence Pike (née Florence Mildred Tew of Falkland, Ontario) served as a nurse at Cordoba, Huete and Valdegunga-Ami. Samuel Abramson of Montréal, Jean Watts and Izzy Kupchik of Toronto, Art Siven, Charles Sim and James Southgate of Vancouver all served as ambulance drivers. Southgate recalls his experiences:

I was eventually transferred to the medical corps on July 28 [1937]. Several of us were sent back to Barcelona . . . to pick up new ambulances. We had to wait nearly a week until our vehicles arrived from France, then back to Tarragona. Already I had travelled nearly a thousand miles along the coast, back and forth, and I was getting impatient for action. It was forthcoming.

I was on my way to the Aragon front. Our army was pushing northward in the hope of taking Zaragoza and the town of Quinto was the first objective. Our base was a few miles away from Quinto.

I drove over to where the fighting took place and found a first-aid location and waited until I had a load. I should mention that my ambulance carried four stretcher cases and twelve sitting up wounded. By the time I got moving it was dusk. I drove to the artillery location but they had left.

I started in what I thought would be the highway location but landed up in the hills. Tanks had churned up the ground into a fine dust which did not help. Finally, through the dust, a tank appeared in front of me. What should I do? Then I noticed a water truck so I drove over to it. Luckily it was ours. The truck driver told me to follow him. Three hours later he led me to our medical base.

Unfortunately I had lost two of our stretcher cases.

A few days later, I found myself at Belchite. Coming back from a trip to an isolation hospital in a heavy downpour I left the road and landed in a soft field where I half buried my vehicle in an effort to get out. It meant staying there for the night for our orders were never to abandon our vehicles. In the morning my absence was reported to headquarters which sent out a tow truck.

I passed from one end of our territory to the other several times, loaned to different military groups, wherever there was a need. I cannot recall when I was transferred to the Garibaldis, but my paybook states I was transferred to the group evacuation, 15th Army Corps on 5th April, 1938. This medical unit was situated in the area of Ciudad Real south towards Cordoba.

I had driven up to the front first-aid post and was waiting for the wounded. Enemy shells were falling in the valley a couple of yards away. I watched them for awhile when their aim was elevated and the shells were going over our heads. Shells were exploding all around me, but I got out OK. I took my load of wounded to our nearest hospital base and then returned to the front.

When it was nearly dark our forces were in full retreat. I had picked up my commanding officer a few miles back who now told me to turn around and go back. This was my first retreat.

I eventually found myself back in Tarragona in time for a move up to the Aragon. We proceeded up the highway towards Zaragoza where action was taking place. Once again I was caught in a retreat. We were heavily attacked by planes. Orders were given to get our ambulances off the roads.[15]

Hans Ibing, a transport driver who had his truck commandeered to carry out the wounded, recalled the retreat:

Thousands of soldiers were streaming by us on the road and both sides of it in a wide swath and there were Franco's planes diving on that mass, circling and diving again and again. With thousands of rifles there was not one turned on those planes to scare them off.

After awhile our group arrived and we followed that retreat after the planes left.

It was miserable to have to listen to the wounded back on the truck being shaken up over the rough road, and the officers urging you on to hurry.[16]

One of the more dangerous and least recognized tasks in the armed forces is that of the stretcher bearers. Bill Beeching recalls an incident during The Retreats which poignantly illustrates the dilemma faced by these men. Beeching and a small group of volunteers were moving through an olive grove when they came upon a large group of wounded, all on stretchers, attended by a Vancouver teacher named Cliff Buckwell. The situation was hopeless, as it was impossible to

158

get the wounded men out. Buckwell knew that he and the wounded would be killed on the spot as soon as the enemy arrived, yet he refused to leave them to their fates unattended, feeling this would be a betrayal of his duties as a first-aid officer. He is listed as "missing" during The Retreats.

Walter Hellund describes efforts to evacuate the wounded during the battle for Gandesa:

> Our losses were heavy and increasing. The order came to retreat 100 yards. A small group took a stand. We were doing good, and kept up a steady stream of fire. But the anti-tank guns had spotted us. Five shells landed among us. In a few seconds our section leader was wounded. Again we retreated. We passed a wounded comrade from the "suicide" squad that had been sent out in front of the position with hand grenades and anti-tank bombs waiting to repel any tanks. He had dragged himself, shot through the chest, along the road. Two of us applied first aid. We had no stretcher, so we carried him, one at a time. A little later we met our company commissar. I gave my rifle to him and went back for another wounded man.
>
> This man was barefooted. He tried to walk but it looked like he was hit through the lung. I applied my bandage. One single plane kept on strafing. I carried him a short distance but he insisted on walking, and asked to be left. We went by a big cook pot full of fresh water which did us a little good.
>
> He was begging and pleading to be put down and left to die. I had put the bandage three times around and a pad over the hole, but he couldn't breath and I had to take it off. He regained consciousness in the truck and shook my arm. He said his name was Cooper.
>
> I came across Tommy Roberts on the road. He couldn't help me because the wounded man was walking barefoot with his arm around my neck. One hour later the truck came up and took the wounded out.
>
> In the truck we held the wounded up in stretcher to ease the vibration.[17]

Marvin Penn and Jerry Glow, two Winnipeg volunteers, were among those Canadians who were with the first-aid services. Penn served with the Lincolns at Jarama, Brunete, Quinto and Belchite, where he drove a water truck. He was then transferred to the medical corps of the brigades in Barcelona where for a time he was the only English-speaking international in the Karl Marx Barracks. Later he escorted wounded volunteers into France.

Glow joined Company Three of the Mackenzie-Papineau Battalion during The Retreats, and took part in the battle in the Sierra Pandolls. The following is his account of the action:

> I remember picking up the wounded, dressing their wounds and helping them all that was possible to get out to the ambulance site where they could be evacuated to field hospitals.
>
> We were fortunate to have a mule and we used it to act as a stretcher bearer. We would sling two stretcher cases on each side of the mule and tote them out to the first aid site, where they would be evacuated . . . The mule was the best means of carrying them out as the stretcher bearers sometimes gave their cases a hard time . . .
>
> The mule, however, never moved, never dodged the shells and as far as we know was never hit. It just waited patiently 'til the drivers reappeared and trundled off with them just as it had done when it was at its legitimate task of pulling a cart or a plough . . .
>
> One day as the German fascist bombers . . . decided to unload their bombs where we were and where the mule was standing patiently waiting . . . all pandemonium broke loose as the deluge of bombs hit around us. So shocking was the explosion of these missiles that it even broke the calm of the mule. It went berserk and took off the Sierra Pandolls. We never saw it again. We never heard any trace of its whereabouts from anybody. The mule had just discharged itself from active duty . . .
>
> Training in first aid consisted of learning what to do in case a wounded person was brought to you as they were bound to be, we were not just being taught about what

might happen, it was happening while we were in school, the idea was to get us out there as fast as possible.

We were supplied with first aid equipment and these kits had been supplied from Canada. Not by the government but bought from donations by citizens . . . during the depression and it wasn't easy.

Our ambulance came from the U.S.A. also donated by its people who also had a depression to contend with.

It even so happened that we captured an enemy ambulance, a fascist one when we crossed the Ebro in that Gandesa offensive. It was taken from a Moorish unit composed of young boys for, by this time, the most vaunted "professional" Moorish veterans that they used to brag about were in short supply . . . We didn't have time to paint out the fascist insignia that was on the sides of the ambulance and to no great surprise when we started to evacuate the wounded in it we came under fire from our side. You may be sure that we rushed to take off those insignias before we made another trip.[18]

One of Canada's most important contributions to the medical services of the republic was the creation of a mobile blood transfusion unit. At the time of the outbreak of the civil war in 1936, Graham Spry, editor of the *New Commonwealth* and chairman of the newly formed Committee to Aid Spanish Democracy, met with the Montréal doctor, Norman Bethune, to explore how Canadians might provide medical assistance to the republican side.

Bethune was already a towering figure in the medical profession.[19] His pioneering work in thoracic and chest surgery had won him an international reputation. His compassion for the poor and a deep sense of social justice had led him to join the Communist party and become an outspoken advocate of socialized medicine. Following meetings with the members of the Committee to Aid Spanish Democracy, Bethune resigned his hospital positions in Montréal and sailed from Québec on 24 October aboard the *Empress of Britain* in order to visit Spain and see first hand what might be done.

He arrived in Madrid on 3 November and took up residence in the Hotel Gran Via. Here he met Henning Sorensen, a Danish journalist and correspondent for the *New Commonwealth*. Sorensen was fluent in a number of European languages and was able to assist Bethune in communicating with Spanish contacts. It did not take long for the two men to determine how they and Canadian sympathizers might be helpful.

Bethune had noticed, during the battle for Madrid, that the mortality rate was very high, not because of lethal wounds, but due to the lack of blood transfusions to the wounded. The practice at the time was to rescue the wounded from the lines and transport them to a hospital or medical aid station in the rear. Men were dying in search of blood. "Let the blood seek out the wounded" was Bethune's answer. It was a simple idea, yet revolutionary in its consequences.

Bethune travelled to Paris and London to make arrangements to organize and equip a mobile blood tranfusion unit. Accompanied by Sorensen, he was joined by two other young men from Montréal—Hazen Sise, an architect, and Ted Allan, a journalist. Bethune named the new unit *Servicio Canadiense de Transfusion de Sangre*. It arrived in Madrid on 12 December and established its headquarters at 36 Principe de Vergara, a well-to-do district in north-central Madrid which had been spared the bombing raids by the fascists.

Dramatic stories are told of the lives saved by the blood unit, and the hope it inspired in the victims of the war, both civilian and military. In a dispatch published in the *Toronto Daily Clarion* in 1937, Bethune wrote:

> Sharp turn left at the top of the hill and there was the 500-bed hospital. No more red crosses now. Last week the fascist planes tried to bomb it so down came the crosses— too easy a mark to hit—500 wounded men, too good a chance to miss.

> The sure signs of an engagement were the low rows of blood-drenched stretchers, propped on end, leaning against the walls, waiting to be washed.

Yes, he needs a transfusion. Two tourniquets in place to check the blood flow from both torn radial arteries. Must have lost a couple of quarts from the look on his face and feeble pulse. Five minutes and we're ready—blood heated to body temperature, grouped, syringe all sterilized. I look at the label: "blood number 695. Donor number 1106. Group Iv. Collected Madrid 6 March." Yes, its OK.

Henning Sorensen bends over him with an anxious distressed air of a father for an only child. They talk. "What did he say?"

Sorensen, quiet, mournful and low: "He said, ten days ago I was in Sweden. I have been in Spain three days. This was my first engagement and now I am no more use to my comrades. I have done nothing for the cause."

One of Bethune's letters, published by the Committee to Aid Spanish Democracy, reads:

As you know, we have withstood the most serious attempt by the fascists to take Madrid by storm since the first and second weeks of November [1936]. Their losses have been terrific. They attacked in dense lines like the Germans in France in 1917. Our machine-guns simply mowed them down. Our losses were one to five of theirs.

The I.B. have suffered badly, of course, as they acted as shock troops. But large reinforcements of French, Germans, English, Polish, Austrians, and Italians, with some Americans and Canadians are arriving.

We have been having two to four raids a day for two weeks now, and many thousands of non-combatants, women and children have been killed.

Yesterday we did three transfusions—this is about the average daily, besides the blood we leave at hospitals for them to use themselves.

This is a grand country and a grand people. The wounded have been wonderful.

After I had given a transfusion to a French soldier who had lost his arm he raised the other to me as I left the room and with his raised clenched fist exclaimed: "*Viva la Revolucion!*" The boy next to him was a Spaniard—a medical student shot through the liver and stomach. When I had given him a transfusion and asked him how we felt, he said "It is nothing—*nada!*" He recovered and so did the Frenchman.

We all feel enormously encouraged by your grand support. You may rest assured and give our assurance to the workers of Canada that their efforts and money are saving many Spanish, French, German and English lives. We will win. The fascists are already defeated. Madrid will be the tomb of fascism.

Bethune was a man with an inventive imagination. A born rebel, he was temperamentally suited to guerrilla warfare. It was no accident that Bethune finally came into his own, both as a man and as a physician, in the service of the Chinese Red Army, in the guerrilla war against the Japanese. Spain, however, was another matter. By the spring of 1937, Bethune was increasingly involved in controversy within the blood transfusion unit and with some of the Spanish doctors in charge of the republic's medical corps. The nature of the disagreements remains a matter of dispute. What is certain is that a consensus was reached that Bethune should return to Canada to undertake a national speaking tour on behalf of the republic's cause. William Kashtan and A.A. MacLeod were asked to go to Spain to arrange his return.

Bethune never thought of himself as a speaker or writer; in fact, he excelled at both. Upon his return to Toronto on 14 June, hundreds gathered to greet him at Union Station. A parade was organized to Queen's Park, where he addressed an open-air rally, electrifying the crowd of some five thousand people. Two days later he returned to Montréal, where one thousand people gathered in Windsor Station to welcome him home. Later, he addressed an overflow crowd of eight thousand at the Mount Royal Arena. The national speaking tour, organized by the Committee to Aid Spanish Democracy, was off to a successful beginning.

Bethune reached and influenced Canadians in another way. While in Spain he undertook a regular correspondence with the *Toronto Daily Clarion*. As well, he wrote a powerful description of the fascist assault upon civilian refugees following Franco's capture of Malaga in January 1937. The southern city had been subjected to an intense bombardment. As resistance crumbled, the civilian population had been ordered to evacuate on foot and head for Almeria. Bethune had travelled to Almeria in February to determine the need for blood transfusion services. Upon his arrival, Bethune immediately left for Malaga, only to run into a sea of human refugees on the coastal road. The civilians needed transportation, not blood, and Bethune ordered his ambulance to ferry the most desperate cases back to Almeria. He wrote a pamphlet on the ordeal which, when it reached Canada, had an unforgettable impact on those who read it. Bethune wrote in part:

> . . . the farther we went the more pitiful the sights became. Thousands of children—we counted five thousand under ten years of age—and at least one thousand of them barefoot and many of them clad only in a single garment. They were slung over their mother's shoulders or clung to her hands. Here a father staggered along with two children of one and two years of age on his back in addition to carrying pots and pans or some treasured possession. The incessant stream of people became so dense we could barely force the car through them.

> . . . it was difficult to choose which to take. Our car was besieged by a mob of frantic mothers and fathers who with tired outstretched arms held up to us their children, their eyes and faces swollen and congested by four days of sun and dust.

> "Take this one." "See this child." "This one is wounded." Children with bloodstained rags wrapped around their arms and legs, children without shoes, their feet swollen to twice their size crying helplessly from pain, hunger and fatigue. Two hundred kilometers of misery. Imagine four days and four nights, hiding by day in the hills as the fascist barbarians pursued them by plane, walking by

night packed in a solid stream of men, women, children, mules, donkeys, goats, crying out the names of their separated relatives lost in the mob. How could we choose between taking a child dying of dysentery or a mother silently watching us with great sunken eyes carrying against her open breast her child born on the road two days ago. She had stopped walking for ten hours only. Here was a woman of sixty unable to stagger another step, her gigantic swollen legs with their open varicose ulcers bleeding into her cut linen sandals. Many old people simply gave up the struggle, lay down by the side of the road and waited for death.

We first decided to take only children and mothers. Then the separation between father and child, husband and wife became too cruel to bear. We finished by transporting families with the largest number of young children and the solitary children of which there were hundreds without parents.

And now comes the final barbarism . . . On the evening of the 12th when the little seaport of Almeria was completely filled with refugees, its population swollen to double its size, when forty thousand exhausted people had reached a haven of what they thought was safety, we were heavily bombed by German and Italian fascist airplanes. The siren alarm sounded thirty seconds before the first bomb fell. These planes made no effort to hit the government battleship in the harbour or bomb the barracks. They deliberately dropped ten great bombs in the very center of the town where on the main street were sleeping, huddled together on the pavement so closely that a car could pass only with difficulty, the exhausted refugees. After the planes had passed I picked up in my arms three dead children from the pavement in front of the Provincial Committee for the Evacuation of Refugees where they had been standing in a great queue waiting for a cupful of preserved milk and a handful of dry bread, the only food some of them had for days. The street was a shambles of the dead and dying, lit only by the orange glare of burning buildings. In the darkness the moans of the wounded children, shrieks of agonized mothers, the curses of the men rose in a massed cry higher and higher to a pitch of intolerable intensity. One's body felt as heavy as the dead themselves, but empty and hollow, and in one's brain burned a bright flame of hate.[20]

Throughout the war the motor transport troops did great work in delivering supplies to the army and troops at the front. They carried enormous amounts of freight in the form of ammunition, combat equipment and military supplies. They also evacuated the wounded and the sick, recovered weapons and equipment, and transported troops; they performed their duty with honour.

There was an *autoparc* (transport) in Albacete, initially commanded by the French. Later, an American section of the *autoparc* was established, and finally a 15th Brigade transport was formed. The *Cuerpo de Sanidad* (sanitary corps) attached to the brigade, originally based in Tarancon, was commanded by an American named Mac Kraus. Its task was to move the wounded, evacuate front-line wounded, and haul supplies. The ambulances and rolling-stock belonged to the international medical units, which were separate from brigade transport.

Dmytro Skavulak drove a water truck, as did Marvin Penn of Winnipeg. Harold Sparks of Toronto drove a truck, and Murray Saunders of Alberta was in transport. After arriving in Albacete on 24 May 1937, Saunders was ordered to drive an ambulance from the French border.

Allen Ross went to Spain in June 1937, at the age of nineteen. He fought as a soldier in the battle for Quinto, was then posted as a mechanic in the truck park, and was finally designated as a driver for the Lincoln Battalion. His job was mainly to transport troops to the various fronts. When the fascists broke through to the Mediterranean in April 1938, his truck was the last to cross the bridge before it was blown up. He was ordered to Barcelona where he was placed in charge of a large garage with eight hundred pieces of equipment.

Joe Hautniemi states that twenty Finnish-Canadians and Finnish-Americans worked as transport drivers, hauling kitchens and equipment and driving ambulances. Some worked with the 13th Brigade and others with the 86th Brigade, including Art Siven.

R.D. Brown went to Spain with Rod Gillis and Perry Hilton. Brown recalls:

> They also asked me [at Albacete] if there were any miners in our group and, as I had worked in mines, I stepped forward. About eight of us made up a unit and we were supposed to be trained as dynamiters, although we weren't trained very much.
>
> Eventually we were sent to the Aragon front, not as a dynamiter, but as a driver in an American transport unit with the 15th Brigade.[21]

Brown was posted to the Mac-Pap as a rifleman in the Third Company. During The Retreats he was attached to the British Battalion and finally, with five other men, took a ship from Barcelona to England.

Hans Ibing volunteered to go to Spain late in 1936. At Albacete he was assigned to the *autoparc* which, he says,

> was a large enclosure equipped with low buildings. This was the *Primero Regimento de Tren de las Brigadas Internationales, V Regimiento.* It was divided into three companies. The first company consisted mostly of Americans and Canadians, with an American lieutenant in charge.
>
> I was attached to the Third Company (mostly Germans, Austrians and some Scandinavians) and, not being a mechanic, was used as a regular driver from the beginning.
>
> We had 75 trucks and auxiliary vehicles, staff cars and one motorcycle dispatch rider.
>
> All our trucks were French Matfords, English Fordsons, with a steering wheel on the wrong side, and American Fords, all mechanically identical. The auxiliary vehicles were French Lantils or Renaults. We also had one water tanker and a gasoline tanker.

Mechanically, the trucks stood up pretty well throughout, but the made-in-Spain wooden bodies were not well made. These trucks were not suitable for transporting troops. The wheelbase was a lot shorter than the length of the bodies called for, but they were the only trucks available.

> With their long overhang and with about 40 soldiers and their equipment, these trucks were hard to handle on the hilly and winding roads. They had no hydraulic brakes and you quickly had to learn how to shift into second or even first gear to hold down the speed on a downhill road. Those gears were hard to shift and especially on the Fordsons, double-clutching was the only way.

> The cab only had room for two but there was [sic] always at least two officers wanting to ride in the cab. On frosty nights during the Aragon battles with three people steaming and icing up the windshield—this was before the heater and defroster days—it became almost impossible to see and very dangerous to drive.

> All the driving at night was done without the use of headlights. I never worked so hard in my life under such miserable conditions, not to mention the danger of getting lost, going through the lines or being shot at. In all this time I never once saw a roadmap.

> This job of driving was one of the most miserable experiences of my life. While the lot of the infantryman was much more dangerous, they had some kind of comradeship and mutual sharing of hardship and danger, and looked after each other, and had their own language of communication. After the central front, most driving missions became single truck operations [for Ibing] and the lot of the driver was isolation and loneliness, at least for me.[22]

ARMOUR, AIRFORCE AND CAVALRY

Edward Reznowski left for Spain in February 1937, with Lionel Edwards, Nels Madsen and a few others, via New York on the SS *President Roosevelt*. When he arrived at Albacete there was a call for volunteers for the armoured car battalion. Reznowski responded, and was later transferred to the armoury.

Only two Canadians are shown as having been in the tank corps, Mykola Tarnawskyi and Bill Kardash. Most of the tanks were Soviet-made, and while reliable, were too few in number to play a decisive role in the war.

A few Canadian volunteers served in the airforce, including Fred Lord and D. Carberry. Douglas Ogle wrote the following account:

> Some sources maintain that Bruno Mussolini, son of the Italian dictator, was involved in a rather colourful combat with a Soviet 1-16. It is said that Mussolini commanded an Italian fighter unit at Palma, Majorca, in August, 1938; and that soon after receiving the new Fiat G.50 monoplane fighter, small numbers of which were used in Spain, he issued a challenge by radio for any five government pilots to meet him in combat. A Republican unit known as the *Alas Rojas* [Red Wings] Squadron was, at that time, based at Castellon de la Plana, equipped with 1-16s and commanded by a Canadian volunteer pilot, Captain Derek Dickinson. Dickinson was told of the Italian pilot's contemptuous gesture, received permission to answer the challenge, and passed his acceptance by radio to the Nationalist base. The two pilots met in the air at 12:00 hours on the 18th of September, 1938, and the ensuing dog fight lasted a little over 22 minutes. Both pilots were slightly wounded; and eventually Mussolini made a signal acknowledging defeat by throwing an article of flying clothing from the cockpit. No less than 326 bullet holes were counted in Dickinson's aircraft when he landed; but his victory in this action with an aircraft powered by an engine of 100 h.p. is a tribute to both his flying ability and his aircraft.[23]

Vasili Ivanovich Hliva served in the 45th Cavalry Brigade for more than two years, was wounded and, after his recovery, returned to his unit. He joined a cavalry unit attached to the Dombrowski Battalion and saw action in Belchite, Villanueva de la Cañada and Teruel. His horse was hit by artillery fire and Hliva suffered a concussion. He was cut off by fascist forces in the south of Spain.

One Canadian, Ed Peneycad (Morgan), is recorded as having been assigned to the Fourth Company Demolition Unit of the Lincoln Battalion. He saw action and was wounded at Teruel, and later was involved in the retreat across the Ebro. Peneycad had some difficulty in returning to Canada, and his experience is illustrative of the attitude of the Canadian government towards the volunteers. He first made his way from Spain to the North African port of Oran, where he was arrested by the French police, interrogated by the American ambassador, and repatriated by ship to Marseilles. There he was taken under escort through France to Le Havre, crossed the channel and took the train to London where the authorities told him to "get lost." Canada House in London would not provide assistance. He worked in two bars in North London to earn passage back to Canada. He landed in Québec, was arrested, and had to swear an oath of allegiance before being released in May 1939.[24]

NOTES
1. Translations from the Finnish press, provided by Sulo Huhtala.
2. Ibid.
3. George Kostoff of Toronto, taped interview.
4. SAB, Fred Hadesbeck, Diary.
5. Ibid.
6. Adapted from Liversedge, "Memoir of the Spanish Civil War."
7. Ibid.
8. Lee Burke, written account in the possession of author.
9. Ibid.
10. Joe Glenn, written account in the possession of author.
11. Fred Mattersdorfer, letters and interviews with author.
12. Ibid.
13. Adapted from Brennan, unpublished account.
14. Ibid.
15. James Southgate, written account to author.
16. Hans Ibing, written account to author.
17. Walter Hellund, written account to author.
18. Cited in Komodowski, *With the Mackenzie-Papineau Battalion*, 2-4.
19. For an account of Bethune's life, see Ted Allan and Sydney Gordon, *The Scalpel, The Sword* (Toronto: McClelland and Stewart, 1952); see also R. Stewart, *Bethune* (Don Mills, Ontario: Paperjacks, 1975).
20. Norman Bethune, *The Crime on the Road: Malaga to Almeria* (Madrid: Publicaciones Iberia, 1937), no page.
21. R.D. Brown, written account to author.
22. Hans Ibing, written account to author.
23. Douglas Ogle to Walter Dent, 20 January 1980.
24. Ed Peneycad, written account to author.

Seven

Atrocities

During the war, right-wing newspapers in Canada attempted to convince their readers that the republican forces had unleashed a "red terror" on Catholic Spain. The more liberal media preferred to suggest that atrocities were committed on both sides, that republicans and fascists alike were equally guilty of "excesses."[1]

It was known that some atrocities had been committed by the republican forces. Age-old bitterness, aggravated by grinding poverty and brutal oppression made restraint difficult to practice when the fortunes of war presented opportunities to mete out rough justice. The republican government was aware of the risk and did everything possible to prevent such acts from occurring. To the Canadian volunteers it appeared that the government was going out of its way to restrain the anger of the Spanish people against those individuals and institutions who had so recently abused and oppressed them.

Dr. O.D. Skelton, Undersecretary of State for External Affairs, came to a similar conclusion. In a memorandum dated 24 January 1939 he wrote:

> Whatever mistakes were made by the anti-fascist forces in Spain in their first angry reprisals, they have shown a surprising growth in moderation, courage, unity and effectiveness. I have followed the record of the Spanish government of recent months with surprise and increasing admiration. When their record is compared with that of most of the most recent governments in France and England, with their endless muddling and lack of foresight, their cold-blooded concentration on their own immediate interests, there is a lot to be said for the conclusion that, if the people of Canada really wanted to

172

get into somebody's European war, they might choose Negrin's instead of Neville's.[2]

The fascist forces in Spain, by way of contrast, made no effort to restrain their troops. Horrible reprisals were not only threatened, but carried out, and atrocities were encouraged as policy. For example, on 28 August 1936 General Queipo de Llano announced that he had issued orders to the effect that for every person killed by the republicans, the fascists would kill five. In his words, "We have struck the word 'pity' out of our dictionary."

The threats of the fascists were deliberately phrased in savage terms to strike fear into their opponents. The *Manchester Guardian* printed a story from Seville in which a fascist leader stated that his followers intended to "grind the blood and bones of the people of Valencia with a pestle and mortar to make cement to rebuild the churches they have burned."[3] A Spanish periodical published in Cordova, known as the *ABC* headlined an article thus: "We shall rip them up like pigs."

The prominent Spanish writer, Miguel de Unamuno, initially supported Franco, but then broke with the fascists. He was then expelled from the presidency of the University of Salamanca, and issued the following statement:

> I am terrified by the violence, the sadism, the inconceivable cruelty of this civil war as it appears from the Nationalist side. All the horrors which have been reported to me as having been committed by the "Reds"—and in which I by no means believe—are pale trifles compared to the cruelty, the systematic and organized sadism which, every day, here accompanies the execution of the most honest and innocent people, irrespective of their party label, simply because they are liberal and Republican. And note well that these brutalities are not here a question of individual terrorist action but result from collective orders given by the general staff which calls itself national. All these crimes are committed in cold blood in response to the slogan implied by the double-edged cry of

this insane general who calls himself Millan Astray: "Death to intelligence and Long Live Death!"[4]

The Times of London reported the storming of Badajoz by the fascists in these words:

All the militiamen and government supporters whom the insurgents [fascists] found with arms in their hands or suspected of having taken part in the fighting were immediately shot. They are said to number 1,200 . . . Throughout the night the "cleaning up" continued in the labyrinths of narrow streets in the older parts of the town. Such prisoners as were taken by the insurgents were escorted in batches to their newly-established headquarters there to be placed against a wall and shot out of hand. When this grim work was finished the pavement in front of the military headquarters ran with the blood of the victims. It dripped into the gutters and congealed there, forming ghastly pools in which lay the caps, torn papers, and small belongings of the massacred men.

Hundreds of terrified people had taken refuge in the Cathedral; among them the insurgents found two government militiamen whom they shot on the steps of the altar.

Many houses were in flames; they burned unheeded, their smoke throwing a pall over the town. The streets were full of dead bodies, broken glass, shattered tiles from the houses, the stench and litter of battle. In the Calle San Juan an eyewitness counted 300 bodies.[5]

The *Manchester Guardian* carried the following report:

The rebels in the districts occupied by them have systematically shot all workers carrying a trade union card. The corpses of the workers left lying in the streets or heaped up in the cemeteries have each the card of a trade union tied to leg or arm. In the town of Seville alone, and independent of any military action, more than 9,000 workers and peasants were executed.

The Moors and Foreign Legionaries went through the streets of humble one-story houses in the workmen's quarters, throwing hand grenades through the windows, killing women and children. The Moorish troops devoted

174

themselves to freely sacking and plundering. General Queipo de Llano in his wireless talks incites these troops to rape and describes scenes of this kind with brutal sarcasm.[6]

Ernest Hemingway, a keen observer of the Spanish civil war, wrote a special article for the Soviet newspaper *Pravda* in which he dealt directly with the issue of atrocities:

> During the last 15 months I saw murder done in Spain by the fascist invaders. Murder is different from war. Men can hate war and be opposed to it, yet become accustomed to it as a way of life when it is fought to defend your country against an invader and for your right to live and work as a free man.
>
> In such a case no man, who is a man, gives any importance to his life because so much more important things are at stake. A man observing this same war and writing of it cares nothing for his life either if he believes in the necessity of what he is doing. He cares only to write the truth . . .
>
> But you have anger and hatred when you see them do murder. And you see them do it almost every day.
>
> You see them do it in Barcelona where they bomb the workers' quarters from a height so great it is impossible for them to have any objective other than the block of apartments where the people live. You see the murdered children with their twisted legs; their arms that bend in wrong directions, and their plaster powdered faces. You see the women, sometimes unmarked when they die from concussion, their faces gray, green matter running out of their mouths from burst gall bladders. You see them sometimes looking like bloodied bundles of rags. You see them sometimes blown capriciously into fragments as an insane butcher might sever a carcass. And you hate the Italian and German murderers who do this as you hate no other people.
>
> You live in Madrid under bombardment for months and while you are there the hotel you live in is hit by artillery fire 53 times. From the window where you live you see

much murder. Because there is a cinema across the street and the fascists time their bombardments for the hours when the people leave the cinema to go to their homes. In this way they know, before the people can seek shelter, that they will have victims . . .

When they shell the cinema crowds, concentrating on the squares where the people will be coming out at six o'clock it is murder.

You see a shell hit a queue of women standing in line to buy soap. There are only four women killed but a part of one woman's torso is driven against a stone wall so that blood is driven into the stone with such force that sandblasting later fails to clean it. The other dead lie like scattered black bundles and the wounded are moaning or screaming.

You see a 9-inch shell hit a street car filled with workers. After the flash and the roar and the dust has settled, the car is on its side. Two people are alive, but they would be better dead, and the others need to be removed with shovels. Before the next shell comes a dog has nosed up to the wrecked car. It sniffs in the dust of the blasted granite. Nobody pays any attention to the dog as the two un-speakably badly wounded are being removed and, as the next shell comes screaming in a descending rush, the dog goes rushing up the street with a four-foot piece of intes-tine trailing from its jaws. He was hungry, as everyone else is in Madrid.

All last spring, last fall and last winter, we saw the fascist artillery doing murder in Madrid and you never see it without hatred and anger . . .

They murder for two reasons: To destroy the morale of the Spanish people and to try the effect of their various bombs in preparation for the war that Italy and Germany expect to make. Their bombs are very good. They have learned much in their experimenting in Spain and their bombing is better all the time.

They are successful as long as they can blackmail countries that fear them. It is when they begin to murder and to fight that they are lost. For the brothers and the fathers of their victims will never forgive and never forget. The crimes committed by fascism will raise the world against it.[7]

Atrocities were not reserved for the civilian population. Despite the assurances issued by Franco's general staff that the fascists would observe the conventions of war, republican soldiers who fell into the enemy's hands were either summarily shot or incarcerated under conditions of severe and deliberate cruelty. At least thirty Canadian volunteers were captured by the fascists, most during The Retreats in March and April of 1938.

SAN PEDRO DE CARDENAS

Jules Paivio was one of the Canadians captured by the fascists. He had attended officer's training school after the battles at Jarama and Brunete, and then joined the topographical section at the base. He was placed in the Mac-Pap as a section commander in Company One when he went to the front in March 1938.

At the end of March, in position along the Gandesa-Alcaniz road, his company received orders that three machine guns were to be moved up with the infantry. Paivio recalls what transpired:

In my opinion a serious blunder. But orders were orders. While the company commander took two guns and crews further to the right flank, I took one gun crew to a ridge top to the right of infantry Company One and Three.

Ahead of me, about 75 metres away, were some more troops on the same ridge. Two soldiers came forward yelling in Spanish to me that there was a better machine-gun position and to come over. This obviously being correct, I walked over to them and, being exceptionally tired, I wasn't as observant as usual.

Suddenly they lifted their guns and "manos arriba! [hands up!]" I looked up, surprised, and discovered they were Italian fascists. I had no arms, not even a revolver, due to the extreme shortage of them and, therefore, could give no resistance.

They invited the Spanish crew to come over also, but I yelled "They are fascists! Get back! Get back!" Then in desperation as they were leading me away: "Shoot! Why don't you shoot them?" to my men again. The two Italians immediately placed me between them and my men. My crew just stared after me with their mouths wide open, completely bewildered. When I saw the formidable array of Italian machine guns along the ridge I was glad they hadn't shot or I would have been mince-meat much too soon.

I was led behind a knoll where I was searched—fortunately not too thoroughly—and given a few clips with the butt of a rifle for luck. The previous day I had taken off my uncomfortable jacket with the bars on it and thus was captured as a plain soldier and, incidentally, my life was saved.

At the enemy headquarters I met about 15 other Canadian prisoners captured while out on patrol five minutes earlier.

We expected to be shot before long. In fact two or three times we were lined up against a wall with firing squads lined up before us. The third time a high ranking officer drove up in a limousine with impressive looking personal guards and, after a hasty consultation, we were shipped farther back to the rear, joining other captured internationals. We were crowded into cold box cars and brought to a jail in Zaragoza.

There we met the 100 English captured on March 30.

On April 7th late at night we arrived at the San Pedro de Cardenas concentration camp where we were to be incarcerated for ten months. It was an old convent and previous to that a palace of the Cid [El Cid] an early king of Spain, situated about 13 kilometres east of Burgos.

Although there were about 700 international prisoners in the camp and from 1000 to 4000 Spaniards we internationals were placed in two long rooms, 350 men to a room. We were forced to sleep on the bare floor. Later most of us were supplied with a straw pallet and a thin blanket.

The place was filthy. Mice ran over our heads. Vermin covered our clothing so thickly that I, for one, had to "read" my pants and shorts twice daily.

For 350 men we had two toilets and one water tap. Sick men slept on the floor at one end of the room until, towards the last, they were given a separate room.

Beatings of at least two or three a day were carried out by the sadist fascist sergeants who, having been wounded at fronts opposite the internationals, hated us intensely and took every opportunity possible to take it out on our hides.

After six Germans escaped by sawing off the bars of a window, one German sleeping near them and suspected of knowing about the escape was beaten so mercilessly that he remained in hospital for a month, and his face was left horribly disfigured for life.

The fascists, in their blind rage at the successful escape, had all of us run down the stairs and through a narrow door singly where we were beaten by the sergeants with loaded whips, while soldiers along the stairs butted and tripped us with rifles. This extreme form of terror lasted for days and had us trembling in apprehension every time we were forced to run down through the gauntlet.

The German Gestapo was in charge of all investigations at the concentration camp. A group of them came down daily from Burgos to investigate us according to nationalities, taking the most detailed information regarding us: photographs, minute description, questioning on our ancestry and even our sexual life. This information was being used to prove the superiority of the Aryan race.

Regardless of the terror, filth and shortage of food, the morale of the prisoners was splendid throughout, with the exception of a few individuals to be found in any group.[8]

The high morale of the International Brigades evident in the field asserted itself among the captured internationals, sustaining the prisoners through the brutal days of captivity.

The prisoners made chess sets out of bread, soap and wood, and held tournaments. Bridge was played with home-made cards. Enough books and magazines were received by the English and American prisoners to establish a prison library and occupy a librarian. Some of the prisoners had been professors and teachers, and therefore classes were conducted on a wide variety of subjects, including languages, geography, algebra, trigonometry, calculus, telegraphy, shorthand and Spanish history, as well as lectures on journalism, philosophy, ecology and other topics.

In January 1939 a group of 106 English and Canadians was sent from San Pedro de Cardenas to San Sebastian in the north, near the French border, where they were to be exchanged. The men were held overnight in the same barn in which they had been held prisoners in transit ten months earlier. Jules Paivio describes the transfer:

> At dawn we set out for Burgos on foot. With sore and blistered feet we still managed to march through the fascist capital like conquerors with our heads up, in good formation, and all in step, looking neither right or left, with haughty tolerance in our glances.

> From there to San Sebastian by train. Arriving there at 8 p.m. we had to march through the main thoroughfare of the city with a sound truck in advance proclaiming: here come the barbaric reds and foreigners who deserted to Franco. The previous evening a radio broadcast had announced our trip through the city for the purpose of getting people to demonstrate against us.

> What an opposite effect! It was obvious that the sentiment of the population was with us.

> We were placed in the basement cells of the San Sebastian Provincial Prison. This was to be the last stage of our confinement. A month-and-a-half in damp and unhealthy quarters on a diet of bread and water mainly soon brought on a recurrence of the dreaded scurvy sores which had broken out among us in San Pedro de Cardenas.

When we were finally released on the fifth of April [1939] our physical condition was unenviable. By bus to the border at Irun and across the International Bridge to Hendaye. France and Freedom! What a sweet word: Freedom!

The English went straight to England while we 35 Canadians stayed three weeks in Le Havre to rest up and recuperate with good food and medical attention. Then through London and Liverpool and across the sea on the *Duchess of Bedford* to Canada and home.[9]

Anthony Mangotic was in the Dimitrov Battalion. In July 1937 he was on patrol with two others; they lost their way and were captured. Mangotic describes what happened:

I hid myself in the long grass. The other two kept on in the direction of the fascists thinking they were ours. They were caught. I walked all night but no trace of my battalion. Next morning I saw that I was surrounded. I was in a large river bed and could see both lines. During the day the fascist planes dropped incendiary bombs. The grass was on fire and driving me towards the fascists.

When I was ten metres away from them they yelled and pointed their guns at me. I had to give myself up. From there the Moors took me to staff headquarters where a wounded Frenchman was also a prisoner.

A fascist major questioned me. He wanted to know if there were Russians driving us forward at the point of a pistol. I told him the reason why we attacked so energetically was because we were disciplined. They took us to a hospital.

They gave us three meals a day, but before each meal, they gave us a beating. They took us into a special room to beat us up. They used a solid rubber thong cut out with sharp corners from a tire. Under the whacks of this strap everyone fell to the ground unconscious.

They brought in a Spaniard who had tried to find his way to the Republican side. For that he received horrible beatings and they smashed his face with the butt of a gun.

They took us to a big church half a kilometre away from town. And we had to pass along the main street so all the world could see us. I had to carry the wounded Frenchman on my back. On my way there I received an awful beating. Under this beating and the weight of the Frenchman I fell to the ground. The lines of people of the town gathered into groups protesting and yelling. As I got up again they kept on beating me. One Spaniard came out into the middle of the street. He was clearly protesting the treatment. They took him away.

In the church the Moors kept on beating the Spaniard. All his teeth were out and his jaw was broken by the butt of a gun. He fell to the ground near the altar in a little alcove. In the corner of the cell there was a bucket of dirty water. After they locked us in I looked at the poor fellow to see what I could do for him.

He seemed to breathe perhaps once in every two minutes. I tore some cloth off my pant leg and washed him. But he did not regain consciousness. Ten minutes later they returned and took us across the church into another room, leaving the Spaniard on the floor.

There I found another two Frenchmen, one Polack [sic], and a platinum blonde American aviator. The American had his hand broken from being twisted and his head was covered in lumps from the beatings. He asked them to write a letter to his wife but they refused. They took him away and we never saw him again.

They took us to the province of Toledo, to Talavera de la Reina. This was July 30, 1937. They put us in a silk factory that had been turned into a prison called Las Sedas [the silks]. There were 1800 prisoners, the majority were sentenced to death or given 30 years. Among them were children of 15.

Every night around eleven the chief of the execution squad came in. He was a captain and carried a strap. A Falangist with him carried a list of names. Usually up to 30 men were called out. Some almost went mad waiting. Everyone stood. Those whose names were called had their hands tied by guards and were sent through a door to a truck.

They used to take them to the banks of the river Tajo and line them up with their backs to the river. When the body crumpled the captain walked from man to man, raised his pistol rhythmically and monotonously and the executed fell into the water. But the monotony sometimes made the captain careless and some corpses, bleeding at the head, dragged themselves up the banks of the Tajo on the Republican side. So they took them to the cemetery and tied them to stakes like in Goya paintings and used a firing squad.

On August 6 in the early morning I awoke to hear the cry of women. I looked through the window. A large mass of people and a big truck full of civilians was ready to be taken to the graveyard. Six were from my prison, among them a boy of fifteen. The women with their children were bidding their last farewells. One with a child in her arms fell on the street before the truck, weeping, "Shoot me, but save my husband."

The truck moved off but the woman kept on crying. One of the Falangists jumped over to her and shoved her away, "Run along! Why do you need a dog!" She fell to the ground. People were murmuring in protest and the prisoners in the truck raised their fists, shouting "*Viva la Republica*" and they sang the International on the way to the graveyard.

An 18 year old boy was sentenced to death. His 60 year old father was sentenced to 30 years. When they called out the son's name the old man took out a razor and cut his own throat.

From this factory I was taken to a place called the Instituto Nacional [The National Institute] where I found a Slovak named Carol Ivanka, who told me he had been a partisan and was sentenced to death.

I was moved to Tinaja where they forced us to dig secondary trenches about four kilometres from the front. I also worked in the garage in the town, thereby getting to know many civilians. They were generous to me. When they found out I was from the International Brigades they tried in every way to help me with wine, food and money. They asked me to their homes. The authorities got wind of it and stopped it, keeping me in prison all the time.

On March 5, I was taken to Burgos. There was great hunger in this prison, also sickness and torture. Many of our comrades died.

Later on we were taken to the Dareta prison at San Sebastian. There they were all British. It was January 23, 1939. It was awful. In Dareta alone there were 2000 prisoners, 300 of whom were women of some 80 years of age. Here, also, 80 Catholic priests were sentenced to death and shot, mostly Basque priests.

When word came of the exchange the English were sent first and the rest of us had to wait half a month. During that time we lived on bread and water. Just before we were supposed to have been exchanged the English Consul came and brought us each a cake of soap![10]

In one of the battles at Gandesa during The Retreats, John Charles Firmin was captured. He was serving in the company commanded by Curly Wilson. He was wounded in the arm and leg. An Italian sergeant picked him up and carried him on his shoulder.

He was put into a big barn where the guards stole all the valuables and personal belongings of the wounded. He was put on a truck and fainted. He ended up in the operating room of a tiny hospital, without even an aspirin to relieve the pain of his wounds. Immediately after the operation he was placed on a train, where he lost consciousness. Firmin had the following comments to make:

An enemy officer was nearby when I opened my eyes. "So you are awake, eh? Thought we'd lost you," he said. We were taken by train to Zaragoza. I was operated on there and they set my arm. At the first hospital they had just slashed off the hanging flesh around the wound. Here they did a proper job. The bone where the bullet had passed was splintered into many fragments and they put me in a cast.

There was a Scotsman who had been wounded in the elbow in the next bed.

Then we went to Bilbao. I was operated on again. In Bilbao we had some freedom. We could go to the bathroom ourselves and walk around. Later on a new administration took over and they cut down on our freedom and put pails in our rooms for latrines and established a more rigid regime.

Our diet consisted of bread and fish, head and all.

I was then moved somewhere else to another prison. But I don't know where it was. It was still in the same area.

It was a huge building. I couldn't tell how many prisoners were there. We used to play games and, during one game, my arm was broken again. I was taken to a small infirmary. The doctor was a prisoner-of-war himself, working without drugs and equipment. He reset my arm and bandaged it with a piece of sheet. Osteomyelitis set in. A Dr. Laird fixed it up in Canada, arranged through the Friends of the Mackenzie-Papineau Battalion.[11]

Firmin states that he and his fellow prisoners often talked about escaping. Before they could do so, however, they were moved to a new prison where the food was the worst of all:

It was soya beans and when they brought them to us the top of the pot containing them was black with bugs. We had no utensils with which to eat. If you had a sardine can that's how much you got. If you had a spoon, then that's what you got.

Then, one day, a guard went around shouting: "Juan Carlos Firmin!" I didn't catch on at first. "Don't you want to go home?" I was asked when I rushed up to the guard. I was turned over to the *Guardia Civil* and was taken to San Sebastian by train. I was taken to a prison and put in a dungeon. There I met Scotty somebody. "What have you heard?" he asked. "That we're going home," I said. "I don't believe it," said Scotty, "Franco won't let us go. I've heard we're all to be shot. But I'm not giving up without a fight."

We were held there about a month, I would guess, and the food was bad. One day the guards walked around shouting "*estranjeros! estranjeros!* [foreigners]" They took enough of us to fill two buses. We were taken to a prison and herded into a room called Salle de Muerte [Room of Death]. We thought, "This is it."

They took us out. "This is it! This is it!" we said to each other. We were loaded into buses again. Where were they taking us? We stopped at a huge building, a monastery. We thought we're here for the last rites. But some members of the religious order came and asked us if we wanted to change our money into francs. We had no money.

We were taken to the border and then over a bridge to the French side. As soon as we were off the buses we thumbed our noses and gave the clenched fist salute to the other side. They were dancing up and down in rage.[12]

NOTES
1. See Peck, *Red Moon Over Spain.*
2. Quoted in John A. Munro, "Canada and the Civil War in Spain," *External Affairs* 23, no. 2 (1971): 58.
3. *Manchester Guardian*, 15 August 1936.
4. Millan Astray was commander of the Spanish Foreign Legion. He had been seriously wounded and the state of his mind appeared to match his physical deformities.
5. *The Times* of London, 17 August 1936.
6. *Manchester Guardian*, 30 October 1936.
7. Reprinted in the *Toronto Star*, 27 November 1982, under the title: "Humanity will not Forget."
8. Jules Paivio, 26 September 1939, written account in the possession of author.
9. Ibid.
10. Anthony Mangolic, written account in the possession of author.
11. Taped interview with author.
12. Ibid.

Eight

The Journey Home

The governments of the western democracies had waged a consistent and successful campaign throughout the civil war to deny aid and assistance to the legitimate republican government of Spain. Now, in 1938, they added to their treachery. Led by the Chamberlain government in Britain, they exerted pressure through the League of Nations to bring a halt to "foreign" intervention in the conflict. Franco, the fascists, and the governments of Germany and Italy would have nothing to do with the proposal. The republican government fell into the trap and favourably considered the British plan.

On 21 September Prime Minister Negrín announced that the government had unilaterally decided to evacuate all foreign volunteers who where serving the republican cause. The announcement was followed by a decree to this effect on 23 September. The League of Nations agreed to establish an International Commission for Verification and appointed a Military Commission to supervise the withdrawals.

The 15th International Brigade held its last parade on the football field at Marsa. The ranks about to be vacated by the foreign volunteers were filled by Spanish soldiers. At the conclusion of the parade the 15th Brigade, now composed entirely of Spaniards, crossed the Ebro once again. The Canadian volunteers would not see their Spanish comrades again.

By 27 September three hundred of the former international volunteers, including Americans and Canadians, had assembled at the Monserrat Monastery north of Barcelona. They then moved on to Ripoll, their final destination before leaving Spain. Here they began their long wait for the journey home.

The volunteers had mixed feelings concerning the Negrín government's decision to withdraw them from the Spanish conflict. The tedium of the camp at Ripoll, and uncertainty whether they would indeed ever get home, added to the general depression. There were, of course, the "farewells," which took many forms. But rather than lifting the men's spirits, these only served to deepen their feelings of anger and helplessness. Many of the men felt guilty, believing that leaving Spain before the forces of fascism had been crushed was tantamount to desertion.

Some of the farewells were of a very personal and touching nature. Bill Beeching, for example, was presented with a letter from a group of Spanish comrades who had only learned to read and write after 1936:

> Dear comrade, the Spanish comrades-in-arms of the 15th International Brigade want to express to you on your discharge their gratitude and affection, born in the joint struggle for the liberties of the Spanish people, that grew out of the heat and difficulties of that struggle, difficulties which are a result of the failure of the democratic peoples, in their isolation from us, to understand why we carry on this struggle for independence.
>
> Our profound sentiments go with you on your withdrawal which is, itself, undertaken because of the wish of our government of national unity to indicate to the world our total spirit of conciliation and peacefulness, and to demonstrate that all of the Spanish people are united, regardless of political or ideological convictions, in a fight for our national independence.
>
> But we have learned well from you and equally from most international comrades with their unlimited organizational accomplishments and discipline and their defence of democratic ideals so that the hole left in our ranks by your departure will be filled with our resolution to ensure that Spain, itself, is free and independent.
>
> It is exceedingly good that you, because of the integrity of your character, will be living proof wherever you go of the truth of our cause and you will testify to the tortures that

fascism has committed against our women and children. You will also tell the democratic people of Canada the truth about our war and how impossible it is for us to tolerate the crimes carried out by fascism in Spain.

Fraternal greetings to you and the cause of peace and democracy in the whole world.[1]

The most memorable farewell was held in Barcelona on 29 October, when volunteers from all the International Brigades held their last parade and marched down the main boulevard of the city. Vast crowds lined the streets, and flowers were thrown on the pavement in front of the marching soldiers. Battle-hardened men wept openly, and no one who was there would ever forget the Barcelonians, nor the singing of "The International" by thousands of voices in many different languages. At the conclusion of the parade the veterans were addressed by Dolores Ibarruri, "La Pasionara." She spoke first to the women:

Mothers! Women! When the years pass by and the wounds of war are staunched; when the cloudy memory of the sorrowful, bloody days returns in a present of freedom, love, and well-being; when the feelings of rancour are dying away and when pride in a free country is felt equally by all Spaniards—then speak to your children. Tell them of the International Brigades. Tell them how, coming over seas and mountains, crossing frontiers bristling with bayonets, and watched for by ravening dogs thirsty to tear at their flesh, these men reached our country as crusaders for freedom. They gave up everything, their loves, their country, home and fortune—fathers, mothers, wives, brothers, sisters, and children—and they came and told us: "We are here, your cause, Spain's cause is ours. It is the cause of all advanced and progressive mankind." Today they are going away. Many of them, thousands of them, are staying here with the Spanish earth for their shroud, and all Spaniards remember them with the deepest feeling.

She went on to address the volunteers:

Comrades of the International Brigades! Political reasons, reasons of state, the welfare of that same cause for which you offered your blood with boundless generosity, are sending you back, some of you to your own countries and others to forced exile. You can go proudly. You are history. You are legend. You are the heroic example of democracy's solidarity and universality. We shall not forget you, and, when the olive tree of peace puts forth its leaves again, mingled with the laurels of the Spanish republic's victory—come back!

The Canadian volunteers were to spend over four months at Ripoll. It was a difficult period; in addition to the boredom of inaction, the news from the front was invariably bad, and although the Spanish personnel did their best, the food was terrible. Every day a scene took place which reminded the volunteers of just how widespread and severe hunger was in Spain. The cooks boiled the bones until they were white and then split them to remove the nourishing marrow. After this, the bones were discarded behind the cook house, where the local inhabitants gathered them up and took them home.

Although discussions on politics and world events were organized, and the local population put on concerts, morale could not be sustained for long. There was no money available to pay for rail and steamship fares, and of greater concern, no one could determine the intentions of the Canadian government. Many volunteers believed that Ottawa was sympathetic to their predicament, but Bert Ramelson put forward a less charitable point of view: "The Canadian Government is not our friend. Mackenzie King is not our friend. You who came to Spain should know and understand that."[2]

The League of Nations Military Commission arrived in Ripoll on 4 November and proceeded to interview the Canadian volunteers. A certain Colonel O'Kelly arrived on behalf of the Canadian government and undertook his own interviews with his fellow countrymen.

O'Kelly was viewed with mixed emotions. In the course of an interview with Bill Beeching, a squadron of Franco's bombers flew overhead. Excited, O'Kelly stopped the interview and ran to the window, exclaiming that he would like to see for himself what a bombing raid was really like. He found out. His car was bombed on the road when he left for his quarters, and O'Kelly and his driver were forced to take shelter under the vehicle. From that day on O'Kelly conducted his business at night; a decision that in no way impressed the Canadian volunteers.

To make matters worse, O'Kelly had a tendency to conduct slow, drawn-out interviews with the Canadians. Unlike the volunteers, he seemed to be in no rush to get things done. A number of impatient, hungry Canadian volunteers raided his private store of food. Fred Mattersdorfer was convinced that once his rations were threatened, O'Kelly would speed matters up. The raid had the intended effect, convincing some of the veterans that even a spot of larceny has its place in the historical process.

Plans for the return of the volunteers to Canada remained up in the air, and rumour fed upon rumour. It was said by some that if Canada refused to permit the volunteers to return home, Mexico would welcome them. Finally, on 15 December, a telegram addressed to Ed Cecil-Smith was received from O.D. Skelton, Undersecretary of State for External Affairs. It recommended contact with the British Consul, who had been advised of steps being taken by the Canadian immigration authorities. The government of Mackenzie King had finally decided to act.[3]

A Canadian Pacific Railway (CPR) agent by the name of Coakley arrived at Ripoll on 29 December. He was a brave and efficient man, businesslike in his determination to see the volunteers return to Canada. He began gathering particulars and in a very short time had won the admiration of the men.

The main obstacle was the lack of money. The Friends of the Mackenzie-Papineau Battalion had until now devoted their efforts to raising money to send volunteers to Spain, and by the December 1938 the Friends had enough money to cover the fares of only 120 volunteers. A.A. MacLeod negotiated with the CPR and concessions were granted to include an additional eighty. MacLeod then launched a campaign to raise the necessary additional funds. In Spain, Tim Buck approached Juan Negrín, only to be told that the Spanish government was bankrupt. The Communist party of Canada mortgaged some of the buildings it owned and undertook its own campaign to raise funds.

Matthew Halton, then a foreign correspondent in London, received a call stating that a large number of Canadian volunteers were stranded and that the French government intended to put them in a concentration camp. The CPR was prepared to transport them back to Canada but required $10,000 in fares. Halton phoned the only two wealthy Canadians he knew in London. The first, described by Halton as a "famous man and a Tory of Tories," refused the request. The second was Garfield Weston. Halton later recalled: "Before I had finished the story he interrupted me: 'I'll send you a cheque for $5,000 in the morning,' he said."[4]

On 25 January 1939 the Canadian volunteers were taken to a small town called Casa de la Selva, where they were quartered in an old cork factory. The highlight of their stay was the call for volunteers to defend Barcelona, which was under attack. The men were in civilian clothes, had turned in all their military equipment, and had received their passports. A meeting was called and the proposition of defending Barcelona was discussed. After a heated debate it was decided that individual volunteers could return to the front if they wished. Many signed the list that was circulated, and some even gave away their personal belongings as they prepared to depart. However, the Canadians were finally told that no one would be going to Barcelona, as the Spanish government remained firm in its decision to repatriate them. Shortly thereafter another meeting was called, where Bob McCallum announced that the Canadians would leave the next morning. That evening Joe Schoen and Bill Beeching hauled down the flag of the Mackenzie-Papineau Battalion for the last time.

The Canadians were put on a train and taken to the border. Sulo Huhtala described the scene in his diary:

Left today on our final journey in Spain. We passed Genora after its rail yards had been heavily bombed and strafed. Franco's planes were searching for our train. Crossing the border into France at 6:05 p.m. Ten minutes later we reached the border town of Cerbere. After a brief medical examination, followed by a light lunch, and at 9:30 boarded a special train. All 290 of us were finally on our way back to the ranks of the unemployed.[5]

Jim Southgate also recalled the trip:

. . . the command received orders for us to delay our departure for one hour. Spies had informed the airfield at Minorca of the time of our departure. The air force came out and bombed the station at Port Bou. We crossed one hour later. If we had kept to the first schedule we would have arrived at Port Bou at the time of the bombing.[6]

Although Southgate and his comrades missed this attack, others were less fortunate. Newspapers carried "the news . . . that 800 volunteers assembled on the railway station at Cardedeu, 23 miles north west of Barcelona, were killed or wounded when Franco's planes bombarded the rail yards. Most of these volunteers were Czechoslovaks, Germans, Italians and other anti-fascists who could not return home."[7]

The train carrying the volunteers passed through Limoges at 6:45 A.M. in a snow storm and the 290 Canadians took a ferry from Dieppe to Newhaven at 7:05 P.M. When they passed through London there was a welcoming committee in Victoria Station which the authorities would not allow them to see. They were kept locked on the train which was to take them to Liverpool. Matthew Halton met them and travelled across Britain with them. He wrote:

No flags waved, no bands played at the little English harbour of Newhaven in the cold darkness of 3 o'clock this morning as some 300 Canadian members of the famous International Brigade which flocked from 30 nations to the defence of democratic Spain, landed in England on the last stage of their odyssey of courage and ideals . . .

Three hundred landed at Newhaven today and I have just left them at an obscure English siding. As I write, they are en route to Liverpool in sealed trains like so many lepers. Another hundred, still waiting for visas allowing them to cross France, had to be left behind and perhaps are among the 800 brigaders killed or wounded by Franco's bombs yesterday ... The other 600 lie forever in the plains of Aragon and Castille.

Three newspapermen, including myself, formed the only reception committee for Canada's returning crusaders at Newhaven. We travelled with them to London, and I had two hours I won't soon forget ...

A few of them, no doubt, are soldiers of fortune and aliens, but most are intelligent Canadians who saw what everyone is beginning to see now, that it is too late; and who had the courage to do something about it. Many of them are even Communists. But today France and Britain wouldn't be so afraid if Spain were Communist instead of fascist.[8]

On 27 January the volunteers boarded the SS *Duchess of Richmond*. After a very rough transatlantic crossing they arrived at Saint John, New Brunswick on 4 February 1939.

For various reasons a few Canadian volunteers did not leave Spain with the main group but went into France and ended up in French concentration camps. In these camps what little food existed was of poor quality, and the inmates suffered from unattended wounds, exposure and dysentery. Under the circumstances, many died. Petro Dolynuik recalls the experience:

I was with 95 leaving Spain. I was with Alex Kabatoff [Alex Forbes] and Mykola Kalieta. It was difficult to make our way because thousands and thousands of civilian Spaniards were fleeing. It was the hardest for the mothers who carried infants in their arms. It seemed that the end of the world had come and there'd be no salvation for anyone.

People were placed in concentration camps behind barbed wire. They were forced to sleep on the sand without shelter over their heads. Powerful winds would often pick up, filling our eyes with burning sand. For two days people were given nothing to eat. On the third day trucks arrived with bread for the starving people. Fascist agitators would arrive at the camps with their loudspeakers appealing to the refugees to return to Spain and a good life. However, they were unsuccessful. People didn't want to return to the fascist hell.[9]

Frank Thirkettle, who was in hospital when the internationals were being repatriated, found that his name was not on the list of those who were to return to Canada. He had to wait for two days after the first convoy had left, and then had to march to San Pedro in the north, as Barcelona had by this time fallen. He remembered the nightmarish trek:

I became too tired. My wounds ached and I was lucky enough to get a ride for the final stage. At last word came for the first batch of us to leave. We marched to Figueras on February 4th to take a train for the border. But the railroad had been bombed and traffic delayed. Figueras was practically in ruins after having suffered several vicious air raids. Towards night a train arrived and, after several days, we arrived at Port Bou early in the morning.

Refugees were fleeing by the thousands—men, women and children struggling along, some barefooted with only a few meagre belongings. Conveyances of every description from coaches to donkeys filled the road to France. It was pitiful to see old men, women and little children struggling up the hills to the border to escape the fascist invaders. All day the fascist planes flew overhead and sirens sounded warnings.

Several times the French anti-aircraft fired warning shots to the planes to warn them off the border line. At 6:00 next morning the French authorities allowed us to cross. In Cerbere we were lined up and marched off. We were given the impression that it was only a few kilometres to our destination.

For two days and nights we had not slept and our total meals had amounted to a little bread and a small can of bully beef to five men. The day was very hot and after marching for about 20 kilometres I became very tired and my legs ached, especially the right one which had been badly wounded.

Although our French guards attempted to force us to march, Red Walsh, Slats McLaren, me and two others, managed to get a ride on a Spanish bus that had come over the border.

The Spaniards were bringing everything possible into France. Trucks full of equipment and refugees passed us steadily. After a while a French guard on the road halted us and turned us out to walk. The French had the whole district under military control and were herding everybody towards the concentration camps.

Our little group were [sic] taken to a village jail and locked up for the night. The jail, a large building like a barn with straw to sleep on, was packed with people. Next to me slept a Spanish family, husband and wife and a little baby. During the night the baby died and the parents sobbed pitifully for a long time.

Next day the French villagers brought us milk and bread and some chocolate. The French people were very decent to us. We were sent to the concentration camp at St. Cyprins.

What a place this was! A sandy beach. No shelter. No food. Barbed wire with French colonial troops to keep us in. Even machine guns were lined up on the camp. Men, women and children were jammed together. Thousands of wounded soldiers as well.

On February 10, Mr. Coakley, the C.P.R. agent who was arranging our fare to Canada, arrived to get us released. On February 12, the Canadians in the camp were taken to the camp at Argeles where the majority of the Canadians were interned. This camp was even worse than the one we had left at St. Cyprins.

Attempts had been made to provide some shelter and a little food, no means of lighting a fire to even cook a mule that was killed on the beach for food.

I believe we were very lucky to have fine weather during this period, although the nights were cold and during the last three days the wind blew hard causing the sand to sift all over us and into our clothes.

At last we were released through the good work of our Paris committee and Mr. Coakley, and boarded the train for Paris, thence to Dieppe and England.

On February 7, we sailed on the *Duchess of York*, landing in St John [*sic*] on February 27. On to Montreal and Toronto, receiving wonderful welcomes at both of these cities.[10]

George Kostoff made his way north with the internationals who had not yet left Spain. They got as far as Port Bou, where they were forced to stay for a few days because the French authorities refused to let them cross into France. Upon receiving permission to enter France, they were immediately placed in a concentration camp. Like other Canadians in the same situation, Kostoff was in the camp for two days before receiving anything to eat. Finally Coakley and someone Kostoff refers to as "Steve of Winnipeg" arrived at the camp, and conveyed Kostoff and his comrades to Paris.

Large crowds turned out in Canada to meet the returning veterans, and receptions and public meetings were held to welcome them home. The newspapers and periodicals of the day were filled with stories such as the following account in *Saturday Night*, entitled "The Soldier's Return":

It is impossible not to feel a great deal of sympathy for the members of the Mackenzie-Papineau Battalion who have this week returned to Canada after a long and not in-glorious campaign on the government side in Spain. Whatever their religious and economic belief, they went gladly and without any necessity into great danger for the sake of what they unquestionably believed to be the best interests of humanity and justice. They may or may not have been in error, but the assumption that they, and all others who fight on the same side as Soviet Russia, are malevolently seeking the destruction of the human race is too much for our credulity . . . a considerable number of them held no communistic theories, and did not regard themselves as fighting for the triumph of the communist system . . . Mayor Day was no doubt right in saying that the City of Toronto can do nothing for them at present in the way of relief, but we question the wisdom and good taste of his remark—if he made it—that they should apply to the Spanish government. We question equally the good taste, and even the wit, of the Montrealers who greeted them with a derisory fascist salute; though men who have fought for a cause, however unsuccessful, are not likely to be much disturbed by gestures of those who have never fought for anything.[11]

Gregory Clark, a well-known columnist, added:

Thus these lads came back from a war in which there were no medals. They helped make history but, without arms of any kind, or uniforms, with oddments of nondescript baggage, like poor immigrants, they looked no more historic than Abraham Lincoln when he was New Salem's postman. They were as unheroic and as little military in appearance as Great Lakes deckhands.

Thus, from the red, raw, quivering crucifixion of Spain, they came back to this chill gray peace of Canada, over 3,000 miles away [from that] tragic land for whose dark masses they had risked their lives to raise them from 500 years of tyranny.

Altogether 1,200 such Canadian boys as these had served a lost cause there. There, under the orange groves, on mesa, and in mountain pass, by bridgehead and in village trench, some 300 of them lie buried. They lie with countless Spanish dead, with dead anti-fascists of many races. They lie in a country where Sir John Moore fell and where many Englishmen, Irish Fusiliers and Highland Scots died fighting Napoleon.

They lie in exile, nameless, unhonoured lads who were part of Canada, breathed its air, went to its schools, sat in its movie shows. Some day it will be remembered to their glory that they served in Spain with the international brigades of many men from many lands. For the "internationals" who fought at Madrid, Brihuega, Teruel and the Ebro will yet become a legend with all men who prize liberty.[12]

198

NOTES

1. Letter to W.C. Beeching, October 1938.
2. Amadée Grenier, written account to author.
3. In doing so, the government rejected the advice of the RCMP to make the return of the volunteers to Canada more difficult than it already was.
4. Matthew Halton, *Ten Years to Alamein* (Toronto: S.J. Reginald Saunders & Co., Ltd., Publishers, 1944), 53. Halton's remark about the "Tory of Tories" probably refers to former Canadian Prime Minister R.B. Bennett, who was living in London at that time.
5. Diary of Sulo Huhtala, in possession of author.
6. Interview with Jim Southgate.
7. Huhtala, Diary.
8. Matthew Halton, *Toronto Daily Star*, 27 January 1939.
9. Petro Dolynuik, translated by Peter Krawchuk from *The People's Gazette*.
10. Frank Thirkettle, written account.
11. *Saturday Night*, 11 February 1939.
12. Gregory Clark, *Toronto Daily Star*, 4 February 1939.

Nine

Their Place in History

The interlude of peace was to be brief. Barely seven months after the Canadian volunteers made their way home, Germany attacked Poland, leading to the outbreak of World War II. Hitler was surprised that the western democracies chose this occasion to declare war, for they had tolerated fascist aggression in other parts of Europe. Many of the Canadians who had fought with the International Brigades had warned that if fascism was not contained in Spain, the inevitable outcome would be another global conflict. Now, their predictions proved to be true, and the world embarked upon the greatest and most devastating conflict in the history of mankind.

Life in Canada had not been easy for the veterans who had fought in Spain. They were subjected to close surveillance by the RCMP, and many were refused employment if they disclosed their role in the Spanish conflict. With the outbreak of war in Europe, however, the struggle against international fascism once again took precedence over personal considerations. The idealism of the veterans was proven by the fact that, in spite of having experienced firsthand the horrors of war, many were prepared to fight again, and perhaps to die, in the struggle for democracy. Indeed, they were the only men in Canada with combat experience in modern warfare. Ed Cecil-Smith, the former commanding officer of the Mackenzie-Papineau Battalion, offered the services of the surviving veterans of the fighting unit to the Canadian government. Stunningly, the offer was refused. Worse was to follow.

In the early years of World War II the USSR was protected by a nonaggression pact with Nazi Germany, during the period known as the "Phony War," when the Allies failed to prosecute the war with conviction, and the Canadian government looked upon supporters of both fascism and communism as enemies.[1] On 6 June 1940, the Communist party and fifteen other organizations were proscribed under the War Measures Act; among those interned were Spanish civil war veterans W.C. Beeching, Bob Kerr, Alick Miller and Orton Wade. This unwarranted suspension of their civil liberties was indeed a bitter pill to swallow, for the veterans who were arrested had already risked their lives in the fight against fascism. They remembered comrades buried in the battlefields of Spain; many had been prepared to enlist in the Canadian army. Although the concentration camps in Canada were not as brutal as those in Nazi-occupied Europe, it was still ironic that men who had fought for the preservation of liberty should be robbed of their own freedom. They were to be remain unjustly confined until the autumn of 1942, well after Germany invaded Russia.

At this point, despite the harassment they had suffered, and the fact that some of them had been imprisoned by their own government, many of the veterans were still prepared to fight for Canada in the war against fascism, and when allowed to do so many enlisted for overseas service. Once again, they incurred heavy casualties.

World War II saw the defeat of Nazi Germany and Fascist Italy. Franco, whose Blue Division had fought alongside the Nazis, managed to avoid the fate of his brother fascist dictators. Shortly after the end of World War II the "Cold War" with the USSR began, and world communism was once again targeted by the western governments as the principal enemy. It was quickly forgotten that fascism was the real threat to civilization—if not to world peace—and Franco was allowed to maintain his brutal dictatorship in Spain. To the veterans who had fought and seen so many close friends die in Spain, this was a bitter realization. They had formed an unbreakable bond with the Spanish people, and continued to work for the reestablishment of democracy in Spain. They supported campaigns to free Franco's prisoners, sent supplies, and protested the suppression of civil liberties in Spain. However, it was only after Franco's death in 1975 that democracy was reborn in the country that many of the veterans had come to consider their second home.

What then is the place of the volunteers in history? For the past fifty years they have been accorded none, at least not by the established historians of the nation. The Spanish civil war is not mentioned in standard histories of Canada and the historic role of the Canadian volunteers and the Mackenzie-Papineau Battalion is conveniently ignored. It is as though the Spanish tragedy never occurred and young Canadians never volunteered to challenge a foe the Canadian government endeavoured to appease. The truth is otherwise. Fascism did arise in Europe over fifty years ago and a large number of young Canadians did volunteer to join others from around the world to challenge and defeat it.

These young men and women were not the dangerous subversives portrayed by officialdom and feared by the police. For the most part, they were working men and women: labourers, machinists, technicians, office workers, loggers, miners, fishermen, farmers, railroaders, seamen, store clerks, nurses, doctors and other professionals. They came from a variety of ethnic backgrounds: French Canadians, Scots, English, Irish, Welsh, Ukrainians, Russians, Poles, Hungarians, Czechs, Bulgarians, Jews, Norwegians, Swedes, Danes, Finns, Germans, Austrians, Dutch and Belgians. Although they came from every region of Canada, a disproportionate number resided on the Prairies and the west coast. There was a large contingent from the lakehead, most of whom were of Finnish background.

Some were politically active in the Communist party of Canada; others in the CCF and Liberal parties. Still others had no political party affiliation at all. By the standards of the day, most had a modest formal education. For many, English was a second language. Yet, these men and women were well informed, self-taught for the most part, and conscious of the larger society and world about them. They shared a common recognition that the establishment of fascism would entail the destruction of democracy, with its attendant rights, obligations and freedoms. This, they knew, was too high a price to

202

pay for the preservation of an economic system that denied work to able-bodied men and women and condemned thousands of families to humiliation and poverty.

The volunteers were young men and women at the time who found it difficult to accept the status quo. They were tough and resilient, and when the Spanish people cried out for assistance, these Canadians knew what the stakes were and what risks were involved. They did what they thought at the time was the right and natural thing—they volunteered in the hope that their contribution to the struggle in Spain would make a difference.

It did, yet in the end it did not. Despite the sacrifices of all the international volunteers, the Spanish people were defeated in their courageous battle against fascism. The veterans who survived and returned to Canada tried to warn their fellow countrymen and women of the consequences; for the most part, the warning was not heeded. Instead, they found themselves the target of harassment by businessmen, the government and the police. In time, they were all but forgotten. When the Veterans of the International Brigades-Mackenzie-Papineau Battalion of Canada petitioned the Canadian government in the 1980s to recognize the surviving volunteers as veterans of Canada's wars, the request was denied.[2]

To the veterans, now scattered across Canada, their ranks dwindling each year through natural attrition, their memories and convictions remain. They know now, in the twilight of their years, that no power can break or diminish the bond that still binds them to the Spanish people. Spain is also their homeland, and Spaniards their special concern. Nor can they ever forget that for a brief moment in their lives they were part of a grand adventure, when men and women from all over the world came together in an attempt to rescue a people they had never known from a terrible evil which sought to arrest and turn back the tide of progress in human history.

Marjorie McKay of British Columbia was really writing about all of the Canadian volunteers when she described her late brother's departure for Spain:

> He worked on Friday and left on Saturday for Spain. He felt it was his duty as a citizen of the world to fight in Spain against the fascist forces. He left quietly without fanfare. Our last letter to him, written in June, 1938 was returned December 24th marked "missing" and "*décédé*."[3]

NOTES

1. The agreement, known as the Molotov-Ribbentrop Pact, was signed by the USSR after the Soviet government failed to persuade the governments of France and the United Kingdom to enter into a defensive alliance against Nazi Germany. The Chamberlain government in particular was of the view that Nazi Germany could be persuaded to turn its aggressive attentions towards the east. It was this intention that persuaded an alarmed Soviet government to seek a nonaggression pact with Germany. For a recent account of these events, see William Manchester, *The Last Lion: Winston Spencer Churchill, Alone 1932-1940* (Boston: Little, Brown and Co., 1988).
2. The campaign to bring official recognition to the volunteers as veterans of Canada's wars was led by Ross Russell of Toronto and began in 1978.
3. Letter written by Marjorie McKay of British Columbia to author, 25 January 1980.

Bibliography

Academy of Sciences of the USSR. *International Solidarity with the Spanish Republic*. Moscow, Progress Publishers, 1974.

Alexander, W. *British Volunteers for Liberty*. London, Lawrence & Wishart, 1982.

Allan, Ted and Sydney Gordon. *The Scalpel, the Sword*. Toronto, McClelland & Stewart, 1952.

Alvarez, Manuel. *The Tall Soldier*. Toronto, Virgo Press, 1980.

Alvarez del Vayo, Julio. *Freedom's Battle*. New York, Alfred A. Knopf, 1940.

Beeching, William and Dr. Phyllis Clarke, eds. *Yours in the Struggle: Reminiscences of Tim Buck*. Toronto, NC Press, 1977.

Bessie, Alvah. *Men in Battle*. New York, Charles Scribner, 1939.

Bessie, Alvah and Albert Prago, eds. *Our Fight*. New York, Monthly Review Press, 1989.

Betcherman, Lita-Rose. *The Swastika and the Maple Leaf*. Toronto, Fitzhenry & Whiteside, 1975.

Biggar Peck, Mary. *Red Moon Over Spain*. Ottawa, Steel Rail, 1988.

Colodney, Robert G. *The Struggle for Madrid*. New Brunswick, New Jersey, Transaction Books, 1958.

Corkill, David and Stuart Rawnsley. *The Road to Spain*. Dunfermline, Fife, England, Borderline Press, 1981.

Cunningham, Valentine, ed. *The Penguin Book of Spanish Civil War Verse*. London, Penguin Books, 1980.

Davis, N. Brian, ed. *The Poetry of the Canadian People*. Toronto, NC Press, 1978.

Ervin, Randy G. "Men of the Mackenzie-Papineau Battalion: A Case Study of the Involvement of the International Communist Movement in the Spanish Civil War." M.A. thesis, Carleton University, Ottawa, 1972.

Fighting Side by Side with Spanish Patriots against Fascism. Moscow, Novosti Press Publishing House, 1986.

Fraser, Ronald. *Blood of Spain: An Oral History of the Spanish Civil War*. London, Penguin, 1979.

Geiser, Carl. *Prisoners of the Good Fight: Spanish Civil War 1936-39.* Westcourt, Connecticut, Lawrence Hill and Company, 1986.

Halton, Matthew. *Ten Years to El Alamein.* Toronto, S.J. Reginald Saunders & Co., 1944.

Hoar, Victor. *The Mackenzie-Papineau Battalion.* Toronto, Copp Clark Publishing Company, 1969.

Ibarruri, Dolores. *They Shall Not Pass.* New York, International Publishers, 1966.

Landis, Arthur H. *The Abraham Lincoln Brigade.* New York, Citadel Press, 1967.

MacLeod, Wendell, Libby Park and Stanley B. Ryerson. *Bethune: The Montreal Years, An Informal Portrait.* Toronto, James Lorimer & Company, 1978.

Matthews, Herbert L. *Half of Spain Died.* New York, Charles Scribner's Sons, 1973.

Maisky, Ivan. *Spanish Notebooks.* London, Hutchinson & Co., 1966.

Monks, Joe. *With the Reds in Andalusia.* London, Nikul Printers, 1985.

Nelson, Steve. *The Volunteers.* New York, Masses & Mainstream, 1953.

O'Riordan, Michael. *Connolly Column.* Dublin, New Books, 1979.

Rolfe, Edwin. *The Lincoln Battalion.* New York, Random House, 1939.

Rust, William. *Britons in Spain.* London, Lawrence & Wishart, 1939.

Ryan, Frank, ed. *The Book of the Fifteenth Brigade.* Madrid, 1938.

Sandoval, José and Manuel Ascarate. *Spain, 1936-1939.* London, Lawrence & Wishart, 1963.

Sheean, Vincent. *Not Peace But a Sword.* New York, Doubleday, Doran & Company, Inc., 1939.

Smith, A.E. *All My Life.* Toronto, Progress Books, 1949.

Stewart, Roderick. *Bethune.* Don Mills, Ontario, Paperjacks, 1975.

Thomas, Gordon and Max Morgan Witts. *Guernica: The Crucible of World War II.* New York, Ballantine Books, 1975.

Thomas, Hugh. *The Spanish Civil War.* New York, Harper and Row, 1977.

Tisa, John. *Recalling the Good Fight.* South Hadley, Massachusetts, Bergin & Garvey Publishers, Inc., 1985.

Index

A

Aalto, William, 141
Abramson, Samuel, 156
Alberti, Rafael, 29
Alfonso XIII, xl
Allan, Ted, 162
Allstop, Geoffrey, 114
Alvarez, Manuel, 133
Amery, L., 115
Anderson, Ivor (Tiny), 23, 25,
    26, 58, 59, 137, 152
Andreef, John, 144
Aranda, M.A. (General), 84
Arcand, Adrian, 4
Armitage, Joe, 47, 48
Astray, Millan, 174
Atanasoff, Nicolas, 144
Aucoin, Thomas, 150
Aviezer, Elias, 42
Azaña, Manuel, xl, xli

B

Bailey, Thomas, 21, 150
Barcena, Frank, 150
Bateman, --, 31
Beeching, William C., xlii,
    108-12, 158, 188, 190, 192,
    201
Bethune, Norman (Doctor),
    xxxviii, 57, 155, 161-65
Bigelow, Howard, 150
Bigras, Alcide, 63
Bilbao, Crescenciano, 78
Bilodeau, Roger, 43
Blackburn, Tom, 117, 118
Bloom, John Oscar, 47, 48
Blum, Léon, 16

Bobby, Frank, 92
Brage, -- (Captain), 103, 105,
    118
Brennan, William, 20, 46,
    49, 52, 54, 56, 64, 155
Brown, Len, 150
Brown, R.D., 168
Buchokowsky, --, 154
Buck, Tim, 1-3, 7, 10, 192
Buckwell, Clifford, 158, 159
Buhay, Beckie, 130
Burke, Ainslee P. (Lee), 17,
    48, 79, 121, 126, 137, 150,
    152
Burton, Yorky, 82, 150

C

Caballero, Francisco Largo,
    120
Caballero, Giminez, 37
Cameron, -- (Lord), xxxvii
Cane, Larry, 136
Cannon, Karl, 137
Carberry, D., 170
Carbonell, George, 124
Cecil, Robert (Lord), 1, 85, 96
Cecil-Smith, Edward, 7, 56,
    78, 80, 88-90, 110, 113, 115,
    123, 124, 130, 191, 200
Chamberlain, Neville, xxxvii,
    187
Chambers, Alex, 151, 152
Christoff, Gregor, 144
Cisneros, Hidalgo de, 34
Clark, James, 128
Clark, Gregory, xxxv, 198
Cluny, --, 154
Coakley, --, 191, 196, 197

207

Hallowell, W., 47, 137
Halton, Matthew, 192, 193
Hanni, Matte, 141
Harbocin, Nick, 49, 50, 52
Hautniemi, Joseph, 167
Hecht, Joseph, 111
Hellund, Walter, 159
Hemingway, Ernest, 175
Henderson, Ray, 117, 118
Henderson, Stanley, 117, 118
Hernden, Milt, 73
Higgins, James, 19, 116, 132, 133
Hilton, Perry, 168
Hitler, Adolf, xxxiv, xxxvii, 1, 2, 5, 16, 33, 200
Hliva, Vasili Ivanovich, 170
Hoshooley, Jack, 68
Hourihan, Martin, 156
Huhtala, Sulo (Sam), 122, 192

I

Ibarruri, Dolores (La Pasionara), 189
Ibing, Hans, 158, 168
Iscziuk, Stepan, 58, 154
Ivanka, Carol, 183
Ivanoff, Anton, 144

J

Jacosta, --, 30, 31
Jimenez, --, 86
Johnson, Arthur, 135

K

Kalieta, M., 194
Kamy, -- (Captain), 98
Kane, Scotty, 47, 48
Kardash, William, 74, 170
Kashtan, William, 57, 164

Keenan, George (Moon), 134, 135
Kelly, Joseph, 56, 134
Kennedy, Joseph, xxxvii
Kerr, Robert, 56, 201
Keto, Reino, 141
King, W.L. Mackenzie, xxxvii, 6, 8, 56, 190, 191
Kiroff, Istvetan, 144
Kleber, Emil, 31
Komodowski, Edward, 85
Korpi, Irgo, 141
Kostoff, George, 144, 145, 197
Kostyk, Fred, 69, 127
Krause, -- (Doctor), 167
Kubenic, Mike, 111
Kuokka, U., 141
Kupchik, Izzy, 156

L

Laaksonen, V., 141
Laird, -- (Doctor), 185
Lane, --, 76
Lapointe, Ernest, 6
Law, Oliver, 49, 51
Lawson, Jack, 65, 145, 146
Lazure, Omar, 76, 77, 129
Leomo, --, 144
Levinson, Leonard, 10, 84
Linton, Arthur (Red), 128, 137
Lister, Enrique, 1, 38
Liversedge, Ronald, 7, 8, 10-12, 22, 57, 71, 75, 78, 147, 149
Llano y Serra, Queipo de (General), 173, 175
Llewellyn, E., 114
Locke, Jacob, 68
Lompik, James, 92
Lord, Fred, 170

Parker, Eric de Witt, 109
Patterson, Harry, 82
Penn, Marvin, 160, 167
Penrod, Jack, 84
Peneycad (Morgan), Ed, 170, 171
Perala, J., 141
Picasso, Pablo, 31
Pike, Florence, 156
Pike, William (Doctor), 155
Polichek, John, 135
Pozas, Sebastian (General), 37
Prieto, Indalicio, 120

R

Ramelson, Bert, 190
Reiss, Dave, 109
Reynault, -- (Mayor of Montréal), 9
Reznowski, Edward, 169
Roberts, Jack, 44
Roberts, Tommy, 117, 118, 159
Roca, Pedro, 124
Rogers, Frank, 90, 109, 124, 141
Rojo, Vicente (General), 39
Rose, Sol, 124
Ross, Allen, 167
Ross, Scotty, 114
Ruskin, James, 102
Ryan, Frank, 39, 116
Ryant, Ruby, 48

S

Saari, Toivo, 141-43
Sankari, --, 25
Sarasola, Luis, 9
Sarvas, George, 23, 24
Saunders, Charlie, 154

Saunders, Murray, 21, 167
Schatz, Isaac, 73
Schoen, Joseph, 25, 26, 58, 91, 128, 138, 192
Schoenberg, Joseph, 86
Schuler, --, 111
Shannon, Danny, 112
Shiveliuk, Oleksa, 129
Shostick, Sydney, 25
Sim, Charles, 156
Sise, Hazen, 162
Siven, Art, 156, 168
Skavulak, Dmytro, 167
Skelton, O.D., 12, 172, 191
Sollenberg, Randall (Doctor), 156
Sorensen, Henning, 162, 163
Southgate, James, 156, 193
Sparks, Harold, 167
Spry, Graham, 4, 161
Steele, Jack, 135
Steele, Ray, 48
Stevens, Russ, 151
Stoloff, Louis, 152
Storgoff, Mike, 127
Swederski, Gregory, 84, 85
Sweeney, Bernard, 150

T

Tapsell, Wally, 116
Tarnawskyi, Mykola, 170
Tate, James, 91, 92
Taylor, Clyde, 82
Taylor, Joe, 155
Telford, Lyle (Doctor), 11, 12
Tellier, Lucien, 64, 150
Thirkettle, Frank, 114, 115, 135, 195
Thomas, Jack, 83
Thompson, Robert, 76, 78
Tough, William, 86
Traynor, Tom, 47, 51, 52

U

Udin, Stan, 128
Unamuno, --, 173

V

Valera, Fernando, 34
Valledor, José, 123
Varela, José (General), 33,
    37, 38
Vassilov, Norman, 144
Veikkola, Vaino, 141
Villeneuve, -- (Cardinal), 5

W

Wade, Orton (Andersen,
    Herman), 16, 17, 59, 201
Walsh, J. (Red), 114, 196
Walter, -- (General), 73, 74,
    90, 100, 110
Walthers, Charles, 71
Wandzilak, John, 135
Watts, Jean, 156
Wellman, Sol, 85, 90, 110,
    113
Werner, Peter, 154
Weston, Garfield, 192
Wheeler, William, 110, 113
Whitehead, --, 76, 78
Wild, Sam, 107
Williamson, E.W., 22
Wilson, Curly, 184
Wintringham, Tom, 38
Wolf, Jim, 68, 71
Wood, S.T., 12

Y

Yardas, Ed, 56

Z

Zamora, --, xl
Zayjak, --, 154

DATE DUE

MAR 10 1993	
MAR 18 1993	
OCT 16 1993	
OCT 28 1993	

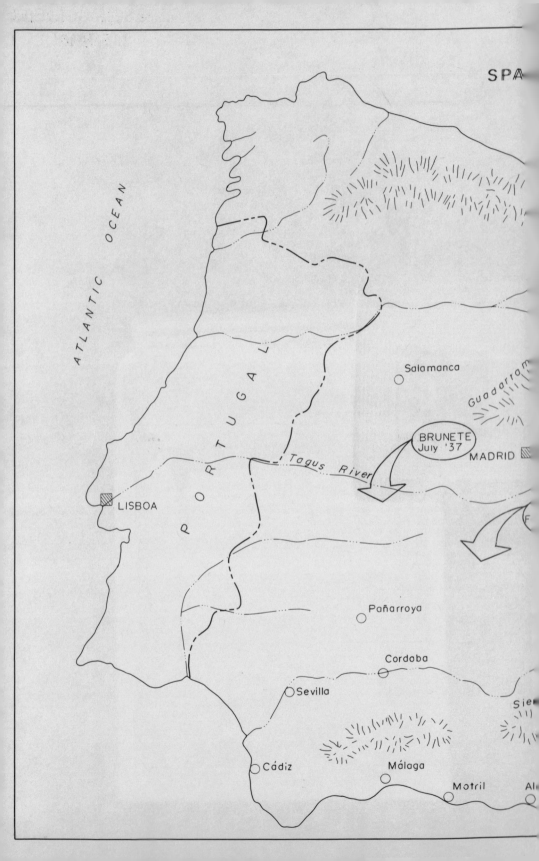